THE
HOME
COOK

Also by Alex Guarnaschelli

OLD-SCHOOL COMFORT FOOD:
THE WAY I LEARNED TO COOK

THE HOME COOK

recipes to know by heart

ALEX GUARNASCHELLI

CLARKSON POTTER/PUBLISHERS

New York

This is for my dad's authentic lemon chicken, Cantonese pork with tofu, and classic Italian tomato sauce mixed with my mom's cheese soufflés, oysters Rockefeller, and strawberry trifles. That glorious celebration of culture through food definitely made me become a chef and pen this book.

———————

All rights reserved.
Published in the United States by Clarkson Potter/Publishers,
an imprint of the Crown Publishing Group, a division of
Penguin Random House LLC, New York.
crownpublishing.com
clarksonpotter.com

CLARKSON POTTER is a trademark and POTTER with colophon is
a registered trademark of Penguin Random House LLC.

Library of Congress Cataloging-in-Publication Data
Names: Guarnaschelli, Alex, 1969– author.
Title: The home cook: recipes to know by heart / Alex Guarnaschelli.
Description: New York: Clarkson Potter/Publishers, 2017
| Includes index.
Identifiers: LCCN 2016045628 (print) | LCCN 2016047577 (ebook)
ISBN 9780307956583 (hardcover) | ISBN 9780307956590 (ebook)
Subjects: LCSH: Cooking, American. | LCGFT: Cookbooks.
Classification: LCC TX715 .G9138 2017 (print) | LCC TX715 (ebook)
DDC 641.5973—dc23
LC record available at https://lccn.loc.gov/2016045628.

ISBN 978-0-307-95658-3
Ebook ISBN 978-0-307-95659-0

Printed in China

Book design by Stephanie Huntwork
Cover photography by Johnny Miller

10 9 8 7 6 5 4 3 2

First Edition

CONTENTS

INTRODUCTION

I think this book began in my head around the summer of 1992. I was cooking at Larry Forgione's restaurant, An American Place, in New York City—my first restaurant job. Someone was making a batch of Parker House rolls, a staple of the bread basket. I remember trays of buttery rolls that made my mouth water. That afternoon, I sat down for the predinner family meal and tore open one of the rolls, still hot from the oven. It tasted like pure butter and salt and yeast all at once. I knew I had to learn how to make it, how to preserve the moment, how to re-create that flavor. When something excites the appetite to that level, it has to be a part of a collection of recipes to know by heart.

When I was growing up, my mother cooked avidly from books. To this day, she retains a voracious appetite for recipes both new and classic alike. But there were always certain books in a category of their own, a small special subset of her whole collection, that she would turn to again and again. We called them by their authors' names: Fannie Farmer. Julia Child. Dione Lucas. James Beard. Craig Claiborne. Diana Kennedy. Marcella Hazan. And, of course, *The Silver Palate Cookbook*. I'd ask her to make cornbread or perhaps some gnocchi and she would reach for a book on this shelf. It was her go-to place for perfect recipes that would deliver on their simple promise. My mother pulls out an encyclopedia of knowledge, experience, and recipes every time she steps into the kitchen. As if that weren't enough, my dad has his own separate bag of tricks in the kitchen, too. Intimidating. Sometimes I think I became a chef just to keep up with my family!

My Parker House roll moment was the first of hundreds of such instances where I began compiling my own go-to recipes for a cookbook to fit on that special shelf, a book that might stop you from flipping through five others to find the recipe you want, a book with reliable recipes for every need and craving: a house vinaigrette for everyday green salads, a whole roasted chicken, a luscious vegetarian main course, a layer cake for your best friend's birthday, a the-bake-sale-is-*tomorrow*? treat that you can get into the oven in minutes with ingredients you most likely already have on hand. Whether you want a recipe that's fast or slow, casual or impressive, healthy or indulgent, hot or cold, winter or summer, day or night—or some combination—you'll find a match in these almost three hundred tried-and-true recipes.

I eventually moved to Paris to cook for a number of years, then back to New York, then on to California before settling in my hometown. This recipe collection has been a constant companion to me throughout my career. To this day, twenty-five years after that first cooking job, I still keep a tiny notebook and pen in my back pocket. When a Parker House roll moment hits, I jot it down, filing away the smells, flavors, and textures to re-create them later. Often a recipe leads me somewhere unexpected, like turning braised short ribs into an even more comforting bowl of soup. Sometimes a seed planted by one recipe morphs into something else.

My needs have also changed over those twenty-five years. My apartment is full of cookbooks; like many chefs, I collect them. I have fancy ones with glossy photos of one scoop of ice cream topped with a lacy gold leaf tuile. There are books that tell me how to pickle skate wings or make elderberry wine. I enjoy this mix of odds and ends—but I can't say I have ever pulled one of them off the shelf and actually *cooked* from it. When I gave birth to my daughter, Ava, who is now nine, I made some changes. You have to remember that while the life of a professional chef is certainly difficult and physically draining, we do enjoy the luxury of a dishwasher who magically replaces all the sauté pans right where we need them. At home, with a baby and no sleep, I turned a corner in my home cooking. Why not have a one-pot meal where the sink is empty and dinner is on the table? I've written this book to strike a balance in my own collection. This is the natural extension of my work and of my life as a parent and daughter.

Generally, books that seek to cover all the bases don't contain much seasonality. After all, there is great comfort

in the evergreen nature of an omelet, pot roast, or rice pilaf. But that's where the professional chef in me steps in. Some of these recipes will pull you toward one season or another, from fresh tomatoes in summer to root vegetables in winter. They will also push you to explore new grains, to seek out and enjoy less fancy cuts of meat, to tackle fish at home. That's what this book seeks to achieve: to give you an entire repertoire for every "occasion"—whether that's a Monday-night dinner or a weekend dinner party—and to have fun while you are doing it.

This book is organized roughly along the lines of an elaborate meal, from starters through sweets and extras—though I really can't imagine anyone preparing a twenty-two-course meal with a recipe from each chapter (nor should anyone have to wait until the very end of the meal for a cocktail); that's not the point. You should feel free to dip into any chapter for that vinaigrette, that roasted chicken, or whatever you need.

We begin with Snacks & Appetizers that range from the simple to one that is almost opulent. And honestly, as the daughter of two Italian Americans who avidly cooked cuisines ranging from Chinese to Indian to French, I can tell you that anything goes in this chapter, including dumplings and ribs. Dips, Crudités & Pickled Vegetables is one-stop shopping for a vegetarian snack, whether creamy or on the healthier side. Lightly pickling veggies that are destined to be dunked is a simple step that takes their flavor to the next level. Dips and pickles can also be prepped ahead of time. My father jokes that his mother would shop for and cook an entire meal from scratch, and, as soon as she was done, she would walk out into the living room as her guests were getting ready to leave. Making some of your appetizers and snacks in advance can buy you more table time with family and friends.

The topic of soup consumes two whole chapters here, with Soups to Start (both chunky and pureed) and Soup for Dinner. One of the ways I feel I really learned to cook was through the art of making soup. It's a great way to keep a meal in the fridge that only improves as it sits for a day or two and can also be a great place to showcase beans and vegetables. My fondness for mom-and-pop red-sauce joints runs through Italian American Pastas & Classics, as does my heritage. The first time I had Pasta Puttan-

esca was at a little joint on Fifty-third Street and Ninth Avenue in Manhattan. It may be my first memory of one of my favorite natural salt bombs: the caper. I didn't know my paternal grandparents well—I met them only a couple of times—but my grandmother's signature lasagna, the layers laced with tiny meatballs, remains with me to this day. It's a masterpiece that tastes just as good reheated and served in a sandwich the next day.

When I became the executive chef at Butter Restaurant in 2003, I went through a few "cheffy" phases, including a "no chicken" rule. I served duck, guinea hen, you name it—but not chicken, which felt *boring*. Then I went out to dinner one Sunday off and I scanned the menu for the comfort of roasted chicken to no avail. And it hit me. If I was looking for it, wasn't everyone? New Chicken Classics aims to fill that void. Because I admire *The Silver Palate Cookbook* so much, tackling my own version of Chicken Marbella seemed a necessary rite of passage. Another favorite here is My Dad's Lemon Chicken: crisp chicken drizzled with a lemony sauce that makes you want to eat twice what you normally would.

In Stand-Alone Main Courses, two standouts are Roast Beef with Dry Sherry Gravy and Cedar-Planked Salmon. Deep flavors are achieved with very few ingredients—one of my favorite ways to cook at home. Great for feeding a few friends or family, these recipes don't really need side dishes and such: just set a platter in the middle of the table and everyone digs in.

For meals that are as comforting as my Lamb Tagine, head straight to One-Pot & Slow-Cooked Meals. These dishes are part of my parenthood revelation. In addition to the lack of pots and pans in the sink after dinner, there is also something magical about smelling something amazing cooking in late afternoon, feeling heat coming from the kitchen as Classic Pot Roast braises stovetop.

My parents instilled in me a love of humble often downright homely ingredients—including root vegetables, supermarket mushrooms, and all kinds of onions—that was reinforced working in professional kitchens in France and in the United States. You might think chefs are all about exotic mushrooms and fiddlehead ferns and, while we love those ingredients, there's something beautiful about taking an ugly vegetable, cooking it simply, and turning it into an insanely tasty dish. How delicious are beets and rutabaga? A simple plate of Buttered Rutabaga or a Summer Beet Carpaccio can round out your repertoire. Raw White Mushroom Salad is such an unassuming yet actually edgy way to begin a meal. I love keeping on hand a batch of recipes like Grandpa Guarnaschelli's Sweet-and-Sour Onions (so good as a quickie condiment or last-minute touch on a dish!) or Dry-Roasted Scallions with Romesco Sauce to round out a meal.

Great salads begin with a great dressing or vinaigrette; you have a couple dozen to choose from here. You've got The Sherry Vinaigrette I Use on Everything all the way to a yummy funky Miso Dressing. Most young cooks start at the salad station (myself included), where nothing is cooked to order, which makes these recipes especially home-cook friendly. Try the Beefsteak Tomato, Bacon, and Red Onion Salad or Fennel and Orange Salad with Walnut Pesto. Then turn to the salads I love as stand-alone meals, such as Thai Beef and Watercress Salad, or as companions to roasted meat or fish, like Crispy Brussels Sprouts Salad or Warm Candied Corn Salad.

I also love grains and beans. Mail-order stores like Kalustyans (kalustyans.com) and SOS Chefs (sos-chefs.com) have helped me change my ingredient game, from wheatberries to French lentils. I love a bean or toasted-grain salad as a make-ahead side dish or even a light dinner. They really satisfy—and I have an appetite!

I am highly invested in the baking recipes in this book, beginning with Italian American Cookies. Two of my favorite recipes, Dark Chocolate Brownies and Thin Crispy Gingerbread Cookies, bridge the gap between afternoon snack and after-dinner dessert (and, if I am being honest, occasional breakfast treat). Cookies, fruit bars, and even chocolate bark are sweets we often buy—until we realize how simply they can be made at home.

The recipes in Berries & Juicy Fruits are all home runs. Some of my favorite fruits are showcased simply, such as Cherries in Red Wine with Frozen Yogurt. Pavlova with Fresh Strawberries is a light, fluffy dessert that doesn't skimp on decadence and dramatic presentation.

Cake is a serious subject for me. It really is my favorite food group. Layer cakes are one of its most excellent subsets (see the classic Yellow Layer Cake with Choco-late Frosting or Carrot Parsnip Cake with Cream Cheese Frosting—it's amazing to me what a few parsnips do to make carrots taste like the best version of themselves). Pies, Tarts & Crisps addresses a cornerstone of American baking and contains recipes made from whatever is in season. I've got you covered on the Thanksgiving classics, of course, but Strawberry Ice Cream Pie with Balsamic ups the ante and Raspberry Crisp with a Crunchy Cinnamon Top celebrates the tang of berries melded with warm spices.

Quick Breads and Jams & Fruit Condiments make a nice pair. These are recipes to make on the weekend when you want your house to smell like Creamy Biscuits and Pumpkin Nutmeg Bread. The jams, jellies, chutneys, and marmalades are good to slather on warm bread you pull from the oven and also make nice accompaniments to other dishes in this book. Some of my favorites are the Lemon Marmalade and the Barely Cooked Blueberry Jam.

And, finally, there are Cocktails. You might think I should have started here, but I am really a cook first and not a professional mixologist. These happen to be some of my favorites to make and drink precisely because they do not require arcane bitters or any professional training. They are timeless and always feel appropriate.

Along the way, in various recipes, I encourage you to "taste for seasoning," my way of reminding you to taste as you go. It's about salt and pepper, for sure, but it's also about spices and acid—whether citrus juice or vinegar. Make sure these ingredients have done enough to make your food punchy and delicious. If not, add more. You may like more tang than I do—or your lemons may be sweeter or more acidic than mine. What you cook should taste good to you.

All of this is preparing you to go and cook these recipes. Be the person who says, "I'm going to make my stuffed mushrooms for the office party" or "I think I'll bake those tangy raspberry cookies for the potluck." There's a wonderful confidence in making great food and sharing it with others. Let these recipes be your guide, with your taste buds giving you additional direction. And please, put this book on your special shelf: the one with the sauce-spattered books that you take down and use all the time. I think it delivers.

Breaded Eggplant Fingers with Balsamic Sauce *11*

Marinated Cerignola Olives *13*

Stuffed Mini Peppers *14*

Extra-Crispy Cheese Straws *15*

Mini Goat Cheese Quiches *16*

Individual Brie Sandwiches with Toasted Sesame Seeds *17*

Warm Bar Nuts *18*

Spicy Spinach Phyllo Triangles *19*

Scallion Pancakes *22*

Spicy Chinatown Pork Dumplings *23*

SNACKS
& APPETIZERS

Glazed Five-Spice Ribs *24*

Veal Meatballs with Tomatoes and Parmesan Cheese *25*

A Basket of Drumsticks and Lemons *26*

Spicy Baked Chicken Wings with Honey Vinegar Glaze *27*

Trout Roe on Tiny Potatoes with Lemon Zest and Sea Salt *29*

Grilled Chicken Satay with Cashew Sauce *30*

Shrimp Toast Sandwiches with Garlic *31*

Tequila-Cured Salmon with Grainy Mustard Sauce *32*

Lobster Rolls *33*

BREADED EGGPLANT FINGERS
WITH BALSAMIC SAUCE

I love eggplant; it's meaty and satisfying. I also love cooking it with the skin on and enjoying the texture and flavor contrasts between skin and flesh. I love to dunk these in a good dip or salsa. They are an adult answer to chicken fingers with way more flavor. The aroma of the eggplant, thyme, and bread crumbs also gives a pizzeria vibe to the kitchen. And that makes everyone hungry. This dish can be prepared in advance and then fried just before serving. The reduction of balsamic coats the eggplant nicely and provides that great balance of tangy and sweet.

1 cup **balsamic vinegar**

2 medium **globe eggplants** (about 1 pound each)

Kosher salt

2 teaspoons dried **oregano**

1 cup **all-purpose flour**

2 large **eggs**

4 large **egg yolks**

¼ cup plus 2 tablespoons **extra-virgin olive oil**

1½ cups plain dried **bread crumbs**

Leaves from 4 sprigs fresh **thyme**

¼ cup **canola oil**

1 Preheat the oven to 375°F.

2 Reduce the balsamic: Pour the vinegar into a small saucepan and bring to a boil. Lower the heat, and cook until it has reduced to ½ cup liquid, 20 to 25 minutes. Set the sauce aside to cool.

3 Prepare the eggplants: Slice the eggplants lengthwise into 1-inch-thick slices. Stack the slices and cut them crosswise into 1½-inch-wide fingers. Season the pieces liberally all over with 2 tablespoons salt and the oregano. In a medium bowl, mix the flour with 1 tablespoon salt. In another medium bowl, whisk the eggs and yolks with the 2 tablespoons olive oil and 1 tablespoon water. In a third medium bowl, mix the bread crumbs with the thyme. One piece at a time, dredge the eggplant in the flour, then in the egg mixture, and finally in the bread crumbs. As the eggplant pieces go through the breading process, arrange them in a single layer on a baking sheet. Note: The eggplant can be frozen at this point and cooked another day.

4 Fry the eggplant: In a large skillet over medium heat, combine the remaining ¼ cup olive oil with the canola oil. When the oil begins to shimmer and smoke lightly, turn off the heat and add some of the eggplant pieces in a single layer. (It's better to cook these in batches than to overcrowd the pan.) Fry on the first side until golden brown, 3 to 5 minutes. Carefully turn them over and fry until golden brown on the other side, 3 to 5 minutes. Transfer the eggplant to the baking sheet, arranging the pieces in a single layer, and season each piece with salt. Note: You can cover the eggplant with plastic wrap and refrigerate for up to 6 hours at this point and bake when ready to serve.

5 Bake the eggplant: Bake until the eggplant is tender when pierced in the center with the tip of a knife, 8 to 10 minutes. Remove the eggplant from the oven and taste for seasoning. Drizzle with the balsamic sauce or serve it on the side for dipping. Serve immediately.

MARINATED
CERIGNOLA
OLIVES

STUFFED MINI
PEPPERS

EXTRA-CRISPY
CHEESE STRAWS

MARINATED CERIGNOLA OLIVES

My favorite olive? Hands down, green Cerignola. They are big and meaty and green, with a large pit that I always roll around in my mouth for a minute after eating off all the olive meat. The flavors of this marinade linger and whet the appetite. I make these in advance so my friends can snack on something while they watch the main course bubble away on the stove. Some grilled or toasted sourdough bread, a couple wedges of cheese or some ricotta, and a bowl of these olives . . . yum. Put out just enough for your friends and watch how much better dinner tastes after a palate opener like this. The longer these sit, the more pronounced the flavors become: whole spices mixed with fresh thyme and orange zest.

¾ cup plus 1 tablespoon fruity **extra-virgin olive oil**

Leaves from 6 large sprigs fresh **thyme**

2 large **garlic cloves**, grated

2 teaspoons crushed **red pepper flakes**

3 light grates of **orange zest** (see Tip)

4 heaping cups green **Cerignola olives**

2 tablespoons **red wine vinegar**

1 tablespoon **yellow mustard seeds**

1 tablespoon **coriander seeds**

1 Start the marinade: In a medium skillet, warm the 1 tablespoon olive oil over medium heat. Add the thyme leaves and cook until they bubble and crisp, 1 to 2 minutes. Remove the skillet from the heat and scrape the thyme into a medium bowl; reserve the skillet. Stir the garlic and red pepper flakes into the thyme. Add the orange zest, remaining ¾ cup olive oil, and the olives to the thyme mixture and toss to combine.

2 Finish the marinade: In the same skillet, combine the vinegar with ½ cup water and warm it over medium heat for 1 minute. Then add the mustard and coriander seeds, and simmer gently for 8 to 10 minutes. Remove the skillet from the heat and allow the spices to sit in the mixture for 20 to 25 minutes.

3 Marinate the olives: Pour the vinegar and spices over the olives and toss to blend. The olives can be served immediately, but their flavor improves if they are left to sit. Pack the olives into a jar, cover them with the marinade, and cover tightly. Refrigerate for 1 to 4 weeks. Bring to room temperature before serving.

TIP: When grating oranges, don't press too hard. Grate lightly to get just the top layer of the floral-scented skin and leave the bitter white pith behind.

STUFFED MINI PEPPERS

These stuffed peppers taste sweet and spicy at the same time. The texture of the pine nuts and the scallions contrasts with that of the creamy goat cheese and makes these little bites exciting to eat. These are a fun way to serve cheese—a change from the usual slabs on a board. I put out thick slices of Italian bread with this and marvel at how quickly the platter empties out.

16 fresh **cherry peppers**
6 tablespoons **extra-virgin olive oil**
Kosher salt
8 ounces creamy **goat cheese**, at room temperature
4 medium **scallions** (green and white parts), thinly sliced
3 tablespoons **pine nuts**, toasted
Grated zest and juice of 1 large **lemon**

1   Preheat the oven to 375°F.

2   **Prepare the peppers:** Lay each pepper sideways on a flat surface and cut off the top so it's like a little hat for the rest of the pepper. Use a paring knife to carefully cut away any seeds that stick to the top. Use a paring knife or a small spoon to scoop any seeds from inside the pepper. In a large bowl, toss the tops and bottoms with 2 tablespoons of the olive oil and 1 tablespoon salt. Heat a large sauté pan over medium heat. When it is hot, drop in the peppers and tops and cook until they are browned and slightly wilted, 3 to 5 minutes. Tilt the pan so the peppers spill out onto a baking sheet. Set aside to cool.

3   **Prepare the filling:** Use a rubber spatula to spread the goat cheese over the bottom and up the sides of a medium bowl so that you can season it evenly. Sprinkle 1 tablespoon salt, the scallions, and the pine nuts all over the cheese. Mix to blend. Taste to make sure the flavors are balanced.

4   **Fill and bake the peppers:** Use a small spoon to stuff the peppers with the cheese mixture, and then arrange them on a baking sheet with room between them. (Reserve the tops.) Bake until the filling is hot in the center, 8 to 10 minutes (test the center with the tip of a knife).

5   **Make the vinaigrette and finish the dish:** In a small bowl, whisk together the lemon zest, lemon juice, and the remaining 4 tablespoons olive oil. Remove the peppers from the oven and drizzle with the lemon vinaigrette. Top each pepper with one of the reserved tops. Serve immediately.

EXTRA-CRISPY CHEESE STRAWS

I infuse these cheese straws with flavors that mimic those of a garlic knot from a New York City slice joint. I usually serve them with some cider, olives, and cheese or with a super-dry white or sparkling wine to get the party going. I love to make this dough by hand. I cut it with a pasta machine because it makes uniform straws, instead of ones in random lengths and shapes. To finish them, I take a page from biscotti bakers and dry the baked straws in a low-temperature oven to make them extra crisp. Arrange them in a single layer on a serving platter and grate additional Parmesan over them for a cheesy touch.

2½ cups **bread flour**, plus more for kneading and rolling

½ teaspoon **active dry yeast**

Kosher salt

2 teaspoons freshly cracked **black pepper**

2 teaspoons **garlic powder**

¼ cup finely grated aged **Provolone cheese**

½ cup finely grated **Parmigiano-Reggiano cheese**

4 tablespoons **extra-virgin olive oil**

1 Make the dough: In the bowl of a stand mixer fitted with the dough hook attachment, combine the flour, yeast, 1¼ teaspoons salt, the pepper, garlic powder, Provolone, and ¼ cup of the Parmigiano-Reggiano and mix to blend. Gradually pour in 1 cup water and mix only until the dough forms a loose ball. Do not mix beyond that or your dough will be tough. Put the dough on a floured surface and knead it gently, 2 to 3 minutes, until the dough feels smooth and cohesive. Add more flour if the dough is wet or won't come together. Grease a large bowl with 1 tablespoon of the olive oil and add the dough. Turn the dough in the bowl so it gets coated with the oil. Cover the top with plastic wrap and leave it at room temperature for 1½ hours or so; then gently press down on the top to deflate it. Leave the dough, covered, for another hour or two. It should double in volume.

2 Preheat the oven to 375°F.

3 Roll the dough: Transfer the dough to a floured flat surface and divide it into 4 equal parts. Roll each portion of dough with a rolling pin and then run it through the thickest setting on a pasta machine. Each portion should now be about ⅛ inch thick. Return the dough to a floured flat surface and use a sharp knife to cut it into ½-inch strips. Arrange the strips of dough, leaving some space between them, in a single layer on two baking sheets.

4 Bake the straws: Brush the dough strips with the remaining 3 tablespoons olive oil and sprinkle with 2 teaspoons salt. Bake until light brown, 13 to 15 minutes. Do not overbake. Remove from the oven and turn off the oven.

5 Finish the straws: Sprinkle the cheese straws with the remaining ¼ cup Parmigiano-Reggiano and return the baking sheet to the warm oven. Let the breadsticks dry out a bit more and the cheese melt slightly over them, 3 to 5 minutes. Serve warm. If you want to make these a few hours ahead, do so through step 4, let them cool, and then when you are ready, proceed with step 5 using a 250°F oven.

MINI GOAT CHEESE QUICHES

I used to make my quiche batter with cream cheese for added thickness and richness. Once, when making it at home, I dropped half a log of goat cheese in the blender as a substitute. I never looked back. The tang of goat cheese adds tremendous depth of flavor to quiche. I always love the effect hot cheese has on people.

One simple finishing touch separates this recipe from the pack: an easy red wine vinaigrette drizzled over the quiches at the last minute takes the flavor to the next level. Sometimes I drizzle some vinaigrette on the quiches and a little on some green leaf lettuce or arugula to go with them.

4 large **eggs**

2 large **egg yolks**

8 ounces fresh **goat cheese**, cut into thick slices, at room temperature

1 cup **heavy cream**

½ cup **whole milk**

Few drops of **Tabasco**

Few drops of **Worcestershire sauce**, preferably Lea & Perrins brand

Kosher salt

30 mini (1½-inch) **prebaked tart shells** or mini phyllo shells

¼ cup finely chopped fresh **flat-leaf parsley**

2 tablespoons **red wine vinegar**

1 small **garlic clove**, grated

6 tablespoons **extra-virgin olive oil**

1 Preheat the oven to 375°F.

2 **Make the quiche batter:** In a blender, combine the eggs, egg yolks, goat cheese, cream, milk, Tabasco, and Worcestershire with 2 teaspoons salt. Blend on low speed (to avoid incorporating too much air) until completely smooth, 1 minute. Scrape down the sides of the blender and blend for an additional minute.

3 **Fill and bake the tart shells:** Arrange the tart shells on a baking sheet with some space between them. Pour the filling into a pitcher, stir in the parsley, and then pour it into each of the tart shells as high as it will go without spilling over. Bake until light brown and just set, 15 to 20 minutes. The filling should not move when you shake the baking sheet gently.

4 **Make the vinaigrette and finish the dish:** In a small bowl, whisk together the vinegar, garlic, and olive oil until combined. Drizzle the vinaigrette over the hot quiches. Serve immediately.

INDIVIDUAL BRIE SANDWICHES
WITH TOASTED SESAME SEEDS

This recipe came about after I tasted a simple quiche made with Brie and leeks. The leeks really amplified the richness of the cheese. Sesame seeds add a nuttiness to round out the trio. I know it's tempting to add a lot of ingredients to a grilled cheese sandwich—like bacon or pancetta and herbs. But these three ingredients are magic enough. And while there are cheeses that are far more distinctive than Brie, none ends up so creamy. These sandwiches can be cut in half to go with a bowl of roasted tomato soup for a warming lunch or quartered and devoured as an addictive starter.

1 medium **leek** (white and light green parts only)
4 tablespoons (½ stick) **unsalted butter**
Kosher salt
8 large (¼-inch-thick) slices **sourdough bread**
16 ounces **Brie cheese**, cut into 16 thick slices
½ teaspoon **hot paprika**
4 tablespoons **canola oil**
2 tablespoons **sesame seeds**

1 Preheat the oven to 350°F.

2 Cook the leek: Quarter the leek lengthwise and then slice it finely crosswise. Rinse thoroughly, as leeks can be sandy, and drain well. In a medium skillet over low heat, melt 2 tablespoons of the butter; then add the leeks and season them with 2 teaspoons salt. Cook, stirring frequently, until the leeks are tender, 3 to 4 minutes. Taste for seasoning. Transfer to a plate and set aside to cool.

3 Prepare the sandwiches: Put 4 slices of the bread on a flat surface and arrange 4 slices of cheese in a single layer on each slice of bread. Sprinkle with 2 teaspoons salt, and use a small strainer to sift an even layer of the paprika over the cheese. Top the cheese with the cooked leeks and the remaining 4 slices bread to make 4 sandwiches. Press down gently on each sandwich to help the ingredients adhere to one another and to the bread.

4 Cook the sandwiches: Heat a large skillet over medium heat. Add 2 tablespoons of the canola oil. When it begins to smoke, add 1 tablespoon of the butter, and arrange half of the sandwiches in a single layer in the skillet. Cook the sandwiches until browned on the bottom, 5 to 8 minutes. Turn them over and cook until browned on the other side, 3 to 5 minutes. Stir in half of the sesame seeds. Stir to coat the seeds with the butter. Remove the pan from the heat. As you remove the sandwiches, try to sponge up the sesame along the way. Transfer to an ovenproof platter and keep warm in the oven. Repeat the process with the remaining sandwiches.

5 Serve the sandwiches: Transfer the sandwiches to a cutting board and cut each one into 4 pieces. Season lightly with 1 more teaspoon salt. Arrange them on a serving platter and sprinkle with any remaining sesame seeds from the pan. Serve immediately.

WARM BAR NUTS

I know it's hard to believe I had close neighbors when I was growing up in bustling and impersonal midtown Manhattan, but I did. My neighbor Francine Pascal, author of the famous Sweet Valley High book series, had an amazing apartment and put out the kinds of snacks I wished we would eat at home. She always had a bowl of nuts, some shelled and some not: crunchy Brazil nuts coated with salt, and hazelnuts and walnuts in the shell. I loved the textures, the taste of the nuts and their skins. This is my adult interpretation of that childhood memory: a mix of nuts tossed together with a fruity and herby note. Warming nuts with herbs, red pepper flakes, and crunchy sea salt makes them even better. Simple yet special.

2 tablespoons **extra-virgin olive oil**

Leaves from 12 sprigs fresh **thyme**

1 cup **peanuts** with the skin on

1 cup whole **almonds** with the skin on

1 cup **pecan halves**

1 teaspoon crushed **red pepper flakes**

4 light grates of **lemon zest**

1 tablespoon **Maldon sea salt**

1 Preheat the oven to 375°F.

2 **Make the nuts:** Heat a large sauté pan over medium heat. Add the olive oil. When the oil begins to smoke lightly, remove the pan from the heat and add the thyme. The leaves will sizzle and fry a little. Immediately stir in the peanuts, almonds, pecans, and red pepper flakes. Mix to coat with the oil. Spread the nuts on a baking sheet and bake until browned, 5 to 8 minutes. Transfer the mixture to a bowl, stir in the lemon zest and salt, and serve immediately—or let cool and then rewarm in a low oven.

SPICY SPINACH PHYLLO TRIANGLES

My secret to a tasty triangle lies in salting both the filling and the exterior of each one. I often make these just through step 4, freeze them, and then bake as needed. Be patient while these are in the oven; even if they look cooked on the outside, the inner layers need time to bake.

8 tablespoons (1 stick) **unsalted butter**, melted, plus more for the baking sheet

2 tablespoons **extra-virgin olive oil**

¾ cup finely chopped **red onion**

1½ teaspoons crushed **red pepper flakes**

Kosher salt

2 (10-ounce) packages frozen chopped **spinach**, defrosted

4 large **eggs**, lightly beaten

1½ cups freshly grated **Parmigiano-Reggiano cheese**

½ teaspoon ground **allspice**

12 ounces creamy **feta cheese**, crumbled (2 cups)

20 (14 × 18-inch) frozen **phyllo sheets** (1 pound), defrosted

Maldon sea salt

1 **lemon**, cut into wedges

1 Preheat the oven to 350°F. Grease a baking sheet with butter.

2 **Start the filling:** In a medium sauté pan, heat the oil over medium-low heat. When it is warm, add the chopped onions and the red pepper flakes. Season with kosher salt and cook until the onions are translucent, 8 to 10 minutes. Set aside to cool.

3 **Finish the filling:** Wrap the spinach inside a kitchen towel and twist the towel to squeeze all of the water from the spinach. Put the spinach in a medium bowl and stir in the eggs, ½ cup of the Parmigiano-Reggiano, the allspice, and the cooked onion. Season with 1 tablespoon kosher salt and gently stir in the feta. Do not overmix. Cover with plastic wrap and refrigerate until cool.

4 **Make the triangles:** Keeping the stack of phyllo dough covered with a barely damp kitchen towel (to prevent it from drying out) while you work with individual sheets, put one sheet of phyllo on a flat surface with a long side closest to you. Brush the dough with a light layer of the melted butter. Sprinkle with a little of the remaining Parmigiano-Reggiano. Put a second sheet on top. Brush with butter and sprinkle with Parmigiano-Reggiano. Make two more layers in this fashion so there are four layers in all. Use a sharp knife to cut the stack in half lengthwise. Scoop about ¼ cup of the filling onto one end of one of the strips, about 2 inches in from the end. Fold the 2 inches of phyllo over the spinach, forming a triangle, so it covers the filling. Now that the spinach is enclosed, continue to fold, as though you're folding a flag, until you have used up all of the dough and you are left with a triangle. Set it, seam side down, on the prepared baking sheet. Repeat with the second strip of phyllo. Then repeat the entire process four more times to make 12 phyllo triangles. Leave a little space between them on the baking sheet.

5 **Bake the triangles:** Bake until the phyllo is golden brown, 40 to 45 minutes. Sprinkle 1 teaspoon Maldon salt over the triangles. Serve immediately, with lemon wedges on the side.

SCALLION PANCAKES

GLAZED FIVE-
SPICE RIBS

SPICY CHINATOWN
PORK DUMPLINGS

SCALLION PANCAKES

I grew up eating scallion pancakes on special occasions and still get a thrill when I tear into one, dip it in sauce, and devour it when it is almost too hot to eat. These little pancakes are great with the dipping sauce or simply with a little soy sauce or spicy mustard. The scallions provide an unusual form of crunch that makes this snack exciting. I use cake flour for that extra fluff factor because a flat scallion pancake is not nearly as much fun as a puffy one.

1½ cups **cake flour**

½ cup **all-purpose flour**, plus more for rolling

Kosher salt

Canola oil

1 cup **boiling water**

4 tablespoons grated fresh **ginger**

4 medium **garlic cloves**, grated

6 tablespoons **dark soy sauce**

1 teaspoon **sugar**

2 teaspoons **red wine vinegar**

2 tablespoons **sesame oil**

2½ cups minced **scallions** (green and white parts; from about 16)

1 **Make the pancake batter:** Sift the cake flour, all-purpose flour, and 1 teaspoon salt into a large bowl. Make a well in the center of the dry ingredients and stir in 2 tablespoons canola oil and the boiling water. Once the ingredients have been mixed, use your hands to work the dough into a ball, taking care that all the ingredients are thoroughly combined. Add a tablespoon or two of additional flour if the dough seems too wet. Spread a sheet of plastic wrap on a flat surface, put the dough in the middle of the plastic, and cover it loosely. Press the dough out so it flattens inside the layer of plastic. Refrigerate for at least 1 hour or overnight.

2 **Make the dipping sauce:** In a medium bowl, whisk together the ginger, garlic, soy sauce, sugar, red wine vinegar, and sesame oil. Set aside.

3 **Roll the dough:** Divide the dough into 4 equal pieces. Working with one piece at a time on a lightly floured work surface and keeping the remaining dough covered, use a rolling pin to roll it out about ¼ inch thick. Sprinkle with ½ cup of the scallions, and fold the dough in half so the scallions are hidden. Roll it out again and then use a glass that's about 2 inches in diameter (or a biscuit cutter) to cut out rounds. Transfer the rounds to a baking sheet lined with parchment paper. Repeat with the remaining dough, using ½ cup scallions for each piece. Note: If you want to make these ahead, cover and refrigerate for up to 4 hours.

4 **Cook the pancakes:** In a large sauté pan, heat ¼ inch of canola oil over medium-high heat. Line a baking sheet with a kitchen towel and set it near the stove. When the oil begins to smoke, use a pair of tongs to lower a few of the rounds into the oil. Fry until lightly browned, 2 to 3 minutes on each side. Use a slotted spoon to transfer the pancakes to the towel-lined baking sheet to drain. Repeat with the remaining pancakes, adding more canola oil as needed and letting it heat up before cooking additional pancakes.

5 **Serve the pancakes:** Sprinkle the pancakes with the remaining ½ cup scallions, season lightly with salt, and serve hot, with the dipping sauce on the side.

SPICY CHINATOWN PORK DUMPLINGS

The zingy taste and textures of a homemade dumpling make the offerings from any dumpling joint seem pale in comparison. Most of all, that wonderful pork and sherry combination is addictive.

12 ounces **ground pork shoulder**

1 tablespoon plus 1½ teaspoons **kosher salt**

4 **scallions** (green and white parts), minced

4 inner (yellow) **celery stalks**, cut into thin slices

2 medium **garlic cloves**, minced

2 tablespoons grated fresh **ginger**

1 teaspoon **sesame oil**

2 large **eggs**

1 tablespoon **cornstarch**

2 teaspoons **dark soy sauce**

2 teaspoons **dry sherry**

1 (16-ounce) package round **dumpling wrappers**, such as Twin Marquis or Twin Dragon brand

My Favorite Dumpling Sauce (recipe follows)

1 Make the filling: In a large bowl, spread the pork over the bottom and up the sides (the meat will be easier to season evenly). Sprinkle the pork with the salt, scallions, celery, garlic, ginger, and sesame oil. In a small bowl, whisk together one of the eggs, the cornstarch, soy sauce, and sherry until smooth. Drizzle over the pork and use your hands to mix it into the meat. Cover with plastic wrap and refrigerate for 1 hour.

2 Make the dumplings: Line a baking sheet with parchment paper. On a flat work surface, arrange a few of the dumpling wrappers in a single layer. In a small bowl, lightly beat the remaining egg. Scoop a generous teaspoon of the pork filling onto the middle of each wrapper and brush the edges of the wrapper with the egg. Keep the remaining pork filling covered with plastic wrap while you assemble the dumplings. Fold the wrapper over the filling and

seal it to form a closed half-moon shape, pushing out any air from inside before sealing. Transfer the dumplings to the prepared baking sheet. Repeat to make 32 dumplings, leaving a little room between the dumplings on the baking sheet. Cover with plastic wrap and refrigerate for at least 15 minutes and up to 6 hours to let the meat filling rest. Note: You can also freeze the dumplings at this point by arranging them in a single layer on a baking sheet lined with plastic wrap.

3 Cook the dumplings: Prepare a steamer by bringing an inch or two of water to a boil in a pot. Arrange as many dumplings as will fit in a single layer in the steamer basket. Insert the basket, making sure the water is not touching the dumplings. Cover and steam over medium heat until the wrappers are tender and moist to the touch but not falling apart, 15 to 20 minutes (a few minutes longer if frozen). Transfer to a serving platter and cover with foil to keep warm. Cook the remaining dumplings. Serve immediately, with the dipping sauce alongside.

MY FAVORITE DUMPLING SAUCE

MAKES ABOUT 1 CUP, ENOUGH FOR 32 DUMPLINGS

½ cup **dark soy sauce**

½ cup **distilled white vinegar**

1 tablespoon **honey**

6 **scallions** (green and white parts), thinly sliced

In a small bowl, combine the soy sauce, vinegar, and honey. Stir in the scallions just before serving.

GLAZED FIVE-SPICE RIBS

I always gravitate toward recipes that make a juicy glazed rib, and this one has become my favorite finger-licking dish for entertaining. I toss the ribs in the vibrant flavors of five-spice: star anise, tingly cloves and Sichuan pepper, toasty cinnamon and fennel seeds. When these spices connect with the soy sauce and mustard, it's dynamite.

2 tablespoons **canola oil**

3 pounds **pork spare ribs** (see Note)

2 medium **shallots**, cut into thin rounds

4 large **garlic cloves**, grated

1 tablespoon plus 1½ teaspoons **five-spice powder**

1 cup **dark soy sauce**

2 tablespoons **Dijon mustard**

2 tablespoons **dark brown sugar**

1 tablespoon grated fresh **ginger**

2 tablespoons **red wine vinegar**

1 Sear and marinate the ribs: Heat a medium saucepan over medium heat, and add the oil. When the oil begins to smoke lightly, add the ribs in a single layer and sear on each side, 3 to 5 minutes. Transfer the ribs to a large bowl. Add the shallots and garlic to the same pan and cook until they become translucent, 3 to 5 minutes. Stir in the five-spice powder, soy sauce, 1 cup water, the Dijon mustard, brown sugar, and ginger, and bring to a simmer. Once the sugar has dissolved, remove the pan from the heat and pour the marinade over the ribs. Toss to coat. Cover and refrigerate for at least 8 hours or, ideally, overnight.

2 Cook the ribs: Transfer the ribs and marinade to a large sauté pan. Simmer them over low heat, stirring from time to time, until the ribs are tender and the meat starts to come away from the bones, about 1 hour. If you are not serving the ribs right away, remove the pan from the heat and let the ribs sit for up to 30 minutes. If longer, refrigerate at this point and reheat when ready to serve.

3 Serve the ribs: When you are ready to serve the ribs, strain the marinade into a saucepan, add the vinegar, and boil over high heat until thickened, 10 to 12 minutes. (Reducing the liquid separately will prevent the ribs from overcooking.) When the sauce is thick, pour it back over the ribs to glaze them. Serve hot or at room temperature.

NOTE: Buy spare ribs on the bone and have your butcher cut them into 1½ × 1½ × 2-inch pieces.

VEAL MEATBALLS
WITH TOMATOES AND PARMESAN CHEESE

My dad always makes the meatballs in my house, and because he makes a lot, there are always leftovers sitting beautifully in the sauce in the fridge. I love unearthing one, like a flavor boulder on the moon, from the sauce and devouring it cold!

SAUCE

¼ cup **extra-virgin olive oil**

2 medium **yellow onions**, halved and thinly sliced

5 large **garlic cloves**, thinly sliced

Kosher salt

2 **plum tomatoes**, cored and thinly sliced

2 teaspoons **sugar**

1 teaspoon dried **oregano**

1 (28-ounce) can whole peeled **San Marzano tomatoes**

MEATBALLS

8 ounces **ground beef** (15% lean)

8 ounces **ground veal**

Kosher salt

½ cup **panko bread crumbs**, toasted

½ cup freshly grated **Parmigiano-Reggiano cheese**

2 large **eggs**, lightly beaten

½ cup roughly chopped fresh **flat-leaf parsley**

1 teaspoon crushed **red pepper flakes**

About ½ cup **canola oil**

½ cup fresh **basil leaves**

1½ to 2 cups freshly grated **Parmigiano-Reggiano cheese**

1 Make the sauce: In a medium skillet, heat the olive oil over medium heat. When it is hot, add the onions, garlic, and 1 tablespoon salt. Cook for about 2 minutes and then add the fresh tomatoes, sugar, and oregano. Stir to blend, and then pour in the canned tomatoes and their juices. Simmer for 5 to 8 minutes over high heat, stirring from time to time. Lower the heat and use a wooden spoon to break up the whole tomatoes. Simmer until the tomatoes are soft, an additional 15 to 18 minutes. Set aside.

2 Make the meatballs: In a large bowl, mix the beef and veal together with your hands. Spread the meat over the bottom and sides of the bowl. Sprinkle with 1 tablespoon salt, the bread crumbs, Parmigiano-Reggiano, and eggs, and then mix again. Sprinkle the parsley, salt to taste, and the red pepper flakes all over the mixture. Use your hands to blend the ingredients completely without overworking the meat. Roll into 20 or so balls, each about 2 inches in diameter.

3 Cook the meatballs: Heat half the canola oil in a large skillet over high heat. When the oil begins to smoke lightly, remove the skillet from the heat (to avoid splattering) and add half of the meatballs in a single layer, spreading them apart a bit so they have a chance to brown instead of steam. Return the skillet to high heat and brown the meatballs on all sides, turning them as needed. Treat them like hamburgers and cook them until they are medium rare, 5 to 8 minutes. Touch them to make sure they are still tender in the center; they should have a little give. Use a slotted spoon or spatula to transfer the meatballs to the pot of sauce. Repeat with the remaining meatballs.

4 Serve the meatballs: When all the meatballs have been added to the sauce, simmer them over low heat for 15 to 20 minutes. Remove from the heat, stir in the basil, and serve hot, with a lot of Parmigiano-Reggiano sprinkled on top.

A BASKET OF DRUMSTICKS AND LEMONS

My mother always fries chicken in corn oil in a cast-iron skillet. As a kid, I had this exhilarating feeling that the taste of the chicken was worth potentially burning the kitchen down. This is that recipe, and it's great every time. I've added fried lemon slices for their wonderful bitter flavor, and lemon juice to cut through some of the richness.

1½ cups **buttermilk**

2 tablespoons **Dijon mustard**

Kosher salt

16 **chicken drumsticks**

3 cups **corn oil**

3 large **lemons**

6 cups **all-purpose flour**

3 tablespoons **hot paprika**

1 Marinate the chicken: In a large bowl, whisk together the buttermilk, mustard, and 1 tablespoon salt. Toss the drumsticks in the marinade, cover with plastic wrap, and refrigerate for at least 8 and up to 12 hours.

2 Fry the lemon slices: Heat a large cast-iron skillet over medium-low heat. Add the corn oil and bring to 300°F, using a deep-frying thermometer to monitor the temperature of the oil as it heats. Meanwhile, slice one of the lemons in half and then into thin half-moons, removing any pits. When the oil reaches 300°F, carefully drop a few of the lemon slices into the oil. Fry until they are crisp and browned, 2 to 3 minutes. (If they get overly browned, lower the oil temperature to 275°F before frying the remaining slices.) Using a slotted spoon, transfer them to a baking sheet lined with a kitchen towel to drain. Repeat with the remaining lemon slices. Reserve the oil in the skillet.

3 Preheat the oven to 375°F. Cut the remaining lemons into wedges.

4 Bread the chicken: Fill a large paper bag with the flour, paprika, and 1 tablespoon salt. In batches, remove the chicken from the marinade, add the pieces to the bag of flour, hold it closed, and shake to coat. Arrange the floured chicken on a baking sheet.

5 Fry the chicken: Heat the reserved oil in the skillet to 375°F. To ensure that the oil is hot enough, test one drumstick first, placing it skin side down in the skillet. If it immediately starts to bubble and fry, use a pair of tongs to gingerly arrange a single layer of drumsticks in the hot oil. If the oil does not bubble, remove the drumstick and heat the oil for a few minutes more before adding the chicken. Do not overcrowd the pan. Fry the drumsticks until you can see the underside browning, 10 to 12 minutes. Carefully turn the drumsticks over and brown the other side for 8 to 10 minutes. Transfer the drumsticks to a baking sheet fitted with a wire rack and season them generously with salt. Repeat with the remaining drumsticks.

6 Finish the dish: Transfer the baking sheet of fried chicken to the oven and bake until cooked through, 10 to 12 minutes. Arrange the drumsticks in a basket with the fried lemon slices on top and serve with the fresh lemon wedges on the side.

SPICY BAKED CHICKEN WINGS
WITH HONEY VINEGAR GLAZE

No one can resist a tasty chicken wing—it brings out the kid in all of us. Here I combine wings with a trifecta of flavors: honey, vinegar, and hot sauce. Those flavors hit the corners of your palate like a pinball. Mix a refreshing cocktail or pour an ice-cold beer to go with this one.

½ cup **honey**

½ cup **red wine vinegar**

1 tablespoon coarsely ground **black pepper**

16 **chicken wings**

Kosher salt

4 tablespoons (½ stick) **unsalted butter**

1 teaspoon crushed **red pepper flakes**

1 tablespoon **Sriracha hot sauce**

6 **scallions** (green and white parts), thinly sliced

1 large **lime**, cut into wedges

1 Preheat the oven to 375°F.

2 **Make the honey vinegar glaze:** In a small skillet, bring the honey to a simmer over medium heat. When it starts to foam and turn light brown, after 5 to 8 minutes, remove the skillet from the heat and pour in the vinegar. Return the skillet to medium heat and simmer for 3 to 5 minutes so the vinegar melds with the honey and the sauce thickens slightly. Stir in the black pepper, remove from the heat, and keep warm.

3 **Prepare the chicken wings:** Cut each chicken wing at each joint to make 3 parts. You will have 48 pieces including the wing tips. Season them with 2 tablespoons salt. In a small saucepan over low heat, melt the butter and stir in the red pepper flakes and Sriracha. Put the wings on a baking sheet and brush them with some of the melted butter mixture. Bake until lightly browned on top, 15 to 18 minutes.

4 **Broil the wings:** Remove the wings from the oven and turn on the broiler. Turn the wings over and brush them with the remaining butter mixture. Broil the wings for 1 to 2 minutes on the first side. Turn them over and broil on the second side until browned, 2 to 3 minutes.

5 **Finish the dish:** Drizzle the chicken wings on all sides with the honey glaze, and sprinkle with the scallions. Squeeze the lime juice over them, transfer them to a platter, and serve immediately.

TROUT ROE
ON TINY POTATOES
WITH LEMON ZEST AND SEA SALT

Imagine this bite: earthy, creamy potato, tangy sour cream, a burst of briny trout roe, a slight tingle from the scallion. The elegance and simplicity bring a fancy restaurant to your table in a humble bite-size package. Don't worry if the potatoes aren't all exactly the same size.

2 pounds medium **fingerling potatoes**

¼ cup plus 2 tablespoons **extra-virgin olive oil**

Leaves from 6 sprigs fresh **thyme**

Kosher salt

¾ cup **full-fat sour cream**

Grated zest and juice of 1 **lemon**

4 ounces **trout** (or salmon) **roe**

2 **scallions** (green and white parts), minced

Maldon sea salt

1 Preheat the oven to 400°F.

2 Cook the potatoes: In a large bowl, toss the potatoes in the ¼ cup olive oil and season with the thyme and about 2 tablespoons salt. Arrange the potatoes on a baking sheet, and bake until the center of the potatoes is tender when pierced with the tip of a knife, 25 to 30 minutes. Remove from the oven and set aside to cool.

3 Prepare the cream: In a small bowl, whisk the sour cream with 1 tablespoon warm water until smooth. Season it with 2 teaspoons salt. In another small bowl, whisk together the remaining 2 tablespoons olive oil, the lemon zest, and lemon juice. Mix half of the olive oil mixture into the sour cream. Reserve the rest.

4 Assemble the potatoes: Put the potatoes on a flat surface and cut them in half lengthwise. Slice off a bit of each rounded underside so the potato halves sit flat. Arrange them on a serving platter, and top each one with a little of the sour cream and roe. Drizzle with the remaining olive oil mixture. Sprinkle with the scallions and Maldon salt.

GRILLED CHICKEN SATAY
WITH CASHEW SAUCE

Chicken satay often cooks unevenly or the stick burns or breaks, which means I find myself more worried about the skewer than about the meat! In this recipe, I marinate the meat, cook it, slice it, and then skewer it. It allows for even cooking and a good dose of vinaigrette on each piece. Additionally, you can use more elegant wooden skewers because they never touch the heat or get scorched. If you don't have a grill, sear the chicken in a single layer in a heavy-bottomed sauté pan or cast-iron skillet until cooked through.

½ cup **extra-virgin olive oil**
½ cup fresh lime juice (about 4 **limes**)
6 medium **garlic cloves**, grated
1 tablespoon dried **oregano**
6 (4- to 5-ounce) boneless, skinless **chicken breasts**
Kosher salt
Cashew Sauce (recipe follows)

1 **Marinate the meat:** In a medium nonreactive bowl, whisk together the olive oil, lime juice, garlic, and oregano. Add the chicken and turn to coat with the marinade. Cover and refrigerate for at least 8 hours or, ideally, overnight.

2 **Cook the chicken:** Heat a grill. Remove the chicken from the marinade. Sprinkle 1 tablespoon salt over the chicken breasts, seasoning both sides. Grill the chicken breasts until they start to char lightly, 3 to 5 minutes. Use a metal spatula to rotate them a quarter turn. Cook for an additional 3 to 5 minutes. Then turn the breasts on their second side and cook, rotating them after a few minutes, for 8 to 10 minutes. The breasts should be cooked through. Check the internal temperature of the thickest piece: it should register 160° to 165°F.

3 **Serve the chicken:** Remove the chicken breasts from the heat and transfer them to a flat surface. Allow the breasts to rest for 10 minutes before cutting them lengthwise into ½-inch-thick slices. Skewer each piece. Taste for seasoning. Drizzle with the cashew sauce.

CASHEW SAUCE
MAKES ABOUT 1 CUP

½ cup **cashew butter**
Juice of 2 **limes**
2 tablespoons **Dijon mustard**
1 tablespoon grated fresh **ginger**
1 tablespoon **honey**
2½ teaspoons **Worcestershire sauce**, preferably Lea & Perrins brand
½ cup roasted, salted whole **cashews**, coarsely chopped

In a medium bowl, whisk the cashew butter, lime juice, mustard, ginger, honey, and Worcestershire sauce with ¼ cup hot water. When ready to serve, stir in the cashews.

SHRIMP TOAST SANDWICHES

WITH GARLIC

This is a tea sandwich on steroids. It looks so cute and innocent, but this little starter is a tasty push-pull between the heat of cayenne, the slight sweetness of fresh ginger, and the richness of mayonnaise and shrimp. My secret to holding the shrimp together in the filling comes from the cornstarch. It makes each bite, and the flavors, even more intense!

1 pound large **shrimp** (16 to 20 per pound), peeled and deveined

Kosher salt

1 tablespoon **cornstarch**

4 large **garlic cloves**, grated

2 tablespoons grated fresh **ginger**

2 tablespoons **Worcestershire sauce**, preferably Lea & Perrins brand

1 teaspoon **cayenne pepper**

2 tablespoons **canola oil**

1 **lemon**, cut in half

8 slices **white bread**

3 tablespoons **unsalted butter**, melted

¾ cup **mayonnaise**, preferably Hellmann's or Best Foods

2 tablespoons **red wine vinegar**

1 tablespoon **Sriracha hot sauce**

¼ cup finely chopped fresh **basil leaves**

1 Preheat the oven to 375°F.

2 Make the shrimp mix: In a food processor, combine the shrimp with 2 teaspoons salt, the cornstarch, garlic, ginger, and Worcestershire sauce. Pulse a few times to blend and chop the shrimp. You want a mixture that holds together but isn't completely mushy. Put the cayenne in a strainer and evenly dust the shrimp mixture with it. Pulse once to combine. Transfer the filling to a bowl.

3 Test the shrimp filling: Heat a small skillet over medium heat and add a drop of oil to it. When the oil begins to smoke lightly, add a teaspoon of the shrimp mixture and sauté on both sides until cooked through, 2 to 3 minutes. Taste the shrimp and adjust the seasoning of the whole batch with more salt if needed.

4 Cook the shrimp filling: Heat a large skillet over high heat and add the remaining oil. When the oil begins to smoke, remove the skillet from the heat and add the filling in a single layer. Cook for 1 to 2 minutes, and then use a large metal spoon or spatula to flip the filling onto the other side. It's okay if it breaks into a few pieces. Cook until just cooked through, 3 to 5 minutes, and then squeeze the lemon juice over it. Transfer the contents of the skillet, including any cooking liquid, to a bowl, cover with plastic wrap, and refrigerate until cold.

5 Toast the bread: Arrange the bread slices in a single layer on a baking sheet, and brush with half the melted butter. Bake until golden brown, 3 to 4 minutes. Turn the bread over, brush with the remaining butter, and toast on the second side, 2 to 3 minutes. Remove from the oven.

6 Make the mayonnaise and finish the sandwiches: In a medium bowl, whisk together the mayonnaise, red wine vinegar, Sriracha, basil leaves, and 1 teaspoon salt. Stir in the shrimp mixture and any cooking liquid. Sandwich the shrimp mixture between slices of the toast. Cut the sandwiches into quarters and serve immediately.

TEQUILA-CURED SALMON
WITH GRAINY MUSTARD SAUCE

Somehow I used to feel that I needed the security blanket of a professional kitchen to cure meat or fish. I had been preparing salmon this way at Butter for more than a decade—flavored with lime, mustard, and coriander—thanks to my colleague Alvaro Buchelly. I know this recipe by heart. So I made it at home, just the same way, and it couldn't have been easier. I serve it with a little mustard sauce on the side and pumpernickel bread. Note: Though I find 48 hours optimal for curing the salmon, try a sliver after 24 hours for taste.

1 (4-pound) center-cut fresh **salmon fillet**, skin on, pin bones removed

Grated zest of 4 large **limes**

1 tablespoon **yellow mustard seeds**

1 tablespoon **coriander seeds**

2 teaspoons **cumin seeds**

1¼ cups **kosher salt**

2 cups packed **dark brown sugar**

½ cup **silver tequila**

¾ cup roughly chopped **cilantro** stems and leaves

Grainy Mustard Sauce (recipe follows)

1 Prepare the salmon: Put the salmon, skin side down, in a pan that is large enough to hold the whole piece in a single layer. Sprinkle with the lime zest.

2 In a small sauté pan over medium heat, combine the mustard seeds, coriander seeds, and cumin seeds. Toast for 2 to 3 minutes to wake up the flavors. Transfer the seeds to a bowl and let them cool for 1 minute. Then press the seeds into the flesh side of the salmon, going down the length of the fillet. In a medium bowl, mix together the salt, brown sugar, and tequila. Coat the whole length of the fillet with the sugar mixture. Top with the cilantro. Wrap tightly in plastic wrap and refrigerate for 48 hours.

3 Clean and serve the salmon: Lightly rinse the surface of the fillet and gently pat it dry with a clean kitchen towel. Use the back of a knife to scrape off any spices remaining on the fillet. Remove the skin and cut the fillet in half down the length of it. Remove the bloodline. Trim until clean. Cut the fillet into ¼-inch-thick (or even thinner) slices. Serve immediately, with the mustard sauce alongside.

GRAINY MUSTARD SAUCE
MAKES ABOUT 1¼ CUPS

¼ cup **red wine vinegar**

2 teaspoons **dry mustard**, preferably Colman's

2 tablespoons **dark brown sugar**

⅓ cup smooth **Dijon mustard**

¼ cup **grainy mustard**

⅓ cup **canola oil**

Kosher salt

6 sprigs fresh **dill**, stems and all, roughly chopped

In a medium bowl, whisk together the vinegar, dry mustard, and brown sugar until smooth. Then whisk in the Dijon mustard, grainy mustard, canola oil, ½ teaspoon salt, and the dill. This can be served immediately or refrigerated for a few hours (or overnight) before using.

LOBSTER ROLLS

While there are many types of fancy bread you could use for a lobster roll, I love the slight sweetness and soft texture of a potato hot dog bun—it brings out the natural sweetness in the lobster and the creamy nature of the mayonnaise. I brown the exterior of the buns so the first taste your mouth gets is of a buttery browned roll. The second, contrasting, texture is the soft bread and lobster inside. I think the most important thing about making a lobster roll taste as though you're biting into the ocean is to strike a good balance between the fresh lemon, the mayonnaise, and the lobster meat.

Kosher salt

4 tablespoons plus 2 teaspoons **Tabasco**, plus more as needed

4 **bay leaves**

3 (1½-pound) live **lobsters**

½ cup **mayonnaise**, preferably Hellmann's or Best Foods

2 tablespoons **sour pickle juice**

Juice of 1 **lemon**, plus more as needed

3 sprigs fresh **tarragon**, stems and all, chopped

2 medium **celery stalks**, diced small

1 tablespoon **canola oil**

4 tablespoons (½ stick) **unsalted butter**

8 **potato hot dog buns**

1 Cook the lobsters: Bring a very large pot of water to a rolling boil. Add ½ cup salt, half of the Tabasco, and the bay leaves. Turn off the heat and stir the water to combine the flavors. Allow the water to sit for 2 minutes until it is more like a hot bath than a boiling cauldron (the meat will be more tender as a result). Plunge the lobsters into the water, taking care they are completely submerged, and turn the heat back on under the pot. Cook over medium heat, so the water is simmering, for 10 to 12 minutes. Use tongs to remove the lobsters from the water and transfer them to a flat surface to cool.

2 Shell the lobsters: When the lobsters have had a few minutes to cool, carefully extract the meat from the tails, claws, and legs, keeping the meat as whole as possible. On a flat surface, slice the tail and claw meat into bite-size chunks.

3 Season the lobster: In a medium bowl, whisk together the mayonnaise, pickle juice, the remaining Tabasco, the lemon juice, tarragon, and 2 teaspoons salt. Gently fold in the lobster meat and celery. Taste to see if the flavors are balanced. More salt, lemon, or Tabasco may be needed.

4 Assemble the rolls: Heat a large skillet over medium heat and add 1 tablespoon of the canola oil. When the oil begins to smoke lightly, add 2 tablespoons of the butter. Put half the rolls on their sides in the butter and brown them for 2 to 3 minutes. Turn the rolls over and brown on that side for 2 to 3 minutes. Season with salt. Repeat with the remaining rolls. Fill each roll with the lobster mix. Cut each roll in half. Serve immediately.

Spinach, Artichoke, and Toasted Pecan Dip 35

Roasted Eggplant Dip with Garlic Butter Naan 36

My Favorite Crudités Platter: Carrots with Quick Brown Sugar Pickle,
Cucumbers with Lemon, and Radishes with Salted Butter 38

Spicy Roasted Peanut Dip with Chilled Celery 40

Curried White Bean Dip with Garlic and Parsley 41

DIPS, CRUDITÉS
& PICKLED VEGETABLES

Black Olive Dip with Chilled Carrots 42

Spicy Blue Cheese Dip with Endive Spears 42

Spicy Chickpea Dip 44

Pickled Green Beans 45

Spicy Pickled Carrots 45

SPINACH, ARTICHOKE, AND TOASTED PECAN DIP

I have to say that my mother never made dips when I was growing up and I have been making up for lost time ever since. This is a rich and slightly chunky artichoke dip, made with tangy sour cream and topped with crunchy pecans. I love steamed and roasted artichokes, served plain with some lemon, and this dip is an enriched version of that great flavor.

2 tablespoons **extra-virgin olive oil**

1 (9-ounce) package frozen **artichokes**, defrosted and coarsely chopped

1 (10-ounce) package frozen chopped **spinach**, defrosted

Kosher salt

½ teaspoon crushed **red pepper flakes**

1 tablespoon **unsalted butter**

2 medium **garlic cloves**, grated

8 ounces **cream cheese**, at room temperature

½ cup **full-fat sour cream**

½ cup freshly grated **Parmigiano-Reggiano cheese**

¾ cup **pecan halves**, toasted

1 whole loaf **sourdough bread**, cut into 24 (2 × 1-inch) rectangles

1 Preheat the oven to 350°F.

2 **Cook the spinach and artichokes:** Heat a medium saucepan over medium heat and add the olive oil. Add the artichokes and cook until some of the liquid evaporates, 2 to 3 minutes. Add the spinach, season with salt, and stir in the red pepper flakes. Cook for 1 to 2 minutes to wilt the spinach. Transfer the mixture to a kitchen towel. Wrap and squeeze to drain off any liquid, and set the mixture aside to cool.

3 **Make the dip:** In a medium saucepan over low heat, melt the butter and then add the garlic. Cook until the garlic softens, 2 to 3 minutes. Off the heat, whisk in the cream cheese, sour cream, and Parmigiano-Reggiano. Stir in the spinach and artichokes. Transfer to a serving bowl. Top the dip with an even layer of the pecans.

4 **Make the toast:** Arrange the bread pieces in a single layer on a baking sheet and toast in the oven until golden brown, 2 to 3 minutes. Turn the bread over and toast the other side for 2 to 3 minutes. Remove from the oven. Serve the toast alongside the dip.

ROASTED EGGPLANT DIP
WITH GARLIC BUTTER NAAN

The silky texture of the roasted eggplant, with a hint of a few little seeds meandering through, combined with the mayonnaise creates a snack that is positively addictive. How does eggplant become so luscious and almost smoky when roasted and combined with a little cumin, paprika, and mayonnaise? It just does. I love it with some lightly buttered grilled or toasted pita bread on the side.

3 medium **globe eggplants** (about 2½ pounds)
Kosher salt and freshly ground **black pepper**
½ cup plus 1 tablespoon **extra-virgin olive oil**
1 teaspoon ground **cumin**
3 medium **garlic cloves**, chopped
1 tablespoon fresh **thyme leaves**, chopped
¼ teaspoon **hot paprika**
½ cup **balsamic vinegar**
2 tablespoons **mayonnaise**, preferably Hellmann's or Best Foods
Garlic Butter Naan (recipe follows), or store-bought pita bread or chips

1 Preheat the oven to 350°F.

2 **Prepare the eggplants:** Cut the eggplants in half and arrange them on a baking sheet flesh side up. Season them with 2 tablespoons salt and 1 tablespoon pepper, and drizzle with the ½ cup olive oil. Put the cumin in a small strainer and sprinkle it evenly over the eggplant. Roast until the eggplant halves are completely tender and yielding when pierced with the tip of a knife, 1 to 1¼ hours.

3 **Make the dip:** Remove the eggplants from the oven. Transfer them to a flat surface and scoop all of the flesh out of the skin. If there is an excess of seeds, you can try to remove some as you scoop. Discard the skins. Heat a medium sauté pan over medium heat and add the remaining 1 tablespoon olive oil and the garlic. Season with salt and cook for 1 to 2 minutes to remove the raw flavor of the garlic. Add the eggplant flesh and the thyme leaves. Cook, stirring with a whisk until the eggplant is smooth and fully blended with the garlic and thyme, 5 to 8 minutes. Sprinkle with the paprika, transfer to a bowl, and set aside to cool.

4 **Reduce the balsamic:** Pour the vinegar into a small saucepan and simmer it slowly over low heat, watching it carefully (balsamic vinegar burns very easily), until it is syrupy, 5 to 8 minutes. Set aside to cool.

5 **Serve the eggplant:** Whisk the mayonnaise into the eggplant and taste for seasoning. Put it in a serving bowl and drizzle with the reduced balsamic. Serve with the naan on the side.

GARLIC BUTTER NAAN

MAKES 6 PIECES

This Indian bread can be used as a utensil to scoop up dips or sauces, and as a cooling element for spicy foods. It is traditionally made with chapati flour, a whole-wheat flour with a fine, powdery texture (available in Indian grocery stores), but all-purpose flour works as well. When rolling the bread, use a pastry brush to remove any excess flour; you don't want to get the semi-cooked flour on the exterior of the bread.

2 cups **all-purpose flour**, plus more for kneading and rolling

Kosher salt

1¼ teaspoons **active dry yeast**

¾ cup **whole-milk plain yogurt**

4 tablespoons (½ cup) plus 2 teaspoons **unsalted butter**, melted

Canola oil

2 medium **garlic cloves**, grated

1 Make the dough: Sift the flour into a large bowl. You want the flour to be completely smooth. Add 1 teaspoon salt and the yeast. Use your fingers to mix and blend the dry ingredients. In a separate medium bowl, whisk together the yogurt, 2 tablespoons of the melted butter, and 1 tablespoon warm water. In the bowl of a stand mixer fitted with the dough hook attachment (or, alternatively, with your hands), combine the flour and yogurt mixture, stirring on medium speed until the dough comes together loosely. Knead the dough with the mixer on low speed until it becomes smooth, 2 to 3 minutes. (Alternatively, knead the dough by hand on a lightly floured flat surface.)

2 Proof the dough: Pour the 2 teaspoons melted butter over the bottom and sides of a bowl that is large enough to hold the dough. Put the dough in the center, turning the dough so it gets coated with the butter. Cover the bowl with a kitchen towel and set it in a warm place. Allow the dough to rise until it doubles in volume, 1 to 1½ hours.

3 Knead the dough: Gently press the air out of the dough and turn it out onto a lightly floured flat surface. Divide the dough in half and roll each half into a ball. Cover the 2 balls of dough with a kitchen towel and let them rest for 10 to 15 minutes.

4 Preheat the oven to 450°F.

5 Put two baking sheets upside down on a flat surface. Using a paper towel, lightly grease the underside of the baking sheets with a touch of canola oil. Put the baking sheets in the center of the oven to heat up.

6 Roll and bake the bread: Divide each half of the dough into 3 equal pieces. Lightly flour a rolling pin and roll each portion into a flat, imperfect oval. When all of the ovals are rolled, brush any excess flour off them and put them, in a single layer, on the baking sheets in the oven. Bake until they become light brown and puffy, 5 to 7 minutes.

7 Finish the naan: Remove the baking sheets from the oven. In a small bowl, stir the garlic into the remaining 2 tablespoons melted butter and season with salt to taste. Pour the butter over the bread, and serve immediately.

MY FAVORITE CRUDITÉS PLATTER:

CARROTS WITH QUICK BROWN SUGAR PICKLE, CUCUMBERS WITH LEMON, AND RADISHES WITH SALTED BUTTER

This crudités platter gives each vegetable a fabulous spa treatment before putting it out on the table. I put a pickled vegetable next to a buttered vegetable next to a bright, citrusy vegetable. You can also have a lot of fun arranging each vegetable in its own bowl or Mason jar. A good dip is welcome here, or even a few wedges of a creamy cheese to contrast with the vibrant lemon and vinegar notes from the vegetables.

¼ cup **Maldon sea salt**, plus more for seasoning

¼ cup packed **dark brown sugar**

1 teaspoon crushed **red pepper flakes**

¼ cup **apple cider vinegar**

12 medium to small **carrots**, tops removed, split lengthwise

A few sprigs fresh **dill**

6 **Kirby cucumbers**, peeled and quartered lengthwise

2 tablespoons **extra-virgin olive oil**

2 **lemons**

1 tablespoon grated fresh **ginger**

10 to 12 **red radishes**, tops intact, split lengthwise

2 tablespoons **salted butter**, melted and kept warm

½ teaspoon **cayenne pepper**

1 **Pickle the carrots:** In a medium sauté pan, combine the Maldon salt, brown sugar, red pepper flakes, and vinegar with 2 cups water and bring to a boil. Simmer until the sugar and salt dissolve, 3 to 5 minutes. Remove the pan from the heat and allow the brine to cool slightly. Then add the carrots and dill. Cover and refrigerate for at least 2 hours or overnight.

2 **Prepare the cucumbers:** In a medium bowl, toss the cucumbers with the olive oil, a few light grates of zest from one of the lemons, and the ginger. Cover with plastic wrap and refrigerate for up to 12 hours.

3 **Prepare the radishes:** Dip the radish halves in the warm butter and arrange them in a single layer on a baking sheet. Dust with the cayenne and Maldon salt to taste. Do not refrigerate.

4 **Serve the crudités:** Remove the carrots from the pickling liquid, drain them carefully, and arrange on a third of the area on a serving platter. Arrange the radishes on another third of the platter. Toss the prepared cucumbers with a generous pinch of Maldon salt, and arrange them on the remaining third of the platter. Serve immediately.

SPICY ROASTED PEANUT DIP
WITH CHILLED CELERY

Imagine the roasted flavor of sesame oil mixed with honey and red wine vinegar. One of the subtle touches I love about my father's cooking is that he is a staunch believer in the added crunch and texture of cold vegetables. I agree. I chill the celery for this dip so that it is juicier than ever and refreshing to eat. I am fussy and tend to peel the outer stalks of celery that are larger and stringier. I love the inner yellow stalks the most because they pack great flavor and are more tender.

1 tablespoon **extra-virgin olive oil**

2 medium **shallots**, minced

2 medium **garlic cloves**, minced

2 teaspoons crushed **red pepper flakes**

Kosher salt

1 tablespoon **sesame oil**

1 tablespoon **honey**

3 tablespoons **red wine vinegar**

¾ cup **smooth peanut butter**

¾ cup roasted salted **peanuts**

Juice of 1 large **lime**

1 small **jalapeño**, cut into thin rounds

12 to 14 **celery stalks**, cut into 2-inch-long pieces, chilled

1 Make the dip: In a medium sauté pan, heat the olive oil over medium heat and add the shallots, garlic, and red pepper flakes. Season with salt and cook until the shallots become translucent, 3 to 5 minutes. Stir in the sesame oil and pour the mixture into a medium bowl.

2 Finish the dip: In a small sauté pan, heat the honey over medium heat until it bubbles, froths, and turns dark brown, 2 to 3 minutes. Remove the pan from the heat and add the vinegar—honey is very hot and will splatter, so be careful. Return the pan to the heat and cook until the vinegar evaporates slightly, 1 to 2 minutes. Whisk in the peanut butter and roasted peanuts. Combine this mixture with the shallot mixture and whisk to blend. Season with additional salt, and add the lime juice and jalapeño. Taste for seasoning. Serve warm or at room temperature with the chilled celery on the side.

CURRIED WHITE BEAN DIP

WITH GARLIC AND PARSLEY

This is a dip that I love just as much at room temperature as cold from the fridge. I just put it out with some slices of toasted baguette or Melba toast—something to act as a crunchy sponge for the garlicky beans. It is also a mixture that I keep in the door of the fridge to save the day when something I'm cooking needs a taste boost and some added thickness at the same time. I have been known to use this as a cool spread for a roasted pork sandwich and even as a thickener for a vegetable soup. If you want to serve it as a light vegetarian side dish, skip the blender and serve as is!

Kosher salt

10 medium **garlic cloves**

1 cup **heavy cream**

1 tablespoon **hot curry powder**

Freshly ground **white pepper**

1 (15-ounce) can **white beans**, such as cannellini, rinsed and drained

2 teaspoons **Worcestershire sauce**, preferably Lea & Perrins brand

¾ cup fresh **flat-leaf parsley leaves**

Juice of 1 large **lemon**

3 **scallions** (green and white parts), thinly sliced

2 tablespoons **unsalted butter**, melted

½ cup **panko bread crumbs**, toasted

1   Blanch the garlic: Bring a medium saucepan of water to a boil. Add a generous pinch of salt. Add the garlic cloves and bring the water back to a boil. Drain. Repeat this process a second time, with fresh water. You are blanching the garlic repeatedly to reduce the bitterness and soften the texture. The extra step here makes a big taste difference.

2   Cook the garlic and beans: Return the garlic cloves to the empty saucepan and add the cream and curry powder. Season with salt and white pepper, and bring to a simmer. Add 1¼ cups of the beans and simmer gently until they start to fall apart, 15 to 20 minutes.

3   Meanwhile, preheat the oven to 375°F.

4   Make the dip: Add the Worcestershire sauce to the cooked beans. Pour the mixture into a blender and puree until smooth. Stir in the remaining beans, the parsley, lemon juice, and scallions. Taste for seasoning.

5   Bake the beans: Scoop the bean mixture into an ovenproof dish. In a small bowl, combine the butter and bread crumbs. Sprinkle over the beans and bake until the bread crumbs brown and the mixture bubbles, 10 to 15 minutes. Serve immediately.

BLACK OLIVE DIP
WITH CHILLED CARROTS

While I love tapenade spread, traditionally made up almost entirely of chopped olives, I really like olives better when they have some other, subtler, flavors to play with in the mix. What better than the sweetness of caramelized onions? And a little cream cheese never hurt a dip. Be patient when cooking the onions: good caramelized onions take time to develop their full flavor.

2 tablespoons **unsalted butter**

2 large **yellow onions**, thinly sliced

2 **bay leaves**

Kosher salt

2 teaspoons **sugar**

¼ teaspoon **cayenne pepper**

1 cup **black olives**, such as Gaeta or Alfonso, pitted and coarsely chopped

4 ounces **cream cheese**, at room temperature

1 cup **full-fat sour cream**

Spicy Pickled Carrots (page 45)

1 Cook the onions: In a medium sauté pan over medium heat, melt the butter and then add the onions and bay leaves. Season with 2 teaspoons salt, and add the sugar and cayenne. Cook until the onions are translucent, 8 to 10 minutes. Turn the heat to low and cook, stirring from time to time, until the onions are golden brown, 15 to 20 minutes more. Remove the bay leaves. Stir in the olives. Let cool.

2 Make the dip: In a medium bowl, whisk together the cream cheese and sour cream until smooth. Stir in the onion mixture. Taste for seasoning. Allow the dip to rest for at least 15 minutes and up to 2 hours before serving with the carrots on the side. I also sometimes like to spread some of the dip on each of the carrots and forgo the bowl of dip altogether.

SPICY BLUE CHEESE DIP
WITH ENDIVE SPEARS

I love the salty taste of blue cheese dip playing against the pleasant bitterness of endive leaves or wedges of grilled radicchio. My two favorite blues for this recipe are a Spanish Cabrales or a Danish blue. I like when the cheese is very savory and not too creamy—leave the creamy aspect to the yogurt and mayonnaise.

8 ounces **whole-milk Greek yogurt**

½ cup **mayonnaise**, preferably Hellmann's or Best Foods

2 teaspoons **Tabasco**

2 teaspoons **Worcestershire sauce**, preferably Lea & Perrins brand

Juice of 1 **lemon**

3 medium **garlic cloves**, grated

Kosher salt

6 ounces **blue cheese**, crumbled

4 **scallions** (green and white parts), minced

3 medium heads **Belgian endive**, pulled apart into leaves

In a medium bowl, whisk together the yogurt, mayonnaise, Tabasco, Worcestershire, lemon juice, garlic, and 2 teaspoons salt until smooth. Crumble in the blue cheese, add the scallions, and stir gently to blend. Cover with plastic wrap and refrigerate for a few hours or overnight to allow the flavors to meld together. Serve in a bowl with the endive leaves on the side.

SPICY CHICKPEA DIP

Nothing brings chickpeas to life more than cayenne, curry, and paprika warmed in butter. This recipe first cooks those flavors together and then finishes with creamy chickpeas, olive oil, and a few meaty olives. I like the evenly cooked canned chickpeas (don't use the liquid in the can), rinsed. The low-sodium ones are sweeter.

2 tablespoons **unsalted butter**

1 teaspoon **cayenne pepper**

1 teaspoon **Madras curry powder**

1 teaspoon **hot paprika**

Kosher salt

3 medium **garlic cloves**, grated

1 teaspoon dried **oregano**

1 (15-ounce) can low-sodium **chickpeas**, rinsed and drained

2 tablespoons **extra-virgin olive oil**

1 **lemon**

Maldon sea salt

12 to 15 green **Cerignola olives**, pitted and coarsely chopped

¼ cup fresh **flat-leaf parsley leaves**

1 **Make the dip:** In a medium sauté pan, melt the butter over medium heat and then stir in the cayenne, curry powder, paprika, and 2 teaspoons salt; cook for 1 to 2 minutes. Set aside to cool to room temperature.

2 Add the garlic and oregano to the spices in the sauté pan. Season with salt and cook over medium heat for 2 to 3 minutes so the garlic mellows slightly. Stir in the chickpeas and cook over medium heat until they become warm and tender, 3 to 5 minutes. Scrape the mixture into a food processor, add 1 tablespoon of the olive oil, a few grates of lemon zest, and the juice of the lemon, and process until the mixture is smooth. Taste for seasoning.

3 **Finish the dip:** Transfer the dip to a serving bowl and drizzle the remaining 1 tablespoon olive oil over the top. Sprinkle with Maldon salt, the olives, and the parsley leaves. Serve warm.

PICKLED GREEN BEANS

I eat these bright crunchy beans as a snack or toss them into a vegetable salad. I use the smaller, more tender haricots verts when they are available because their sweetness, tenderness, and complex flavor are the perfect match for the star anise and mustard seeds.

1 cup **distilled white vinegar**

¼ cup **sugar**

1 medium **garlic clove**

1 small **bay leaf**

12 whole **black peppercorns**

1 teaspoon **yellow mustard seeds**

1 small **star anise pod**

1 medium **red onion**, thinly sliced

8 ounces **haricots verts**

1 In a medium saucepan, combine the vinegar, sugar, garlic, bay leaf, peppercorns, mustard seeds, and star anise. Add ½ cup water and bring to a simmer. Simmer for 2 to 3 minutes to combine the flavors and dissolve the sugar.

2 Put the onion slices and haricots verts in a heatproof container, pour the hot pickling mixture over them, and stir gently to combine. Cover and refrigerate for up to a few weeks before serving. The brine is also a delicious substitute for vinegar in salad dressings.

SPICY PICKLED CARROTS

I was at Tartine Bakery in San Francisco, making my way through a few plates of savory and sweet pastries, when I stumbled upon some spicy pickled carrots on the edge of one of the plates. A vegetable in the midst of all these baked goods? Hmm. It was delicious. Cold, bright, spicy. The perfect touch. These are wonderful on their own, as part of a crudités platter or a salad, or even with a piece of grilled meat or fish.

⅔ cup **cider vinegar**

¼ cup **honey**

1 **bay leaf**

12 whole **black peppercorns**

1½ teaspoons crushed **red pepper flakes**

1 small **star anise pod**

1 small **jalapeño**, halved and thinly sliced

4 medium **carrots**, quartered lengthwise

1 In a medium saucepan, combine the vinegar, honey, bay leaf, peppercorns, red pepper flakes, and star anise. Add ½ cup water and bring to a simmer. Simmer for 2 to 3 minutes to combine the flavors.

2 Put the jalapeño slices and carrots in a heatproof bowl, and pour the hot pickling mixture over them. Stir gently to combine, then cover and refrigerate for up to a few weeks before serving.

SOUPS
TO START

PURE CORN SOUP

My grandmother used to make her creamed corn with a little cornmeal in it to add body, and I love what that trick does to this soup. It also reinforces the pure, intense taste of the corn. You can crumble some crispy bacon over the bowls as you serve this for a smoky note, but it's also great as is.

4 tablespoons (½ stick) **unsalted butter**
1 small **yellow onion**, thinly sliced
Kosher salt
2 tablespoons **yellow cornmeal**
12 ears (about 4½ pounds) **fresh corn**, shucked
1 quart **half-and-half**
1 tablespoon **light brown sugar**
Freshly ground **black pepper**
1 tablespoon **red wine vinegar**

1 **Make the soup base:** In a medium soup pot, melt 2 tablespoons of the butter over medium heat. Add the onion and 1 tablespoon salt, and cook over medium-low heat until the onion becomes tender and starts to brown, 8 to 10 minutes. Stir in the cornmeal and 3 cups water, and simmer over low heat so the cornmeal gets integrated, 12 to 15 minutes.

2 **Prep the corn:** Hold an ear of corn upright with one end on the cutting board and the other in your non-cutting hand. Use a sharp chef's knife to slice down, shaving the rows of kernels off the cob. Cut close to the core so that the kernels remain relatively whole but not so close that you end up taking fibrous pieces of the cob with you. Repeat with all of the corn. Gather the kernels in a bowl and reserve the cobs.

3 **Cook the corn:** In a medium pot, bring the half-and-half to a simmer and add the cobs. Simmer gently over low heat until they start to flavor the half-and-half, 15 to 20 minutes. Meanwhile, in another medium pot, heat the remaining 2 tablespoons butter and add all of the corn kernels. Season with salt, and stir in the brown sugar and a generous pinch of black pepper. Cook over medium heat until the corn becomes tender, 8 to 10 minutes.

4 **Finish the soup:** Remove and discard the cobs. Pour the half-and-half over the cooked corn and simmer on low heat for 10 to 12 minutes. Taste for seasoning. Puree about 2 cups of the soup in a blender until smooth, and then pour the puree back into the rest of the soup. Stir in the vinegar to wake up the flavor, and taste for seasoning. Serve hot.

PEPPERED CORN AND MISO SOUP

Prepare the Pure Corn Soup, replacing the cornmeal with 2 tablespoons blond miso paste and the red wine vinegar with rice vinegar. Season the finished soup with the rice vinegar and 1 tablespoon freshly ground black pepper.

MIDTOWN MANHATTAN
CLAM CHOWDER

I love a cup of this with enough oyster crackers to fill the bowl two to three times over. The salt from a good cracker plus the brightness of the tomatoes and the natural sweetness of the celery is one of my all-time favorite soup combinations. The cooked clams, clam juice, and raw fresh clams make this tasty and briny enough for the discerning Midtown crowd. I like to make the soup in a pot that has the maximum amount of surface area for efficient cooking. I keep the skin on the potatoes for that earthy taste and swear by the bacon in the base of the soup. After all, pork and potatoes are what make chowder in the first place!

2 tablespoons canola oil

4 ounces slab bacon, cut into ½-inch dice

2 medium onions, diced

6 medium garlic cloves, grated

1 teaspoon crushed red pepper flakes

Kosher salt

2 medium celery stalks, diced

1 (28-ounce) can whole peeled San Marzano tomatoes

2 (8-ounce) bottles clam juice

2 bay leaves

1 cup cooked chopped clams

3 medium Idaho potatoes, cut into 1½-inch chunks

1 teaspoon hot paprika

2 dozen littleneck clams, scrubbed

½ cup fresh flat-leaf parsley leaves

1 **Make the soup base:** Heat a large, heavy-bottomed pot over medium heat and add the oil and the bacon. Add ½ cup water and cook the bacon until all of the water evaporates and the bacon starts to brown, 8 to 10 minutes. Then add the onions, garlic, red pepper flakes, and 1 tablespoon salt and cook until the onions are translucent, 5 to 8 minutes. Stir in the celery, tomatoes with their juices, clam juice, bay leaves, and chopped clams. Bring the soup back to a gentle simmer over medium-low heat.

2 **Cook the potatoes and clams:** In a medium sauté pan, cover the potatoes with water and bring to a simmer over medium heat. Season with salt to taste. add the paprika, and simmer until the potatoes are somewhat tender but still al dente, 10 to 12 minutes. The liquid in the pan will be slightly thick and starchy. Add the liquid and the potatoes to the soup in the pot. Taste for seasoning.

3 **Finish the soup:** In another medium sauté pan, heat ¼ cup water and add the whole clams. Cook over medium heat until they open, 10 to 12 minutes. Add the clams and any liquid to the soup (discard any clams that do not open), and stir in the parsley and remove the bay leaves. Taste for seasoning. Add salt, if needed, and serve hot in wide soup bowls.

NEW ENGLAND CLAM CHOWDER

FROM THE DAUGHTER OF A NEWTON, MASSACHUSETTS, GAL

There is a thread of Portuguese culture that runs through Rhode Island and made its way onto my mother's Massachusetts childhood table. It comes in many forms, but my favorite is the distinct smoky and sweet flavor of chorizo sausage in clam chowder. And while you may imagine chorizo and red pepper flakes pairing better with the tomato base of Manhattan clam, they are a wonderful contrast to the creamy soup. My mother loves cream more than anything. In New England, cream could probably be its own food group. This soup is no exception. I add some fresh dill, an almost imperceptible yet semi-sacrilegious touch, as a little bit of freshness.

2 tablespoons **unsalted butter**

2 large **leeks** (white and light green parts), diced and well rinsed

2 medium **garlic cloves**, grated

2 teaspoons crushed **red pepper flakes**

Kosher salt

2 (8-ounce) bottles **clam juice**

1 cup cooked chopped **clams**

2 tablespoons **canola oil**

8 ounces **Spanish chorizo**

2 green **celery stalks**, sliced ½ inch thick

4 medium **Yukon Gold potatoes**, cut into ¾-inch dice

2 **bay leaves**

3 cups **heavy cream**

2 cups **half-and-half**

Freshly ground **black pepper**

1 tablespoon **Worcestershire sauce**, preferably Lea & Perrins brand

2 teaspoons **Tabasco**

2 pounds **littleneck** or **Manila clams**, scrubbed

4 sprigs fresh **dill**, stems and all, coarsely chopped

1 Make the soup base: In a large, heavy-bottomed pot, melt the butter over medium heat. Add the leeks, garlic, and red pepper flakes. Season with salt and cook until the leeks are translucent, 5 to 8 minutes. Add the clam juice and chopped clams. Bring to a simmer, then remove from the heat and keep warm.

2 Cook the chorizo and celery: Heat a large sauté pan over medium heat. Add 1 tablespoon canola oil and the chorizo and cook until crispy, 5 to 8 minutes. Using a slotted spoon, transfer the chorizo to a paper towel to drain. Heat the residual fat in the pan, add the celery, and sauté for 2 to 3 minutes. Season with salt. Remove with a slotted spoon.

3 Meanwhile, cook the potatoes: In another pot, combine the diced potatoes, bay leaves, cream, and half-and-half with 2 teaspoons salt and 1 teaspoon pepper. Bring the mixture to a gentle simmer and cook until the potatoes are tender, 10 to 12 minutes. Add the Worcestershire and Tabasco. Stir to blend.

4 Cook the clams: Put a large, heavy-bottomed pot on the stove, add the remaining 1 tablespoon canola oil, and heat it over medium heat. Add the clams, cover the pot, and cook until they pop open, 8 to 10 minutes (discard any that do not open). Put the clams in a colander and reserve the cooking liquid.

5 Finish the soup: There is a good chance there will be grit in the clam cooking liquid. Strain it through a double layer of cheesecloth or a coffee filter into a bowl, and add it to the leek mixture. Combine with the potato mixture. Add the clams in their shells, the celery, and the dill. Discard the bay leaves. Taste for seasoning. Top with the chorizo just before serving.

SPRING MINESTRONE

I had the privilege of working a series of short stints in Provence. The huge, bustling markets at Vaison-la-Romaine and Avignon changed me for life. The vegetables there seemed to be alive. Often when I came back from the market, this minestrone was the next natural step. You likely won't be able to eat just one bowlful. It's like cereal with cold milk in the middle of the night: you have to give in to how delicious it is. The peppery arugula-basil pesto thickens the texture and adds a touch of heat and sweetness.

½ cup plus 2 tablespoons **extra-virgin olive oil**

1 medium **yellow onion**, thinly sliced

4 medium **garlic cloves**, thinly sliced

1 medium **carrot**, thinly sliced

Kosher salt

1 (28-ounce) can whole peeled **San Marzano tomatoes**

2 cups loosely packed fresh **arugula leaves**

1 cup fresh **basil leaves**

1 teaspoon **sugar**

1 (15½-ounce) can **cannellini beans**, rinsed and drained

2 small **green zucchini**, quartered lengthwise and sliced into ½-inch pieces

½ cup freshly grated **Parmigiano-Reggiano cheese**

1 **Start the soup:** In a large soup pot, heat the 2 tablespoons olive oil over medium heat, and then add the onion, garlic, and carrots. Season with salt to taste, and cook until the vegetables become tender, 8 to 10 minutes. Add the tomatoes and their juices and 2½ cups water, and simmer over low heat for 30 to 35 minutes.

2 **Meanwhile, make the arugula-basil pesto:** Bring a medium pot of water to a rolling boil in a saucepan. Have ready a large bowl of ice water. Add a generous handful of kosher salt to the boiling water, and then about half of the arugula and all of the basil leaves. Stir to blend. Cook for 1 minute and then quickly drain the arugula and basil in a strainer and immediately plunge the strainer into the ice water. Leave the strainer in the ice water until the arugula and basil are cool, 3 to 5 minutes. Then drain the leaves slightly, put them in a blender, and add the uncooked arugula, the sugar, and the remaining ½ cup olive oil. Blend only until almost smooth. Taste for seasoning.

3 **Finish the soup:** Stir the beans and zucchini into the soup and simmer until tender, 8 to 10 minutes. Taste for seasoning. Put a dollop of the arugula-basil pesto in the bottom of each soup bowl and sprinkle with some Parmigiano-Reggiano. Ladle the soup over the pesto. Serve immediately.

QUICKIE "WHITE" MINESTRONE

So many minestrone recipes are loaded with tomato. While I love that, I often want a vegetable soup that has a touch of fall and winter in it. I also love the taste of celery root and rutabaga cooked together—it's sweet and almost creamy at the same time. I add basil, garlic, and Parmesan at the end for a burst of both freshness and richness.

2 tablespoons **extra-virgin olive oil**

2 medium **yellow onions**, diced

1 medium **carrot**, cut into 1-inch pieces

1 large **celery stalk**, cut into 1-inch pieces

Kosher salt

2 medium **celery roots**, peeled and cut into 1-inch chunks

1 medium head **rutabaga**, peeled and cut into 1-inch chunks

4 cups **vegetable broth**

1 cup fresh **basil leaves**

1 medium **garlic clove**, grated

1 cup freshly grated **Parmigiano-Reggiano cheese**

1 Start the soup: Heat a large soup pot over medium heat. Add the olive oil, onions, carrot, celery, and 1 tablespoon salt. Cook, stirring with a wooden spoon, until the vegetables become tender, 10 to 12 minutes. Add the celery root and rutabaga, lower the heat, and add the vegetable broth. Simmer until the pieces of celery root and rutabaga are tender when pierced with the tip of a small knife, 15 to 20 minutes.

2 Finish the soup: Puree about 2 cups of the liquid and just about half the vegetables in a blender until smooth, and then stir the puree back into the soup. (This will create a thicker, silkier texture.) Taste for seasoning. Stir the basil leaves, grated garlic, and Parmigiano-Reggiano into the soup to finish. Serve immediately.

SHRIMP BISQUE

This is a classic French bistro soup. I like to put it on the table and then watch everyone breathe in the aromas of shrimp, fennel, and that hint of saffron. Chop the saffron threads a few times to break them into smaller pieces so the flavor blends more seamlessly into the soup. I cut all of the vegetables about the same size so they have a similar cooking time. The soup gets its sublime texture from the rice that's cooked into the base with the onions, garlic, and wine. You don't even know it's there, but it adds body and a hint of sweetness. I like to leave the skin on the potatoes for flavor. Serve the bisque piping hot.

¼ cup **extra-virgin olive oil**

1 teaspoon **saffron threads**, roughly chopped

2 small **yellow onions**, diced

4 medium **garlic cloves**, minced

1 large **fennel bulb**, outer layers removed, bulb diced

½ cup **basmati rice**

Kosher salt

2 tablespoons **cognac**

1 large **Idaho potato**, diced

2 cups **dry white wine**

1 (28-ounce) can whole peeled **San Marzano tomatoes**

1 quart store-bought **shrimp stock**

1 (6-ounce) piece skinless **sea bass** or **halibut**

1½ pounds extra-large **shrimp** (10 per pound), shelled, deveined, and cut into ½-inch pieces

Juice of 1 medium **lemon**

2 teaspoons **Tabasco**

6 sprigs fresh **tarragon**, stems and all, minced

1 **Make the soup:** In a Dutch oven, heat the olive oil over medium heat. Add the saffron, onions, garlic, fennel, rice, and 1 tablespoon salt. Stir to blend and cook, stirring from time to time, until the vegetables become tender and start to brown slightly, 5 to 8 minutes. Stir in the cognac and potato and cook until the flavors smell like they are melding together, 2 to 3 minutes. Add the white wine and continue to simmer over medium heat until the wine reduces by at least half, 12 to 18 minutes. Add the tomatoes with their juices and the shrimp stock, and cook for 15 to 20 minutes. Finally, stir in the fish and allow it to cook so it falls apart and flakes into the soup, 10 to 12 minutes; it's there to give body and add to the fish flavor.

2 **Finish the soup:** Taste the soup and adjust the seasoning. Bring it to a simmer over medium heat and then remove the pot from the heat. Season the shrimp with 2 teaspoons salt, and stir them into the soup. Allow the soup to sit for 10 to 12 minutes so the shrimp cooks gently. The shrimp should be tender but cooked through and no longer translucent. Stir in the lemon juice, Tabasco, and tarragon, and serve.

HOT-AND-SOUR BARLEY SOUP

I cannot tell you how many bowls of hot-and-sour soup I enjoyed in Chinese restaurants throughout my childhood. But I never once made it myself. It turns out that it is simple and delicious to make at home. I like the barley in here because it adds a pleasantly chewy texture and makes the soup even more satisfying. Some of the ingredients, like lily buds, are readily available online or in Asian markets—and the lily buds are optional.

20 dried **wood ear mushrooms**

10 dried **lily buds**, broken into small petals (optional)

½ cup **pearl barley**

8 ounces boneless **pork loin**

4 cups **chicken stock**

3 tablespoons **cornstarch**

½ cup **dark soy sauce**

½ cup **rice vinegar**

2 tablespoons **red wine vinegar**

1 large **egg**, thoroughly beaten

2 teaspoons coarsely ground **black pepper**

2 teaspoons **sesame oil**

4 ounces firm **tofu**, cut into small cubes

4 **scallions** (green and white parts), minced

1 Prepare the mushrooms and lily buds: In a small heatproof bowl, combine the wood ear mushrooms with the lily bulbs, if using. In a small saucepan, bring 2 cups water to a simmer; then pour it over the mushrooms and lily buds. Allow it to sit until the mushrooms become tender and hydrated, 15 to 20 minutes. Strain, reserving the soaking liquid separately. Trim any tough stems from the mushrooms.

2 Cook the barley: In a medium saucepan, bring the barley and 2 cups water to a boil. Simmer until tender, 30 to 35 minutes. Make sure there is always enough liquid to cover the barley; add water as it cooks if needed. Drain the barley and set aside.

3 Cut the pork: Slice the pork into 1-inch-thick pieces and then crosswise into 1½-inch strips. Set aside.

4 Make the soup: Strain the mushroom soaking liquid through a fine-mesh strainer into a soup pot, and add the chicken stock. Bring to a simmer over medium heat and then add the mushrooms. In a medium bowl, whisk the cornstarch with ½ cup water until completely smooth. Whisk in the soy sauce, rice vinegar, and red wine vinegar. Stir the pork slices into the cornstarch mixture and pour everything, whisking as you go, into the simmering stock. Return to a simmer and cook over low heat until the pork is cooked through, 15 to 18 minutes.

5 Finish the soup: Using a large spoon, stir the simmering soup while you swirl in the egg so it cooks as soon as it hits the hot liquid and resembles little rags. Stir in the cooked barley, the black pepper, sesame oil, tofu, and scallions. Taste for seasoning. Serve immediately.

ROASTED SWEET POTATO SOUP
WITH TOASTED CURRY

To enrich the flavor of squash soup, I often roast a few sweet potatoes until they are completely soft and blend the flesh into the soup. One day it dawned on me: these potatoes need a soup of their own. The most important thing is to cook the sweet potatoes until they are completely tender through and through. Otherwise, the soup can be stringy and taste like undercooked sweet potatoes. The warm heat of curry and smoky Aleppo pepper brings out the sweetness of the potato and keeps you spooning this up to the bottom of the bowl.

4½ to 5 pounds medium **sweet potatoes**

8 tablespoons (1 stick) **unsalted butter**

2 medium **yellow onions**, thinly sliced

2 tablespoons **Madras curry powder**

1 teaspoon **Aleppo pepper flakes**

Kosher salt

2 tablespoons **dark brown sugar**

2 tablespoons **blackstrap molasses**

2 teaspoons **Worcestershire sauce**, preferably Lea & Perrins brand

Juice of 1 small **orange**

1 teaspoon **ground ginger**

2 tablespoons grated **fresh ginger**

3 cups **half-and-half**

1 Preheat the oven to 450°F.

2 Roast the sweet potatoes: Put the sweet potatoes on a baking sheet in the center of the oven and bake until they are completely yielding when pierced in the center with the tip of a knife, 1 to 1½ hours, depending on their size.

3 Start the soup: In a medium soup pot, melt the butter over medium heat. When it starts to turn a light brown color, add the onions, curry powder, Aleppo pepper, and 1 tablespoon salt. Cook until the onions become translucent, 5 to 8 minutes. Then stir in the brown sugar and molasses. Turn off the heat.

4 Finish the soup: When the potatoes are cooked, put them on a flat surface and cut them in half. Use a large spoon to scoop out the flesh. Discard the skins and transfer the flesh to a medium bowl. Whisk vigorously to remove any large lumps (but not for too long or it will make the puree gummy in texture), and season with 1 tablespoon salt. Stir in the Worcestershire sauce and the orange juice. Finish by whisking in the ground ginger, fresh ginger, and half-and-half. Transfer the mixture, in batches, to a blender and blend until smooth. Do not overblend or the soup can become gummy. Stir the mixture into the soup pot and bring to a simmer over medium heat, whisking constantly. Add a little water if the soup is too thick. Taste for seasoning. Serve immediately.

BEEF MEATBALL SOUP
WITH PAPRIKA AND ISRAELI COUSCOUS

You can see it when you take a spoonful of this soup: the little meatball, poached gently in the broth, the zing of fresh serrano chile, and the pleasantly chewy couscous. It's a great first course that can double as a meal.

MEATBALLS

8 ounces **ground beef** (chuck or sirloin)
2½ cups freshly grated **Parmigiano-Reggiano cheese**
½ cup plain dried **bread crumbs**, toasted
⅛ teaspoon grated **nutmeg**
2 medium **garlic cloves**, grated
Kosher salt
1 large **egg**, lightly beaten

SOUP BASE

1 tablespoon **canola oil**
2 medium **carrots**, cut into 1½-inch pieces
2 large **celery stalks**, cut into 1½-inch pieces
1 medium **yellow onion**, halved and sliced
2 large **garlic cloves**, grated
2 teaspoons **hot paprika**
1 teaspoon **cayenne pepper**
Kosher salt
1 small bunch fresh **thyme**, tied with string
4 cups **chicken stock**

COUSCOUS

½ cup Israeli **couscous**
Kosher salt
1 tablespoon **unsalted butter**
½ cup finely chopped fresh **flat-leaf parsley leaves**

¼ cup finely grated **Parmigiano-Reggiano cheese**
1 tablespoon **red wine vinegar**
1 small **serrano chile**, cut into thin rounds

1 Make the meatballs: Spread the beef out over the bottom and sides of a medium bowl. (Having more of the beef exposed in a thin layer in the bowl will make it easier to season the meat evenly.) Sprinkle with the Parmigiano-Reggiano, bread crumbs, nutmeg, and garlic and season with salt. Add the egg and use your hands to blend the ingredients, but do not overmix. Then roll the mixture into small meatballs, each about the size of a small cherry tomato. You should have about 24 meatballs. Arrange the meatballs in a single layer on a baking sheet. Refrigerate.

2 Make the soup base: In a large, heavy-bottomed pot, heat the canola oil over medium heat. Add the carrots, celery, onion, garlic, paprika, cayenne, and 1 tablespoon salt. Cook until the vegetables become translucent, 8 to 10 minutes; then add the thyme and chicken stock. Bring to a gentle simmer over low heat and skim the surface with a ladle, discarding any oil or foam that floats to the top. Simmer until the vegetables are tender, 15 to 18 minutes.

3 Cook the couscous: In a medium soup pot, bring 3 cups water to a simmer over medium heat and add the couscous. Season the water with 2 teaspoons salt and add the butter. Cook, stirring from time to time, until the couscous is al dente but cooked, 10 to 12 minutes. Drain the couscous in a colander. In a medium bowl, combine the couscous with the parsley leaves and season with 1 teaspoon salt.

4 Finish the soup: Taste the soup base and adjust the seasoning. Discard the thyme. Drop the meatballs into the soup, return it to a simmer, and cook until the meatballs are cooked through, 5 to 8 minutes. Stir in the couscous, Parmigiano-Reggiano, the vinegar, and the slices of fresh chile. Taste for seasoning, and serve.

VICHYSSOISE

This quick, creamy leek soup is actually good hot or cold. I find that if I make it and chill it completely before serving, the subtle layers of flavor that exist in the scallions and leeks really come to the forefront. You can make this the day before and refrigerate it until ready to serve the next day. I prefer this soup really cold. That's the classic way!

3 tablespoons **unsalted butter**

1 large **Idaho potato**, thinly sliced

6 large **leeks** (white part only), minced and thoroughly rinsed

4 bunches (about 30) **scallions** (green and white parts), minced

Kosher salt and freshly ground **white pepper**

3 cups **half-and-half**

½ cup sliced fresh **chives**

In a soup pot, heat the butter over medium heat, and add the potato slices and ½ cup water. Cook until the potatoes are tender, 8 to 10 minutes. Add the leeks, scallions, 1 tablespoon salt, and 2 teaspoons white pepper. Cook over high heat until the leeks and scallions become translucent, 3 to 5 minutes. Add the half-and-half and 1 cup water and simmer, stirring from time to time with a wooden spoon, for 10 to 15 minutes. Puree the soup, in batches, in a blender until smooth. (Do not allow the soup to cool before blending or the texture could be gummy.) Taste for seasoning. Serve hot, or chill and serve cold, topped with the chives.

CHILLED CARROT AND GINGER SOUP

With the exception of vichyssoise, in my mind a chilled soup is best when made without dairy or any of the other usual soup suspects like onions and garlic. When vegetable juice forms the backbone of the soup, it's refreshing and light to eat. Carrots and ginger make a bracing, irresistible combination. I often add a fresh seasonal herb at the end: basil in spring or summer and some crisped sage leaves in fall.

2 tablespoons **extra-virgin olive oil**

6 large **carrots** (2 pounds), thinly sliced

Kosher salt

2 tablespoons **honey**

2 teaspoons **ground ginger**

2 teaspoons freshly ground **black pepper**

6 cups freshly squeezed **carrot juice**

Grated zest and juice of 1 **orange**

¼ cup grated **fresh ginger**

1 Make the soup: In a medium sauté pan, heat the olive oil over medium heat, and then add the carrots. Season with salt and cook, stirring frequently, until they start to soften, 5 minutes. Stir in the honey, ground ginger, and pepper. Continue simmering until the carrots are fully cooked and falling apart, 15 to 20 minutes.

2 Finish the soup: Add the carrot juice and bring back up to a simmer. Taste for seasoning. Stir in the orange zest and juice and the fresh ginger. Puree the soup, in batches, in a blender until smooth. Chill for at least 2 hours or overnight before serving.

SECRET WATERCRESS SOUP

I have been making this beautiful soup at the restaurant for years. If we don't tell anyone what's in it, we sell it like hotcakes. We generally tell the customers it's a "mixed green" soup with greens from the local market. But it's time for people to stop being afraid of watercress. While I make this soup year-round, it has the biggest impact in spring, when watercress has peppery heat and grassy freshness.

8 tablespoons (1 stick) **unsalted butter**

6 large **shallots**, thinly sliced

2 inner **celery stalks**, thinly sliced

Kosher salt and freshly ground **white pepper**

3 medium **garlic cloves**, grated

3 large **Idaho potatoes**, thinly sliced

2 cups **heavy cream**

1 cup **whole milk**

4 large bunches (about 1½ pounds) **watercress**, stems trimmed, plus 1 cup leaves

1 **Start the soup:** Heat the butter in a large sauté pan over medium heat, add the shallots and celery, and season them with about 1 tablespoon salt and 1 teaspoon white pepper. Stir in the garlic. Cook until the shallots become translucent, 6 to 8 minutes. Add the potato slices and 2 cups water. Cover and cook over low heat until the potatoes become tender, 15 to 20 minutes.

2 **Meanwhile, heat the cream:** In a medium saucepan, combine the cream and milk and bring to a light simmer over low heat. Season with salt and white pepper.

3 **Finish the soup:** Add the watercress to the celery mixture and stir to wilt the leaves. Remove the pan from the heat and stir in the cream mixture. Blend three-fourths of the soup, in batches, in a blender until smooth. Return the pureed soup to the pot, stir it into the remaining chunky soup, and return to a simmer. Taste for seasoning. Top with the reserved watercress leaves, and serve immediately.

TOMATO AND FENNEL SOUP

My soup education really began with this one: sweet tomatoes and licoricey fennel with dry vermouth as a bridge between them. This begs for toasted buttered bread or a grilled cheese sandwich for dunking.

2 tablespoons **canola oil**

12 medium **plum tomatoes**

½ cup **dry vermouth**

Kosher salt

1 tablespoon plus 1 teaspoon **sugar**

¾ cup **extra-virgin olive oil**

10 medium **garlic cloves**, grated

3 large **shallots**, thinly sliced

3 medium **fennel bulbs**, outer layers removed, bulbs thinly sliced, fronds reserved

1 teaspoon **fennel seeds**

½ teaspoon crushed **red pepper flakes**

Freshly ground **black pepper**

1 tablespoon dried **oregano**

1 (28-ounce) can whole peeled **San Marzano tomatoes**

1 tablespoon **red wine vinegar**

2 tablespoons **panko bread crumbs**, toasted

½ cup freshly grated **Parmigiano-Reggiano cheese**

Grilled Cheese Sandwiches on the Side (recipe follows; optional)

1 Char the plum tomatoes: Heat a large cast-iron skillet over medium heat and add the canola oil. When the oil begins to smoke lightly, add the tomatoes in a single layer. You want to blister the skin slightly, drawing out the liquid from the tomatoes, to intensify their flavor. Turn them as needed until they are charred all over, 10 to 12 minutes. Add the vermouth to the skillet, season with salt and 1 tablespoon sugar, and lower the heat. Continue cooking over low heat, breaking the tomatoes apart with a spoon as they cook. Simmer gently until the tomatoes are broken down and the flavor of the vermouth is integrated, 10 to 15 minutes. Set aside.

2 Build the soup base: In a soup pot, heat 1 tablespoon of the olive oil over medium heat and add the garlic, shallots, fennel bulbs, fennel seeds, and red pepper flakes. Season with salt and pepper. Stir in the oregano and the remaining 1 teaspoon sugar. Cook over low heat until the shallots and garlic become tender and translucent, 3 to 5 minutes. Add the canned tomatoes and their juices along with 2 cups water. Turn the heat down to medium-low and simmer until the tomatoes start to lose their shape, 30 to 35 minutes. At this point, the soup should be mushy and blender-ready. If there are still some hard pieces, don't be afraid to add an additional 1 cup of water and cook for a few more minutes. Taste for seasoning.

3 Finish the soup: Put about half of the tomato soup in a blender and puree until smooth. Stir the puree into the remaining soup in the pot. Next, puree the roasted plum tomatoes in the blender until smooth, adding the remaining olive oil through the top in a slow, steady stream. Taste for seasoning. Pour the roasted tomato puree into the soup pot. Bring the soup to a simmer and taste for seasoning. On a flat surface, finely chop some of the reserved fennel fronds. Add them to the soup. Stir in the vinegar and bread crumbs. Ladle the hot soup into bowls and finish with a generous grating of Parmigiano-Reggiano cheese. Serve the grilled cheese sandwiches alongside, if desired.

GRILLED CHEESE SANDWICHES ON THE SIDE

SERVES 4 TO 6

Only sharp cheddar achieves a good enough melt while retaining that almost tangy flavor that goes so well with this soup. Once the soup is cooked, assemble and cook these sandwiches. Serve them piping hot, tucked next to the soup bowls.

8 large (¼-inch-thick) slices **sourdough bread**
8 ounces sharp **cheddar cheese**, cut into 16 slices
Kosher salt
4 tablespoons (½ stick) **unsalted butter**

1 Assemble the sandwiches: Put 4 slices of the bread on a flat surface and arrange 4 slices of cheese in a single layer on each slice of bread. Sprinkle with salt to taste, and put the remaining 4 slices of bread on top to make 4 sandwiches. Press down gently on each sandwich so the cheese is more firmly encased in the bread.

2 Cook and serve the sandwiches: Heat a large skillet over medium heat. Add 2 tablespoons of the butter, and when it is hot, put half of the sandwiches in a single layer in the skillet. Cook the sandwiches on one side until browned, 3 to 5 minutes. Turn them over, and cook until browned on that side, 3 to 5 minutes. Keep the first 2 sandwiches warm on a platter by covering them with aluminum foil. Repeat with the remaining butter and sandwiches. Transfer the sandwiches to a flat surface and cut each one in half. Season lightly with salt, and serve hot.

CREAMIEST OF THE CREAMY BROCCOLI SOUP

Roasting broccoli gives it a wonderful sweetness and crunch, making it a welcome side dish to any meal. Add in flavorful garlic and the spicy heat of red pepper flakes and you have a dish that will make even the biggest broccoli skeptic ask for seconds. Go one step further and turn this into the foundation for a vibrant creamy soup and you will blow minds.

4 tablespoons **extra-virgin olive oil**

3 medium **garlic cloves**, thinly sliced

1 teaspoon crushed **red pepper flakes**

Kosher salt and freshly ground **black pepper**

1½ to 2 pounds **broccoli**, cut into 2-inch florets

2 cups **chicken stock**

2 tablespoons **unsalted butter**

2½ cups **heavy cream**

¾ to 1 cup shredded sharp **cheddar cheese**, to taste

2 tablespoons **full-fat sour cream**

1 Preheat the oven to 425°F.

2 Roast the broccoli: In a medium bowl, combine the olive oil, garlic, and red pepper flakes, and season with salt and black pepper. Add the broccoli florets and toss to coat. Transfer the broccoli mixture to a baking sheet, spreading it out in a single layer.

(Keeping the florets in a single layer increases their exposure to the heat, which allows for even caramelization and a sweet, nutty flavor.) Put the baking sheet in the hot oven and roast the broccoli for 10 to 15 minutes. Check the broccoli and if certain florets are beginning to brown faster than others, toss gently to prevent burning. Roast until all the edges of the broccoli are beginning to brown and become tender, another 10 minutes. Remove from the oven. Season to taste with salt and black pepper.

3 Make the soup: In a soup pot, heat the stock, butter, and cream over medium heat until simmering. Add the broccoli and simmer for 3 to 5 minutes. Puree the soup, in batches, in a blender until smooth. Return the soup to the pot, taste for seasoning, and stir in the cheddar and sour cream until melted. Serve immediately.

ASPARAGUS SOUP

WITH TOASTED WALNUTS

I like using the whole asparagus spears in this soup, and roasting them separately allows the flavor to come through. Asparagus is grassy with a sweet note reminiscent of fresh peas or basil. This soup harnesses all those dimensions and adds richness with walnuts and fresh basil at the end.

¼ cup **extra-virgin olive oil**

2 pounds fresh **pencil asparagus**, trimmed

Kosher salt

2 tablespoons **sugar**

2 tablespoons **unsalted butter**

2 medium **yellow onions**, thinly sliced

6 sprigs fresh **thyme**, tied with a string

4 cups **half-and-half**

½ cup fresh **basil leaves**

½ cup **walnut halves**, toasted and lightly crushed

1 Preheat the oven to 400°F.

2 Prepare the asparagus: In a large bowl, toss the olive oil and asparagus together with 1 tablespoon salt. Arrange the asparagus in a single layer on a baking sheet, and roast until the spears become tender and start to brown, 12 to 15 minutes. Remove from the oven. Sprinkle with the sugar.

3 Make the soup: In a large soup pot, melt the butter over medium heat. Add the onions, thyme, and 1 tablespoon salt and cook over medium heat until the onions brown and are completely soft, 12 to 15 minutes.

4 Meanwhile, prep the asparagus: Put the roasted asparagus (all facing in the same direction) on a cutting board, and starting at the stem end, cut the spears into 2-inch pieces, reserving the tips for the garnish. Drop everything except the tips into the onions in the soup pot, and add the half-and-half. Simmer gently until the asparagus becomes soft, 8 to 10 minutes. Discard the thyme.

5 Finish the soup: Then puree the soup, in batches, in a blender until smooth. Taste for seasoning. Reheat the soup in the same soup pot over medium heat until hot again. Stir in the basil leaves, reserved asparagus tips, and walnuts. Serve immediately.

SOUP
FOR DINNER

BEEF CHILI

I like two different cuts of beef for my chili to give it different degrees of richness, fat, texture, and flavor. The cubes of beef chuck are one texture and size, and the ground beef is another. The flavor of store-bought chili powder takes me back to my childhood, but I like to temper it with Aleppo pepper, which is smoky with a slow-burning heat. I know we think chili should languish romantically on the stove all day, but better not to let it. Cook it. Let it rest off the heat for a bit. Then reheat and serve.

4 tablespoons **canola oil**

1½ pounds boneless **beef chuck**, trimmed and cut into ½-inch cubes

1½ pounds **ground beef**

Kosher salt

3 tablespoons **Aleppo pepper**

2 tablespoons **chili powder**

3 medium **red onions**, minced

12 medium **garlic cloves**, minced

2 (28-ounce) cans whole peeled **San Marzano tomatoes**

6 **jalapeños**, seeded and minced

2 tablespoons **red wine vinegar**

1 (15-ounce) can **red kidney beans**, rinsed and drained

1 cup grated extra-sharp **cheddar cheese**

1 cup **full-fat sour cream**

1 Brown the meats: Heat 2 large skillets over medium-high heat and add 2 tablespoons of the canola oil to each skillet. Season the chuck and the ground beef generously with salt (on all sides for the cubes). When the oil begins to smoke lightly, remove the skillets from the heat (to reduce splattering), and add the beef chuck in a single layer to one skillet and the ground beef to the other. Brown the chuck on the first side over medium heat, 3 to 5 minutes, and then turn the pieces over; sprinkle with the Aleppo pepper. Brown the ground beef over medium heat, stirring with a wooden spoon from time to time to avoid burning the meat, 5 to 8 minutes. Add the chili powder to the ground beef. Use a slotted spoon to remove the cooked beef from both skillets and combine them in a large pot.

2 Make the chili: Combine the cooking fat from both skillets into one and set it over medium heat. Add the onions and garlic, season with salt, and cook until the onions are translucent, 5 to 8 minutes. Pour the tomatoes and their juices over the onions, and simmer for 8 to 10 minutes, crushing some of the tomatoes with a wooden spoon. Pour the entire contents of the skillet into the pot of beef. Add the jalapeños, red wine vinegar, and kidney beans. Continue cooking gently for 15 to 18 minutes to allow the flavors to meld. Remove the pot from the heat and allow the chili to rest for at least 15 minutes. This is like resting a cut of meat before slicing.

3 Serve the chili: Return the pot to the heat and simmer over medium heat for 3 to 5 minutes. Serve with the grated cheese and sour cream on the side.

WHITE BOUILLABAISSE

I really love a fish soup that doesn't need tomato to make it feel whole—and that uses the cheapest varieties of fish and some shellfish to create a dish that tastes far more expensive. I serve this with loaves of bread on a tablecloth I don't care about because people tend to get really into it: it turns into a dunk fest with the bread and aioli.

2 tablespoons **canola oil**

2 pounds skinless **hake** or **pollock fillets**, cut into 1-inch-thick slices

Kosher salt

2 pounds **mussels**, scrubbed

1½ cups **dry white wine**

32 **littleneck clams**, scrubbed

3 tablespoons **extra-virgin olive oil**

3 bunches (about 18) **scallions** (green and white parts), minced

4 medium **garlic cloves**, minced

4 sprigs fresh **thyme**, tied with a string

½ teaspoon **saffron threads**, lightly chopped

5 cups store-bought **fish stock**

Aioli (recipe follows)

Toasted sliced **sourdough bread**

1 Sear the fish and cook the shellfish: Heat a large skillet over medium heat and add the canola oil. When the oil begins to smoke, season the fish pieces with an even layer of salt. Sear the fish in a single layer in the hot oil for 2 minutes. Use metal tongs to turn the fish over, and cook on the other side for 1 minute. Remove the fish and set it aside on a baking sheet. Add the mussels and ½ cup of the white wine to the skillet. Cover, and simmer the mussels for about 3 to 5 minutes, removing them as they open. Next add the clams and the remaining 1 cup wine to the skillet. Cover and cook the clams, removing each one as it opens, 8 to 10 minutes. Reserve the cooking liquid in a bowl.

2 Make the soup: In the same skillet, heat the olive oil over medium heat, and add the scallions, garlic, thyme, and saffron. Season with salt and cook until the scallions become tender and the garlic is translucent, 5 to 8 minutes. Pour in the fish stock and bring to a gentle simmer over low heat. Shell almost all of the mussels and clams (leave a few in the shells for garnish and discard any that have not opened). Add the reserved shellfish cooking liquid, taking care to leave any grit behind, and the mussel and clam bodies to the soup. Then add the mussels and clams in their shells as well. Discard the thyme. Gently add the pieces of fish. Taste for seasoning.

3 Serve the soup: Ladle the soup into bowls and top with a generous dollop of aioli. Serve with slices of toasted sourdough bread on the side.

AIOLI

MAKES ABOUT 1 CUP

2 large **egg yolks**

3 medium **garlic cloves**, grated

2 teaspoons **kosher salt**

¾ cup **extra-virgin olive oil**

Juice of ½ **lime**

In the bowl of a food processor, combine the egg yolks, garlic, salt, and 2 tablespoons warm water. Blend on medium speed. With the machine still running, pour the olive oil and lime juice through the top in a steady stream. The aioli can be kept covered in the refrigerator overnight.

WHITE BEAN CHILI
WITH SPICED CHEDDAR

I know chili is a dish we associate with a pot bubbling on the stove, or with a slow cooker simmering on the counter all day long. However, for this chili I like to cook the white beans almost all the way before adding them to the other cooked ingredients, and then I let everything sit so the flavors can meld. I don't want the vegetables waiting on the beans to finish cooking or vice versa. If all the ingredients are being ruled by one, you risk overcooking the ones that are going along for the ride. White beans don't have the intensely sweet and earthy notes of black or kidney beans. That leaves more room for the white beans to have the starring role along with the robust chili powder, jalapeño, and cheddar cheese.

2 cups **great white northern beans**

2 tablespoons **extra-virgin olive oil**

4 medium **garlic cloves**, minced

1 large **yellow onion**, minced

Kosher salt

2 tablespoons **hot paprika**

1 tablespoon **chili powder**

1 (28-ounce) can whole peeled **San Marzano tomatoes**

1 medium **red bell pepper**, seeded and finely chopped

1 **jalapeño**, thinly sliced

6 **scallions** (green and white parts), minced

2 cups grated extra-sharp **cheddar cheese**

1 cup **full-fat sour cream**

1 Soak the beans: Put the beans in a large bowl and add enough water to cover by at least 2 inches. Let soak overnight.

2 Cook the beans: Drain the beans and put them in a medium pot. Add 4 cups water, bring it to a simmer over medium heat, and continue cooking until the beans are tender, 40 to 45 minutes. Drain and toss with 2 tablespoons of the olive oil, reserving any cooking liquid.

3 Make the foundation of the chili: In a large skillet, heat the remaining 2 tablespoons olive oil over medium heat. When the oil begins to smoke lightly, add the garlic and onion. Season with salt and cook, stirring from time to time, until the onion softens slightly, 3 to 5 minutes. Stir in the paprika and chili powder. Cook for 1 minute, so the spices melt together with the onion.

4 Finish the chili: Stir in the tomatoes with their juices and bring to a simmer. Stir in the bell pepper and jalapeño. Taste for seasoning. Allow the mixture to simmer for 20 to 25 minutes, crushing some of the tomatoes with a wooden spoon. Then stir in the white beans, and if the chili is dry, stir in some of the reserved bean cooking liquid. Simmer so the beans absorb the flavors, 12 to 15 minutes. Remove the pot from the heat and allow the chili to rest for at least 15 minutes. This is like resting a cut of meat before slicing.

5 Serve the chili: Return the pot to the heat and simmer over medium heat for 3 to 5 minutes. Taste for seasoning. Stir the scallions into the chili, and ladle the chili into individual bowls. Serve the cheddar and sour cream on the side.

CHICKEN AND COCONUT MILK CURRY SOUP

Honestly this recipe is not so much about loving chicken soup in all forms as it is about my not-so-secret love affair with coconut milk. When I cook with it, I open the can and catch that first smell of rich coconut and my heart beats faster. While we think of chicken as rich, it actually screams for some added creamy richness. This soup is the answer.

4 cups **chicken stock**
2 (13.5-ounce) cans **unsweetened coconut milk**
Kosher salt
2 small **jalapeños**, seeded and thinly sliced
1 **Thai (bird's-eye) chile**, thinly sliced
3 tablespoons **fish sauce** (nam pla)
1 tablespoon **honey**
4 boneless, skinless **chicken breasts** (about 1 pound), cut into 1-inch pieces
Juice of 1 **lime**
1 tablespoon minced fresh **ginger**

In a medium pot, bring the chicken stock to a boil over high heat and cook until it has reduced by one-fourth; there should be about 3 cups liquid remaining. This will take 5 to 8 minutes. Add the coconut milk and 1 tablespoon salt, and simmer over medium heat until the flavors integrate, 3 to 5 minutes. Stir in the jalapeños, Thai chile, fish sauce, and honey. Simmer for a few minutes, and then stir in the chicken. Simmer gently over medium-low heat until the chicken is cooked through, 15 to 20 minutes. Taste for seasoning. Add the lime juice and ginger. Remove the pot from the heat and allow the soup to sit for 8 to 10 minutes before ladling it into individual bowls.

ZUCCHINI AND PARMIGIANO-REGGIANO SOUP

Zucchini is so delicious when briefly cooked and served with support from earthy thyme and fresh basil. This soup is surprisingly light and tastes just like springtime. Resist the urge to cook it any longer than described.

2 tablespoons **unsalted butter**
1 tablespoon **extra-virgin olive oil**
2 bunches (about 12) **scallions** (green and white parts), sliced
4 sprigs fresh **thyme**, tied with a string
Kosher salt and freshly ground **white pepper**
5 medium **zucchini** (about 2 pounds), thinly sliced
1 cup fresh **basil leaves**
1 cup freshly grated **Parmigiano-Reggiano cheese**

1 Make the soup: In a medium pot, heat the butter and olive oil over medium heat. Add the scallions, thyme, 1 tablespoon salt, and 2 teaspoons white pepper. Add the zucchini and season again with salt and pepper. Cook until softened, 5 to 8 minutes. Add 2 cups water and simmer, stirring from time to time with a wooden spoon, until the zucchini is tender when pierced with the tip of a knife, 10 to 15 minutes.

2 Finish the soup: Discard the thyme and transfer the soup to a blender. Add the basil and puree until the soup is smooth. Taste for seasoning. Ladle the soup into bowls and sprinkle liberally with the Parmigiano-Reggiano.

BEEF BRISKET SOUP

WITH QUICKIE PARMIGIANO-REGGIANO DUMPLINGS

I love brisket when it's simply roasted with carrots, but I always find it to be a cut of meat that is hard to serve juicy. The best way to balance this? Serve it as a soup with cheese dumplings. And I love the concept of developing the flavor of a soup by braising it in the oven. I prefer the second cut of brisket, which is wonderfully marbled with fat; the first cut is far more lean.

SOUP

3 tablespoons **canola oil**

3½ to 4 pounds **beef brisket**, preferably all second cuts

Kosher salt and freshly cracked **black pepper**

4 medium **garlic cloves**, grated

4 medium **red onions**, thinly sliced

6 sprigs fresh **thyme**, tied with string

1 cup **dry red wine**

1½ quarts **beef stock**

2 medium **carrots**, thinly sliced

6 **scallions** (green and white parts), thinly sliced

DUMPLINGS

4 tablespoons (½ stick) **unsalted butter**, softened

4 large **eggs**, lightly beaten

1 cup **all-purpose flour**

1 teaspoon **kosher salt**

1 teaspoon coarsely ground **black pepper**

1 cup freshly grated **Parmigiano-Reggiano cheese**

1 Preheat the oven to 350°F.

2 Cook the brisket: In a large ovenproof pot, heat the canola oil over medium heat. When the oil begins to smoke lightly, season both sides of the brisket pieces with salt and cracked black pepper. Use metal tongs to add the meat to the pot. Cook, undisturbed, on the first side until browned, 12 to 15 minutes. Turn the meat over onto the other side and cook until browned, another 12 to 15 minutes. Lower the heat and add the garlic, onions, thyme, and wine. Simmer until the wine evaporates, 10 to 12 minutes. Add 1 quart of the stock and 4 cups water and bring to a boil. Use a ladle to skim any impurities from the top. Transfer the pot to the oven and cook, uncovered, until the brisket is tender and the meat flakes easily with a fork, 1¾ to 2 hours.

3 Make the dumplings: In a medium bowl, whisk the butter until it is smooth and then whisk in the eggs. Use a wooden spoon to stir in the flour, salt, pepper, and ¾ cup of the Parmigiano-Reggiano. Do not overwork the mixture.

4 Cook the dumplings and finish the soup: Remove the pot from the oven and put it on a burner over medium heat. There should be about 1½ quarts liquid remaining. If there is less than that, add the remaining 2 cups beef stock and bring to a simmer. Discard the thyme. Remove the meat from the pot and set it aside on a platter to rest. Season the meat with salt. Drop teaspoonfuls of the dumpling dough into the simmering liquid. Stir in the carrots. Simmer gently until the dumplings and carrots are cooked, 6 to 8 minutes. Note: The dumplings float to the top when they are cooked. Then break the meat apart slightly and return it gently to the pot. Stir in the scallions and taste for seasoning.

5 Serve the soup: Ladle the soup into individual bowls, sprinkle with the remaining ¼ cup Parmigiano-Reggiano, and serve immediately.

ROASTED ROOT VEGETABLE SOUP

This is the kind of soup in which all of the ingredients come together to make something greater than the sum of their parts. I simmer the soup base on the stove while the vegetables roast in the oven. The roasted flavor mingles nicely with the pleasantly sour notes of the apple and vinegar.

1 large **celery root**, peeled and quartered

1 medium **rutabaga**, peeled and quartered

1½ pounds medium **parsnips**, peeled and halved lengthwise

¼ cup **extra-virgin olive oil**

Kosher salt and freshly ground **white pepper**

2 tablespoons **dark brown sugar**

4 tablespoons (½ stick) **unsalted butter**

4 medium **garlic cloves**, grated

4 **scallions** (green and white parts), minced

2 **Granny Smith apples**, cored and thinly sliced

1 teaspoon **ground allspice**

2 cups **heavy cream**

2 tablespoons **rice vinegar**

1 Preheat the oven to 350°F.

2 Cook the root vegetables: In a large bowl, toss the celery root, rutabaga, and parsnips with the olive oil, 1 tablespoon salt, 2 teaspoons white pepper, and the brown sugar. Spread the mixture out on two baking sheets and roast until completely tender when pierced with the tip of a knife, 1 to 1¼ hours. Note: The parsnips will likely cook more quickly than the other vegetables.

3 Meanwhile, make the soup base: In a large pot, heat the butter over medium heat and then add the garlic and scallions. Stir to blend with a wooden spoon, and season with 1 tablespoon salt and 1 teaspoon white pepper. Cook over medium heat until tender, 5 to 8 minutes. Add the apple slices and allspice. Cook, stirring from time to time, until the apples become tender, 5 to 8 minutes.

4 Finish the soup: Add 3 cups water and the cream to the pot and bring to a simmer. Add the roasted root vegetables and the rice vinegar. Transfer the soup, in batches, to a blender and puree. Return the puree to the pot and bring to a simmer over medium heat. Taste for seasoning. Serve immediately.

ALL-DAY, LOW-MAINTENANCE CHICKEN BROTH
WITH PEPPERED CARROTS

This hands-off recipe is as easy as making stock, but you get a chicken soup for dinner instead. The broth flavors itself simply from the long cooking. Prepping the carrots separately with the acidic wine, dark brown sugar, salt, and black pepper, and then stirring them into the soup at the end, gives the whole soup a deeper flavor.

SOUP
4 slices **bacon**, thinly sliced crosswise
2 medium **carrots**, cut into 1-inch pieces
2 **celery stalks**, cut into 1-inch pieces
2 cups **pearl onions**
Kosher salt and freshly ground **black pepper**
1 **whole chicken** (3 to 4 pounds)
1 small bunch fresh **thyme**, tied with string
4 cups **chicken stock**

CARROTS
1½ cups **dry red wine**
4 medium **carrots**, peeled and cut into ½-inch pieces
2 tablespoons **dark brown sugar**
Kosher salt and freshly ground **black pepper**

½ cup fresh **flat-leaf parsley leaves**
Splash of fresh **lemon juice**

1 **Start the soup:** In a pot that is large enough to hold the chicken, brown the bacon over medium heat until crispy, 5 to 8 minutes. Use a slotted spoon to transfer the bacon pieces to a kitchen towel to drain. Add the carrots, celery, and pearl onions to the bacon fat in the pot, and season with 1 tablespoon salt and 1 teaspoon pepper. Cook over medium heat until the vegetables become translucent, 12 to 15 minutes.

Add the chicken, thyme, stock, and 4 cups water. Bring to a boil, skim the surface with a ladle to remove any impurities, and then lower the heat and simmer the chicken, slowly and gently, until the chicken is completely cooked, about 1 hour.

2 **Cook the carrots:** In a medium sauté pan, bring the red wine to a simmer over medium heat. Add the carrots and brown sugar. Season with salt and a generous pinch of pepper, and cook over medium heat until the carrots are tender when pierced with the tip of a knife, 12 to 15 minutes. Note: If all of the liquid evaporates and the carrots are not tender, add ½ cup water and cook for an additional 5 to 8 minutes.

3 **Finish the soup:** Taste the chicken broth and adjust the seasoning as needed with salt and pepper. Remove the chicken and allow it to cool for a few minutes. Remove and discard the thyme sprigs. Pull the breast, thigh, and drumstick meat off the chicken, discarding all the skin and bones. Tear the meat into bite-size pieces and return them to the broth. Don't flake or break up the chicken too much or the soup will become mushy. Stir in the carrots and parsley. Taste for seasoning. Just before serving, add a touch of lemon juice and the reserved bacon.

SPICY CHICKEN AND FARRO SOUP
WITH CILANTRO

When I make a slow-cooking chicken soup, I expect the chicken meat to provide great taste and texture. I also expect it to flavor the broth as the soup simmers on the stove. You know how cooking something changes the aromas and energy of the kitchen: "What's cooking?" and "When will it be ready?" are what's heard when I cook this. The wonderfully chewy farro and fresh chile make this unique.

SOUP

1 tablespoon **canola oil**

1 medium **yellow onion**, thinly sliced

2 medium **carrots**, cut into 1½-inch-thick rounds

2 teaspoons crushed **red pepper flakes**

Kosher salt

1 **whole chicken** (3 to 4 pounds)

2 **bay leaves**

5 cups **chicken stock**

FARRO

1 tablespoon **extra-virgin olive oil**

1 cup **farro**

Kosher salt

½ cup fresh **cilantro leaves**

Juice of 1 to 2 **limes**, to taste

½ small **serrano chile**, cut into thin rounds

1 **Make the broth:** In a pot that is large enough to hold the chicken, heat the canola oil over medium heat. Add the onion, carrots, red pepper flakes, and a generous pinch of salt. Cook, stirring from time to time, until the vegetables become tender, 10 to 12 minutes. Then add the chicken, bay leaves, and chicken stock along with 3 cups water. Bring the liquid to a gentle simmer and skim the surface with a ladle, discarding any oil or foam that rises to the top. Sprinkle with salt, lower the heat, and finish cooking the chicken at a gentle simmer, 45 minutes to 1 hour.

2 **Meanwhile, cook the farro:** In a medium skillet, heat the olive oil over medium heat and add the farro. Cook, stirring constantly, to toast the farro, 3 to 5 minutes. Season it generously with salt, cover it with 2 cups water, and cook, stirring from time to time, until all of the water has been absorbed or evaporated and the farro is pleasantly chewy but tender, 35 to 40 minutes.

3 **Finish the soup:** Use a large spoon and a pair of tongs to remove the chicken from the soup. Transfer it to a baking sheet and allow it to cool for a few minutes. Then pull the breast and thigh meat off the chicken, discarding the skin and bones. Tear the meat into bite-size pieces. Stir the chicken, farro, and cilantro into the broth. Taste for seasoning. Allow the soup to sit on the stove for 10 to 15 minutes. Discard the bay leaves. Finish with a squeeze of lime juice and the serrano chile slices.

PORK SHOULDER SOUP
WITH SAVOY CABBAGE

Roasted or braised, pork shoulder is a cut of meat that keeps on giving: rich, but not particularly fatty. The pork is the star of the soup and flavors the broth at the same time. While the flavor of the soup usually drives the bus, here you want the meat to be tasty and fully cooked. Cook the cabbage in the soup while the meat rests on the side.

1 tablespoon **canola oil**

1 (3-pound) piece boneless **pork shoulder**

Kosher salt

1 teaspoon **caraway seeds**

12 medium **garlic cloves**, grated

½ cup **dry Marsala**

3 tablespoons **honey**

2 quarts **beef stock**

1 small head **Savoy cabbage**, cored, leaves torn into bite-size pieces

6 **scallions** (green and white parts), minced

1 Preheat the oven to 350°F.

2 Make the soup: In an ovenproof pot that is large enough to hold the pork shoulder, heat the oil over medium heat. Season the pork generously on all sides with 2 tablespoons salt and the caraway seeds. When the oil begins to smoke lightly, add the pork and brown it on the first side, 12 to 15 minutes. Use metal tongs to turn the shoulder over, and brown it for 12 to 15 minutes on that side. Lower the heat and stir in the garlic. Cook for 1 to 2 minutes, stirring so the garlic doesn't burn. Add the Marsala and honey, and simmer for 2 minutes. Pour in 6 cups of the beef stock along with 4 cups water. Bring the liquid to a simmer and skim off any impurities that rise to the surface. Put the pot in the oven and cook, uncovered, until the pork is tender and flakes easily with a fork, 2 to 2½ hours. Note: This is a soup, so we want to end up with enough delicious cooking liquid to make it so. Add water or more stock as the meat cooks so that it finishes cooking with 6 to 8 cups of tasty liquid at the end.

3 Finish the soup: When the pork is cooked, remove the meat from the pot. Stir the cabbage into the broth in the pot and simmer over medium-low heat until it becomes tender, 8 to 10 minutes. Taste for seasoning. Flake the meat gently into bite-size pieces and stir them into the soup. Top with the scallions and serve.

MY FAVORITE PHO

Oxtails are so beefy and almost sweet when browned. The bones and the meat really build the foundation for this pho. The warm spices—cinnamon and star anise—give this pho an aroma that makes my stomach growl as the soup cooks. Let the pho sit for a bit before you serve it (if you can resist). It's all about the beef . . .

2 tablespoons **canola oil**

4 pounds **beef oxtails**, cut into 3-inch pieces (ask your butcher to do this)

Kosher salt

2 small **yellow onions**, thinly sliced

4 medium **garlic cloves**, minced

1 (3-inch) **cinnamon stick**

5 **star anise pod**s

1 tablespoon **dark soy sauce**

3 tablespoons **sugar**

10 cups **beef stock**

12 ounces dried **flat rice stick noodles** (banh pho)

8 ounces **boneless beef round steak**, cut into ½-inch-thick slices

2 small **serrano chiles**, thinly sliced

¼ cup tightly packed fresh **cilantro leaves**

1 cup tightly packed fresh **basil leaves**

4 **scallions** (green and white parts), minced

1½ cups fresh **bean sprouts**

1 tablespoon **red wine vinegar**

1 Preheat the oven to 350°F.

2 Brown the oxtails: Heat a large ovenproof skillet over medium heat and add the canola oil. Season the oxtails on all sides with 2 tablespoons salt. When the oil begins to smoke lightly, remove the skillet from the heat and add the oxtail pieces in a single layer. Return it to medium heat and brown the oxtails on one side, 5 to 8 minutes. Use a pair of metal tongs to turn the oxtails over, and brown on the other side for 5 to 8 minutes. Add the onions and garlic, and continue cooking until the onions become tender, 3 to 5 minutes.

3 Build the broth: Add the cinnamon, star anise, soy sauce, sugar, beef stock, and 2 cups water to the meat. Bring to a boil, and then lower the heat and simmer for 8 to 10 minutes, skimming off any impurities that rise to the surface. Put the skillet in the oven, uncovered, and cook until the oxtail meat is tender and falling away from the bone, 2½ to 3 hours. Check the oxtails at the 1½-hour mark as cooking time may vary depending on the thickness and size of the meat.

4 Soak the noodles: After the oxtails have cooked for about 2½ hours, submerge the noodles in a large bowl of cold water. Fill a medium pot with water, add ¼ cup salt, and bring the water to a boil.

5 Prepare the beef and aromatics: When the oxtails are completely cooked, combine the beef round steak, chiles, cilantro, ½ cup of the basil leaves, the scallions, bean sprouts, and red wine vinegar in a large bowl. Use a pair of metal tongs to carefully transfer the oxtails to the bowl. Pour the broth over the vegetables.

6 Cook the noodles and finish the soup: Drain the noodles from the cold water and add to the pot of boiling water. Boil the noodles until they become tender, 1 to 2 minutes, and then immediately drain them. Add the noodles to the soup. Allow the soup to sit for a few minutes and taste for seasoning. Ladle it into bowls and top with the remaining basil leaves.

ITALIAN AMERICAN
PASTAS &
CLASSICS

MY MOM'S LINGUINE
WITH CLAMS

This is my mother's absolute favorite pasta dish, and I have watched her eat it everywhere from a diner to the finest Italian restaurants. Something magical happens when you combine the sweet and salty clams with a plate of cooked pasta. You don't need much else, though you could add a pinch of red pepper flakes if your taste runs to spicy. The only crime you can commit here is not thoroughly rinsing and soaking the clams to make sure grit isn't an ingredient in your final dish.

Kosher salt
1 cup bottled **clam juice**
1 cup **dry white wine**
1 **bay leaf**
Juice of 1 large **lemon**
4 dozen **littleneck clams**, scrubbed
¼ cup **extra-virgin olive oil**
4 large **garlic cloves**, minced
1 pound dried **linguine pasta**, preferably De Cecco brand
4 tablespoons **unsalted butter**
¼ cup fresh **flat-leaf parsley leaves**

1 Bring 6 quarts water to a boil in a large pot over high heat. Season with ½ cup salt. The pasta water should taste like seawater.

2 Cook the clams: Heat a large skillet over medium heat. Add the clam juice, white wine, 1 cup water, and the bay leaf, and simmer to reduce the liquid by about half, 2 to 3 minutes. Add half of the lemon juice. Rinse the clams one final time to make sure they are free of any sand or grit. Add the clams to the skillet in a single layer and cook, uncovered, until they open, 5 to 8 minutes. Be patient. Sometimes littleneck clams take a surprising length of time to open. As they open, use a pair of metal tongs to transfer the clams to a large bowl (discard any that do not open). Strain the cooking liquid through a double layer of cheesecloth or a coffee filter into a bowl; reserve the liquid.

3 Make the sauce: Wipe out the pan you used to cook the clams, and add the olive oil and garlic. Cook over low heat until the garlic becomes translucent, 5 to 8 minutes. Meanwhile, shell the clams. Add the clams and their reserved cooking liquid to the pan. Simmer over low heat. Taste for seasoning.

4 Cook the pasta: Add the pasta to the boiling water and stir so it doesn't stick to the bottom as it cooks. Cook the pasta until al dente, chewy but not hard or raw tasting, 8 to 10 minutes. Drain the pasta in a colander, reserving some of the pasta water in case you need it to adjust the sauce.

5 Finish the dish: Add the pasta to the pan containing the clams and sauce. Add the butter and parsley and toss to blend. Taste for seasoning. Add a little pasta water if needed to create a sauce that lightly coats the pasta. Stir in the remaining lemon juice. Serve immediately.

BUCATINI

WITH GARLIC AND OIL

I love the flavor of olive oil, and this dish celebrates that as opposed to making it a background note. That's why I use butter to work the garlic and finish with the olive oil so it is not cooked and remains more pronounced. The result is luxurious—all from five humble ingredients.

4 tablespoons (½ stick) **unsalted butter**

8 medium **garlic cloves**, grated

Kosher salt

1 pound dried **bucatini pasta**, preferably De Cecco brand

2 tablespoons good-quality **extra-virgin olive oil**

1   Make the sauce: In a large skillet, melt the butter over low heat and add the garlic. Season with salt and cook gently until the raw garlic flavor cooks out, 5 to 8 minutes. Remove the pan from the heat.

2   Meanwhile, cook the pasta: In a large pot, bring 6 quarts water to a rolling boil and season it with ½ cup salt. The pasta water should taste like mild seawater. Add the pasta to the boiling water and stir so it doesn't stick to the bottom as it cooks. Cook until the pasta is al dente (chewy but not hard or raw tasting), 10 to 12 minutes. Drain the pasta in a colander, reserving 1 cup of the pasta water in case you need it to adjust the sauce.

3   Finish the dish: Add ½ cup of the reserved pasta water to the garlic, put the skillet over high heat, and stir to blend. Toss in the pasta. Drizzle with the olive oil. Taste for seasoning. Add the remaining pasta water if needed to make a sauce that lightly coats the pasta. Serve immediately.

SPICY WEEKNIGHT MARINARA SAUCE

WITH BUCATINI

This is my family's weeknight sauce. While we do not believe in simmering sauce all day long, there are some differences of opinion in my parents' kitchen. My dad is all about tomato paste and a pinch of sugar with the tomatoes. My mother goes in a different direction, calling upon a little bit of carrot to add natural sweetness. I borrow from both in this recipe, adding sugar for my dad and carrots for my mom. This sauce tastes fresh and really complex despite how quickly it comes together. I like long, toothsome pasta for this dish.

Kosher salt

2 tablespoons **extra-virgin olive oil**

1 small **yellow onion**, thinly sliced

1 medium **carrot**, grated

5 medium **garlic cloves**, grated

1 teaspoon crushed **red pepper flakes**

1 teaspoon **sugar**

1 (28-ounce) can whole peeled **San Marzano tomatoes**

½ cup fresh **basil leaves**

1 pound dried **bucatini pasta**, preferably De Cecco brand

2 cups freshly grated **Parmigiano-Reggiano cheese**

1 In a large pot, bring 6 quarts water to a boil over high heat. Season with ½ cup salt. The pasta water should taste like seawater.

2 Meanwhile, make the sauce: In a medium skillet, heat the olive oil over medium heat. Add the onion, carrot, and garlic, and season with salt and the red pepper flakes. Cook until the onion becomes translucent, 5 to 8 minutes. Add the sugar and the tomatoes with their juices. Use a wooden spoon to break up some of the tomatoes. Cook, stirring from time to time, until the tomatoes are tender when pierced with the tip of a knife, 8 to 10 minutes. Add 1 cup water and continue cooking until the tomatoes fall apart, another 8 to 10 minutes. Taste for seasoning and stir in the basil leaves.

3 Cook the pasta: Add the pasta to the pot of boiling water and stir so it doesn't stick to the bottom as it cooks. Cook the pasta until it is al dente (chewy but not hard or raw tasting), 10 to 12 minutes. Drain the pasta in a colander, reserving some of the pasta water in case you need it to adjust the sauce.

4 Assemble the dish: In a large bowl, toss the pasta with half of the Parmigiano-Reggiano. (Tossing the pasta directly with the cheese before adding the sauce gives the pasta a richness and saltiness.) Stir the sauce into the pasta. Taste for seasoning. Add a little of the reserved pasta water if needed to create a sauce that lightly coats the pasta. Serve immediately with the remaining Parmigiano-Reggiano on the side for sprinkling.

PASTA PUTTANESCA

This classic Italian puttanesca sauce originated as a simple combination of ingredients that were on hand: a late-night sauce. When I was working at restaurants in Paris, I used to get off work really late—as did a whole group of other young cooks, all of us ironically starving after cooking food all night. I think because we made such austerely French food, our tastes went in a different direction. Give us some pasta and flavors of Italy: capers, olives, anchovies, and red pepper flakes! This was a dish I often made for my fellow cooks after rifling through my kitchen cabinets. I loved juxtaposing sophisticated three-star Michelin cuisine with this Italian peasant dish.

½ cup **extra-virgin olive oil**

2½ teaspoons drained **capers**

2 teaspoons crushed **red pepper flakes**

8 medium **garlic cloves**, minced

6 small canned **anchovy fillets**, finely chopped

1 cup **black olives**, such as Ligurian or Gaeta, pitted and roughly chopped

1 (28-ounce) can whole peeled **San Marzano tomatoes**

Kosher salt

1 pound dried **linguine pasta**, preferably De Cecco brand

1 **Make the sauce:** In a large skillet, heat the olive oil over medium heat. When it starts to get hot, add the capers and let them bubble and fry gently in the oil, 2 to 3 minutes. The capers will be mellowed from the frying and develop a crispy texture. When the capers start to float, add the red pepper flakes and garlic. Cook until the garlic is translucent, 2 to 3 minutes. Stir in the anchovies and olives. Pour the tomatoes, with their juices, over the mixture and crush some of the tomatoes with the back of a wooden spoon. Allow the sauce to simmer over medium heat until all of the flavors meld together, 10 to 15 minutes.

2 **Meanwhile, cook the pasta:** In a large pot, bring 6 quarts water to a rolling boil and add ½ cup salt. The pasta water should taste like seawater. Add the pasta to the boiling water and stir so it doesn't stick to the bottom as it cooks. Cook the pasta until it is al dente (chewy but not hard or raw tasting), 8 to 10 minutes. Drain the pasta in a colander, reserving a little of the pasta water in case you need it to adjust the sauce.

3 **Assemble the dish:** Transfer the sauce to a warmed serving bowl and add the pasta. Toss to blend. Add some of the reserved pasta water if needed to create a sauce that lightly coats the pasta. Taste for seasoning. Serve immediately.

ORECCHIETTE

WITH BACON, LEMON, AND CREAM

I love orecchiette pasta because it has great personality without taking over the whole dish. It is small enough that other ingredients (like bacon in this case) can hitch a ride to make a perfect bite. The sour cream mixed with the heavy cream tastes surprisingly light, especially when punctuated with the lemon and chives.

12 slices **bacon**, cut into 2-inch strips

1½ cups **heavy cream**

¼ cup **full-fat sour cream**

Kosher salt and freshly ground **black pepper**

Grated zest and juice of 1 **lemon**

2 teaspoons **Worcestershire sauce**, preferably Lea & Perrins brand

1 pound dried **orecchiette pasta**, preferably De Cecco brand

½ cup minced fresh **chives**

1 Cook the bacon: Heat a medium skillet over medium-high heat, and add ½ cup water and the bacon slices. Cook until all of the water evaporates and the bacon becomes crispy, 8 to 10 minutes. Transfer the bacon to a kitchen towel to drain, reserving the fat in the pan.

2 Make the sauce: In a large skillet, whisk together the heavy cream and sour cream. Season with 2 teaspoons salt and 1 teaspoon pepper. Simmer the cream mixture over medium heat, whisking, until it thickens, 5 to 8 minutes. Add the lemon zest, lemon juice, and Worcestershire sauce. Set aside.

3 Cook the pasta: In a large pot, bring 6 quarts water to a rolling boil and season with ½ cup salt. The pasta water should taste like seawater. Add the orecchiette to the boiling water and stir with a slotted spoon to make sure it does not clump or stick to the bottom as it cooks. Cook until the pasta is al dente (chewy but not hard or raw tasting), 6 to 8 minutes. Drain the pasta in a large colander, reserving ½ cup of the pasta water in case you need it to adjust the sauce.

4 Finish the dish: Reheat the pasta sauce over medium heat until it simmers gently. Add the pasta to the skillet and toss to coat it with the sauce. Remove the skillet from the heat and allow the pasta to rest for 2 minutes. Taste for seasoning. Stir in the bacon, some of the reserved bacon fat, chives, and pasta water if needed to make a sauce that lightly coats the pasta. Serve immediately.

GRANDMA GUARNASCHELLI'S LASAGNA

WITH MINI BEEF MEATBALLS

I did not grow up with an Italian grandmother who was always around the house cooking. I saw her only on special occasions—but then she would cook everything under the sun. Even as a kid, I was so impressed that she went to such painstaking trouble to roll and brown little meatballs and layer them throughout her lasagna. It's worth it. When making classic lasagna bolognese, the ground beef and tomato work beautifully together, but there is something about getting a bite of beef in a little meatball and then the burst of flavor from the tomato sauce that makes this dish even more delicious.

TOMATO SAUCE

½ cup **extra-virgin olive oil**

1 medium **yellow onion**, finely chopped

5 **garlic cloves**, minced

Kosher salt

1 teaspoon crushed **red pepper flakes**

2 teaspoons **sugar**

1 (28-ounce) can whole peeled **San Marzano tomatoes**

2 teaspoons dried **oregano**

1 cup tightly packed fresh **basil leaves**

MEATBALLS

12 ounces 90% lean **ground beef**, preferably chopped sirloin

4 ounces **ground veal**

Kosher salt

½ cup **panko bread crumbs**, toasted, plus more if needed

¾ cup freshly grated **Parmigiano-Reggiano cheese**

½ cup finely chopped fresh **flat-leaf parsley leaves**

1 large **egg**

3 medium **garlic cloves**, grated

⅓ cup **canola oil**

Kosher salt

1 pound dried **lasagna** sheets, preferably De Cecco brand

1 pound **whole-milk mozzarella cheese**, thinly sliced

1 pound **whole-milk ricotta cheese**

3 cups freshly grated **Parmigiano-Reggiano cheese**

1 **Make the sauce:** In a medium skillet, heat the olive oil over medium heat. Add the onion and garlic and season with 1 tablespoon salt. Stir in the red pepper flakes and sugar, and cook for about 2 minutes. Then add the tomatoes, with their juices, and the oregano. Cook for a few minutes over high heat, stirring from time to time. Taste for seasoning, add the basil leaves, and remove from the heat.

2 **Make the meatballs:** Put the beef and veal in a large bowl and spread the meat all over the bottom of the bowl and up the sides a little. (This will help you to distribute the seasonings evenly through the meat.) Sprinkle with 2 teaspoons salt. Then sprinkle the bread crumbs, Parmigiano-Reggiano, and parsley all over the meat and use your hands to mix the ingredients together. In a small bowl, whisk together the egg and garlic. Drizzle the egg mixture over the meat. Mix the meat thoroughly with your hands.

(recipe continues)

3 **Test a meatball:** Form 1 small meatball (about 1 inch in diameter) with your hands. Heat a splash of the canola oil in a small skillet over high heat. When the oil begins to smoke lightly, add the meatball, lower the heat, and cook it over medium heat for 2 to 3 minutes. Taste for seasoning and texture. If it seems too wet, add some more bread crumbs to the mixture in the bowl. If it is too dry, add a splash of water. Adjust the seasoning of the mixture in the bowl as needed. Roll the remaining meat into balls; you should have about 40 very small meatballs.

4 **Cook the meatballs:** Heat a large skillet over medium heat and add half of the remaining canola oil. When the oil begins to smoke lightly, remove the pan from the heat and add half of the meatballs in a single layer, spreading them apart somewhat so they have a chance to brown instead of steaming. Return the pan to high heat and brown the meatballs, turning them so they brown all around, until medium-rare, 2 to 3 minutes. Use a slotted spoon or spatula to transfer them to a baking sheet lined with a kitchen towel to drain. Wipe out the skillet and repeat the process with the remaining canola oil and meatballs.

5 **Cook the pasta:** Bring 6 quarts water to a rolling boil in a large pot over high heat and season with ½ cup salt. The pasta water should taste like seawater. Add the lasagna sheets, stirring with a slotted spoon to make sure they do not clump or stick to the bottom, and cook for 4 minutes. Drain in a colander, rinse under cold water, and drain again. The pasta should still be very firm to the touch. Separate the sheets carefully so they don't stick together.

6 Preheat the oven to 350°F.

7 **Assemble the lasagna:** Spoon a thin layer of the sauce over the bottom of a 9 × 13-inch baking pan. Arrange a layer of pasta sheets over the sauce. Sprinkle one-fourth of the mozzarella, ricotta, and Parmigiano-Reggiano over the pasta, and then add another thin layer of sauce. Dot the surface with about one-third of the meatballs, spacing them evenly. Repeat the layering process two more times. Add a final layer of pasta and top it with the remaining sauce and cheese.

8 **Bake the lasagna:** Cover the dish tightly with foil and put it in the center of the oven. Bake for 45 minutes. Then raise the oven temperature to 450°F and remove the foil. Bake the lasagna until the top browns slightly, 10 to 15 minutes. Remove the lasagna from the oven and allow it to cool for 15 minutes or so before serving.

CREAMY MUSHROOM LASAGNA

Mushrooms and Marsala come together so nicely with cream and cheese that meat and tomatoes are not even missed in this vegetarian dish. I love using portobellos for their deep earthy notes and cremini and white button for their clean flavor and great texture.

¾ cup **extra-virgin olive oil**

10 medium **garlic cloves**, minced

Kosher salt

6 sprigs fresh **thyme**, tied with string

6 medium **portobello mushrooms**, stemmed and thinly sliced

8 ounces **white button mushrooms**, thinly sliced (1 cup)

8 ounces **cremini mushrooms**, thinly sliced (1 cup)

Freshly ground **white pepper**

4 tablespoons **all-purpose flour**

1 pound dried **lasagna sheets**, preferably De Cecco brand

1 cup **dry Marsala**

2 cups **heavy cream**

8 ounces (1 cup) **mascarpone cheese**

1 cup fresh **basil leaves**

Grated zest of ½ **lemon**

1 pound **whole-milk mozzarella cheese**, thinly sliced

8 ounces **whole-milk ricotta cheese**

2 cups freshly grated **Parmigiano-Reggiano cheese**

1 Cook the mushrooms: Heat 2 large skillets over medium heat. Add half of the olive oil and garlic, and 1½ teaspoons salt to each. Cook until the garlic is translucent, 2 to 3 minutes. Add half of the thyme and mushrooms to each. Season each with an additional 1½ teaspoons salt and ½ teaspoon white pepper. Stir in half the flour to each skillet and cook until the mushrooms are tender and a lot of the liquid has evaporated, 12 to 15 minutes. Discard the thyme sprigs. Set the mushrooms aside, in one of the skillets.

2 Cook the pasta: Bring 6 quarts water to a rolling boil in a large pot over high heat and season with ½ cup salt. The pasta water should taste like seawater. Add the lasagna sheets, stirring with a slotted spoon to make sure they do not clump or stick to the bottom, and cook for 4 minutes. Drain in a colander, rinse under cold water, and drain again. The pasta should still be very firm to the touch. Separate the sheets carefully so they don't stick together.

3 Finish the sauce: Add the Marsala to the mushrooms, return the skillet to medium heat, and cook until the flavor of the alcohol has mellowed considerably and the liquid reduces to a couple of tablespoons, 10 to 12 minutes. Stir in the cream and simmer gently over medium heat until it coats the mushrooms, 5 to 8 minutes. Then stir in the mascarpone, basil, and lemon zest. Remove from the heat.

4 Preheat the oven to 350°F.

5 Assemble the lasagna: Spoon a thin layer of the sauce over the bottom of a 13-inch baking pan. Arrange a layer of pasta sheets over the sauce. Layer one-fourth of the mozzarella, ricotta, and Parmigiano-Reggiano cheeses over the pasta, and top with another thin layer of sauce. Repeat the layering process two more times. Add the final layer of pasta and top it with the remaining sauce and cheese.

6 Bake the lasagna: Cover the dish tightly with foil and bake for 45 minutes. Raise the oven temperature to 450°F and remove the foil. Bake until the top browns slightly, 10 to 15 minutes. Allow the lasagna to cool for 15 minutes or so before serving.

GNOCCHI MACARONI AND CHEESE

This is one of the top dishes at the restaurant, and it's easy to make at home. There is something about combining supple gnocchi with cream and melted cheese that is irresistible. While I could consider adding some crispy bacon bits for smoky flavor and texture, this dish by itself is a major crowd-pleaser.

2½ pounds **Idaho potatoes**

Kosher salt and freshly ground **black pepper**

1¼ to 1½ cups **all-purpose flour**, as needed

Pinch of grated **nutmeg**

2 large **eggs**, lightly beaten

1 cup freshly grated **Parmigiano-Reggiano cheese**

1 quart **heavy cream**

2 tablespoons **Dijon mustard**

2 cups grated **Gruyère cheese**

1 cup grated extra-sharp **cheddar cheese**

2 teaspoons **Worcestershire sauce**, preferably Lea & Perrins brand

½ teaspoon **Tabasco**

½ cup **panko bread crumbs**, toasted

1 Preheat the oven to 375°F.

2 Cook the potatoes: Bake the potatoes in the oven until they are tender when pierced with the tip of a knife, 1 to 1¼ hours. Let cool for 5 minutes. Lower the oven temperature to 350°F.

3 Make the gnocchi: Split the potatoes lengthwise and scoop the flesh into a potato ricer. Rice the potatoes and spread them out on a baking sheet. Season with salt and pepper. Sift 1¼ cups of the flour and the nutmeg over the potatoes. Add the eggs and ½ cup of the Parmigiano-Reggiano. Lightly knead the mixture together with your fingers. It should be fairly firm. Add additional flour if needed.

4 Cook the gnocchi: Bring a medium pot of salted water to a boil. Meanwhile, roll the potato dough into cylinders about ½ inch wide. Cut them into ½-inch-long pieces and roll them into small oval shapes. Add the gnocchi to the boiling water and cook for 1 minute or until the gnocchi float. With a slotted spoon, transfer the gnocchi to a baking sheet. Drain the water and set the pot back on the heat.

5 Make the sauce: In the same pot, bring the cream to a simmer over medium heat. Add the mustard, Gruyère, cheddar, and remaining ½ cup Parmigiano-Reggiano. Season with 2 teaspoons salt and 1 teaspoon pepper. Simmer gently, stirring constantly, until the cheese has integrated with the cream, 3 to 5 minutes. Stir in the Worcestershire and Tabasco. Taste for seasoning.

6 Bake the gnocchi: Add the gnocchi to the cheese sauce and stir gently to blend. Allow the gnocchi to rest in the pot, off the heat, for 5 to 10 minutes. Then transfer the gnocchi, with all the sauce, to a 9 × 13-inch baking dish and top with the panko. Bake in the oven just until hot, 8 to 10 minutes. Serve immediately.

EGGPLANT PARMIGIANA

This is, hands down, my all-time Italian American favorite, inspired by one of those casual sauce joints that lined Ninth Avenue in New York's Hell's Kitchen. Served volcanically hot, it encompasses everything I love about a hearty vegetarian meal.

SAUCE

¼ cup **extra-virgin olive oil**

3 medium **yellow onions**, thinly sliced

6 large **garlic cloves**, grated

Kosher salt

2 tablespoons crushed **red pepper flakes**

1 tablespoon **sugar**

3 (28-ounce) cans whole peeled **San Marzano tomatoes**

EGGPLANT

1 cup **all-purpose flour**

Kosher salt

6 large **eggs**

5 tablespoons **whole milk**

6 cups Italian-seasoned dried **bread crumbs**, toasted

1 tablespoon dried **oregano**

1 tablespoon fresh **thyme leaves**

3 medium **globe eggplants** (about 2½ pounds), cut into ½-inch-thick rounds

1½ to 2 cups **canola oil**, as needed

1½ pounds **whole-milk mozzarella cheese**, cut into 1-inch slices

1 cup freshly grated **Parmigiano-Reggiano cheese**

1   Make the tomato sauce: In a large skillet, heat the olive oil over medium heat. Add the onions and garlic and season with salt and the red pepper flakes. Cook until the onions become translucent, 3 to 5 minutes. Add the sugar and the tomatoes with their juices. Use a wooden spoon to break up some of the tomatoes, and cook, stirring from time to time, for 10 to 15 minutes. The tomatoes should be fairly broken down and the flavors coming together. Taste for seasoning. Set aside to cool.

2   Bread the eggplant: Put the flour in a medium shallow bowl and season it with salt. In another bowl, whisk together the eggs and milk. In a third bowl, combine the bread crumbs with the oregano and thyme. One by one, making sure to coat both sides, dip an eggplant slice in the flour and shake off any excess. Then dip it in the egg mixture and finally in the bread crumbs. Arrange the eggplant in a single layer on baking sheets.

3   Preheat the oven to 425°F.

4   Cook the eggplant: In a large skillet, pour canola oil to a depth of about ½ inch. Heat the oil until it begins to smoke lightly (alternatively, test with a thermometer and wait until it registers between 360° and 380°F). Working in batches, use a pair of kitchen tongs to add a single layer of the eggplant slices to the pan. Cook until they are golden brown, about 2 minutes on each side. Transfer the slices to a baking sheet lined with a kitchen towel to drain, and season them lightly with salt. Before adding another batch of slices to the pan, take care to reheat the oil.

5   Assemble the lasagna: In an 11 × 17-inch baking dish, spoon a thin layer of the tomato sauce over the bottom. Top with a layer of the eggplant (the slices can overlap slightly), one-third of the mozzarella slices, and one-fourth of the Parmigiano-Reggiano. Spoon another thin layer of sauce over the cheese, and repeat the layers two more times. Top with the remaining sauce and Parmigiano-Reggiano.

6   Bake the lasagna: Bake until the cheese is melted and bubbly, 15 to 20 minutes. Just before serving, put the dish under a hot broiler for a minute or two to get an extra-brown cheesy top.

NEW CHICKEN CLASSICS

CHICKEN CUTLETS

WITH PROSCIUTTO AND SAGE

This is an excuse for me to combine two of my favorite dishes: chicken cutlets and saltimbocca. Piney sage leaves and salty prosciutto give the cutlets a real boost of energy and flavor. I like to use finely ground bread crumbs and bread the cutlets twice. I simply put store-bought crumbs into the food processor to grind them into a finer texture. I love biting through that added layer of breading and then tasting the lemon and red wine vinegar in one moment and the prosciutto and sage in the other. It's like bright and vibrant combined with salty and earthy.

4 thin skinless **chicken cutlets** (about 4 ounces each)

1 tablespoon dried **oregano**

Kosher salt

4 large **eggs**, lightly beaten

3 cups plain finely ground dried **bread crumbs**

¾ cup **canola oil**

8 slices **prosciutto** (3½ to 4 ounces), torn into bite-size pieces

16 to 24 fresh **sage leaves**

2 large **garlic cloves**, grated

1 tablespoon **red wine vinegar**

Juice of 1 **lemon**

2 tablespoons **extra-virgin olive oil**

Freshly ground **black pepper**

1 **Prepare the cutlets:** Season both sides of the chicken cutlets with the oregano and with salt to taste. Put the eggs in a medium shallow bowl and the bread crumbs in another. Dip each piece of chicken in the egg (on both sides) and then in the bread crumbs, shaking off any excess. Arrange the cutlets on a baking sheet lined with parchment. Refrigerate for about 20 minutes, reserving the bowls of eggs and crumbs. Repeat the breading process with the cutlets. Refrigerate again.

2 **Cook the prosciutto and the sage:** In a large skillet, heat 1 tablespoon of the canola oil over medium heat. Reduce the heat to low and add half of the prosciutto pieces and cook over low heat until crispy, 8 to 10 minutes. Using a slotted spoon, transfer the prosciutto to a plate lined with a kitchen towel. Add another tablespoon of the canola oil and repeat with the remaining prosciutto. Add the sage leaves to the skillet and cook until they turn pale in color and become crispy, 2 to 3 minutes. Transfer them to the towel-lined plate and season with salt. Off the heat, stir the garlic into the cooking oil and season it with salt to taste. Allow the garlic to simmer in the warm oil for 1 to 2 minutes to cook off the raw flavor, and then transfer the garlic and oil to a medium bowl.

3 **Cook the chicken cutlets:** Heat the remaining canola oil in a large skillet over medium heat. When it starts to smoke lightly, add the chicken cutlets in a single layer and cook on their first side until golden brown, 3 to 5 minutes. Turn them over onto the other side and cook for 5 to 7 minutes. Transfer the cutlets to a kitchen towel to drain. Note: It's better to cook these in batches than to overcrowd the pan.

4 **Make the vinaigrette and finish the dish:** In the bowl containing the reserved garlic and oil, whisk together the red wine vinegar, lemon juice, and olive oil. Season with salt and pepper. Arrange the cutlets on a serving platter and drizzle with the vinaigrette. Top with the sage leaves and prosciutto.

CHICKEN CUTLETS WITH
PROSCIUTTO AND SAGE

MOM'S CHICKEN CACCIATORE

Cacciatore means "hunter's style," and I always imagine a group of hunters gathered around a fire while digging into bowls of this belly-warming braise. It's the same way I imagine the crew from a fishing boat gathered on the dock for some fish stew. This dish also tastes great the next day. While I add thyme and bay leaves to the braise early on, I like to treat rosemary with more care; it has a medicinal flavor when cooked too long. Instead of letting the rosemary cook in the skillet the whole time, I steep it for a few minutes only, then remove and discard it.

2 tablespoons **canola oil**

1 **whole chicken** (3½ to 4 pounds), cut into 10 pieces

Kosher salt

1 tablespoon crushed **red pepper flakes**

2 medium **yellow onions**, thinly sliced

6 large **garlic cloves**, grated

8 ounces **white button mushrooms**, thinly sliced

1 cup **dry white wine**

1 (28-ounce) can whole peeled **San Marzano tomatoes**

2 **bay leaves**

4 sprigs fresh **thyme**

1 sprig fresh **rosemary**

1 Brown the chicken: Heat a large skillet over high heat and add the canola oil. Arrange the chicken pieces in a single layer on a baking sheet, and season them with salt and the red pepper flakes. Turn the pieces over and season on the other side. When the oil begins to smoke lightly, reduce the heat to medium. Use a pair of metal tongs to carefully add the chicken, skin side down, to the skillet. Do not overcrowd the pan. Sauté, resisting the temptation to move or turn the pieces, until they have browned on the first side, 5 to 8 minutes. Turn the chicken pieces over and brown on that side, 5 to 8 minutes. Transfer the chicken pieces to a rimmed baking sheet and set aside.

2 Make the sauce and cook the chicken: In the skillet where you browned the chicken, add the onions and a pinch of salt and cook until the onions become translucent, 3 to 5 minutes. Add garlic and mushrooms and cook over medium heat, until the vegetables turn light brown, 10 to 12 minutes. Add the white wine, season with salt, and simmer until almost all the liquid is gone, 5 to 8 minutes. (Cooking the wine out first is important so there won't be any raw alcohol flavor in the sauce.) Add the tomatoes with their juices and bring to a simmer. Add the bay leaves and thyme sprigs. Arrange the chicken pieces in a single layer in the pan and pour any accumulated juices into the sauce as well. Simmer over low heat until the chicken is cooked through, 40 to 45 minutes. Use a wooden spoon to break up some of the tomatoes. Remove the pan from the heat and add the rosemary. Allow the chicken to rest on the stove off the heat for about 10 minutes, and then remove and discard the rosemary sprig, thyme sprigs, and bay leaves. Taste for seasoning, and serve.

CHICKEN MARBELLA 2.0

The flavors of Chicken Marbella are a wonderful combination that doesn't seem to make sense on paper but makes all the sense in the world when you take that first bite. Prunes and olives? Only the Silver Palate could have made such a brilliant combination. Think about the deep sweetness of prunes against the salt and brine of the olives and oregano and the flavor starts to take shape. In my little tweak, I exchanged the capers and brine for mustard to ramp up the acidity, reduce the salt, and give the marinade (and therefore the sauce) more body. It's now a simpler dialogue between olive and prune with mustard as the mediator. The chicken takes these flavors and runs with them.

4 tablespoons **Dijon mustard**

½ cup **red wine vinegar**

1 cup **dry vermouth**

2 **whole chicken**s (3 to 3½ pounds each), quartered

3 tablespoons **dark brown sugar**

15 medium **garlic cloves**

1 tablespoon dried **oregano**

½ cup pitted **prunes**, coarsely chopped

¼ cup **green Cerignola** or **Castelvetrano olives**, pitted

2 **bay leaves**

½ cup coarsely chopped fresh **flat-leaf parsley leaves**

1 Marinate the chicken: In a large, wide bowl, whisk together the mustard, vinegar, and vermouth. Add the chicken pieces to the bowl along with the brown sugar, garlic, oregano, prunes, olives, and bay leaves. Flatten the chicken pieces so they are as close as possible to submerged in the marinade, and cover the bowl tightly with plastic wrap. Refrigerate for at least 4 hours, rotating the pieces at some point in the process so the marinade coats every part, and preferably overnight.

2 Preheat the oven to 375°F.

3 Cook the chicken: Remove the pieces of chicken from the marinade and arrange them in a single layer in a 2-inch-deep baking pan lined with foil. Put the chicken in the oven and bake until the meat is cooked through and the juices run clear, 40 to 45 minutes.

4 Finish the sauce: Pour the marinade into a small saucepan and bring to a boil over high heat. Then reduce the heat and simmer the marinade gently until the liquid has reduced by a little more than half, 10 to 12 minutes. Taste for seasoning. Stir in the parsley.

5 Finish the dish: When the chicken is cooked and has had a few minutes to rest, arrange the chicken pieces on a serving platter, and spoon the juices, olives, and prunes around them (discard the bay leaves). Taste for seasoning and add salt if needed. Pour the marinade over the chicken, and serve.

SWEET-AND-SOUR CHICKEN

"Sweet-and-sour chicken" means a dish that you will make and then eat double what you normally would. In one bite you get the sweetness tempered by the sour, and in the next you get the sour tempered by the sweet. Add a little chicken and bacon in the middle for the balance of richness, and you have a winner. This is a two-pan meal with onions and seasonings simmering away in one pot and then the tomatoes and white wine simmering in delicious chicken drippings in the other.

2 tablespoons **canola oil**

1 (3½ to 4-pound) **chicken**, cut into 10 pieces

Kosher salt and freshly ground **white pepper**

4 slices **bacon**, cut into ½-inch pieces

1 tablespoon **unsalted butter**

1 pound **pearl onions**, peeled

½ cup **dry white wine**

2 tablespoons **golden raisins**, coarsely chopped

2 tablespoons **dark brown sugar**

2 tablespoons **red wine vinegar**

1 pint **cherry tomatoes**, halved

1 Preheat the oven to 375°F.

2 Brown the chicken: Heat a large skillet over medium heat and add the canola oil. Arrange the chicken in a single layer on a baking sheet and season with salt and white pepper. Turn the pieces over and season again. When the oil begins to smoke lightly, use a pair of metal tongs to carefully add the pieces, skin side down, to the skillet. Do not overcrowd the pan. Resist the temptation to move or turn the pieces, until they have browned on the first side, 5 to 8 minutes. Turn the chicken over and brown on the second side, 5 to 8 minutes. Transfer the chicken to a baking sheet and bake in the oven until cooked through, 15 to 18 minutes.

3 Cook the bacon: Add the bacon to the skillet you used to cook the chicken and cook until browned and crispy, 12 to 15 minutes. Transfer the bacon to a kitchen towel. Reserve the skillet.

4 Make the sweet-and-sour sauce: In a medium saucepan, melt the butter over medium heat and add the onions. Cook, stirring from time to time with a wooden spoon, until they brown and become tender, 5 to 8 minutes. Add the white wine, raisins, brown sugar, red wine vinegar, and ½ cup water. Simmer until the liquid reduces and the onions are cooked through, 12 to 15 minutes. Season with salt and white pepper.

5 Finish the dish: In the skillet you used to cook the bacon, pour off any excess grease and add the tomatoes. Simmer over medium heat until almost all the liquid is gone, 5 to 8 minutes. Pour the sweet-and-sour sauce into the skillet and then add the pieces of chicken. Bring to a simmer over medium heat and toss to coat the chicken with sauce. Taste for seasoning. Arrange the chicken in a single layer on a serving platter. Top with the bacon. Serve immediately.

SESAME CHICKEN DRUMSTICKS

My daughter refers to chicken drumsticks as "microphones." I love to watch her latch on to one of these. Lightly coated in sesame and a little paprika, these chicken legs are a great way to introduce the concept that a spice can add tingle, zing, and amplified flavor without burning your mouth. The acidity of the lime also keeps this dish light. "I don't like spicy food, Mom," says my daughter as she devours a few of these drumsticks. I can even get away with putting a couple of them in her lunch for school . . .

2 tablespoons **white sesame seeds**

2 pounds **chicken drumsticks**

Kosher salt

1 teaspoon **hot paprika**

1 tablespoon **dark sesame oil**

Juice of 1 large **lime**

1 Preheat the oven to 400°F.

2 Toast the sesame seeds and prepare the chicken: Spread the sesame seeds in an even layer on a rimmed baking sheet, and put it in the center of the oven. Toast until the seeds are light brown, 3 to 5 minutes, and then remove from the oven. In a medium bowl, toss the drumsticks with salt to taste, the paprika, and the sesame oil. Arrange the drumsticks on a baking sheet lined with foil, spacing them far apart.

3 Bake the chicken and finish the dish: Bake the drumsticks for 15 to 18 minutes. Rotate the baking sheet in the oven and bake for an additional 15 to 18 minutes. In a large bowl, toss the chicken with the lime juice and toasted sesame seeds. Transfer to a serving platter. Serve immediately.

STICKY FINGERS BAKED CHICKEN WINGS

I keep a stash of this sauce in the refrigerator. I tend to forget about it and then one day when I find myself standing in front of the open fridge, racking my brain for something to coat my chicken, I remember it's there: just toss the wings in it and bake. Make a double batch of the sauce and store it in the fridge for a few weeks. I like to broil the wings for a few minutes at the end so that the tips burn slightly. There is no way to eat one of these and emerge clean-handed.

1½ cups **ketchup**, preferably Heinz brand

1 cup **cider vinegar**

2 tablespoons **Worcestershire sauce**, preferably Lea & Perrins brand

¼ cup **dark soy sauce**

1 cup packed **dark brown sugar**

1 tablespoon **dry mustard**, preferably Colman's

1 tablespoon **Dijon mustard**

½ cup **chili powder**

6 medium **garlic cloves**, grated

1 (4-inch) knob fresh **ginger**, peeled and finely grated

2 **lemons**, cut into ½-inch-thick slices

24 **chicken wings** (2 to 2½ pounds)

Kosher salt

1 **Make the sauce:** In a large saucepan, combine the ketchup, cider vinegar, Worcestershire sauce, soy sauce, dark brown sugar, dry mustard, Dijon mustard, and chili powder. Whisk to blend. Bring to a simmer over medium heat, and add the garlic, ginger, and lemon slices. Simmer until the vinegar mellows slightly and the flavors start to meld together, at least 20 to 25 minutes. Keep warm.

2 Preheat the oven to 375°F.

3 **Season and cook the wings:** In a large bowl, toss half of the sauce with the chicken wings until they are evenly coated. Season them lightly with salt. Arrange the chicken wings on a baking sheet lined with foil, placing them as far apart as possible for better browning. Bake the wings until they start to brown, 15 to 18 minutes. Then rotate the pan and bake until the juices run clear and the wings are nicely browned, 18 to 20 minutes more. If you like, run them under a hot broiler for 2 to 3 minutes for maximum browning.

4 **Serve the wings:** Arrange the chicken wings on a serving platter and drizzle with the remaining sauce (or serve with a bowl of the sauce for dunking).

WHOLE ROASTED CHICKEN
WITH BACON

This is the kind of recipe that my mom would pull out of her notebook from time to time. She would wrap the chicken in the bacon slices and I'd watch as the bacon browned and crisped and hardened into a smoky shell as it cooked. The bacon just gives the chicken the kind of skin and moistness we wish every roast chicken had!

1 **whole chicken** (3 to 3½ pounds)
Kosher salt and freshly ground **black pepper**
6 sprigs fresh **thyme**
2 **lemons**, each cut into 8 wedges
12 slices **bacon**
1 tablespoon **Dijon mustard**

1 Preheat the oven to 500°F.

2 **Prepare the chicken:** Season the outside of the chicken with salt and pepper. Fill the cavity with the thyme sprigs and lemon wedges. Turn the chicken so the cavity is facing you. Put one end of a bacon slice squarely over the left thigh, run it over the breast meat, and finish by covering the right thigh. Repeat with 9 more strips of bacon, slightly overlapping, so the thighs and all of the breast meat are covered. Then wrap one strip, slightly overlapping, around each drumstick.

3 **Cook the chicken:** Transfer the chicken to a shallow baking pan fitted with a roasting rack and put it in the center of the oven. Roast for 20 minutes, and then lower the oven temperature to 350°F. Cook until the juices run clear or the internal temperature reaches 160°F, another 40 to 50 minutes. Remove the chicken from the oven and allow it to rest for 15 minutes before carving. The bacon should form a hard shell over the breast meat. Take care to use a sharp knife when carving so the bacon stays on top of the white meat.

4 **Finish the dish:** Make a sauce by pouring the juices from inside the cavity (along with the thyme and lemon wedges) into the roasting pan. Put the pan over medium heat and bring to a simmer. Whisk in the mustard, add 2 tablespoons water, and simmer for 2 to 3 minutes to allow the sauce to come together. Strain, pressing down on the lemon wedges to get the juice into the sauce, and season with salt and pepper. Taste for seasoning. Discard the lemon wedges. Serve immediately.

WHOLE
SPICE-RUBBED CHICKEN
WITH ROASTED GARLIC AND LEMONS

I have a beautiful roasting pan that I pull out when I make a roast beef or Thanksgiving turkey. I leave it in the cabinet when I roast a chicken. Instead, I like to use a rimmed baking sheet with a rack or a shallow roasting pan—anything with low sides that allow for maximum browning of the skin. The cinnamon sticks and pleasantly bitter cooked lemon in the sauce amplify the flavors from the garlic and paprika. It reminds me of when I eat rye toast with marmalade and get that balanced bite of caraway, butter, and marmalade. So good.

1 **whole chicken** (3½ to 4 pounds)

Kosher salt

1 tablespoon **hot paprika**

1 tablespoon **dry mustard**

4 medium heads **garlic**, unpeeled, halved widthwise

2 tablespoons **extra-virgin olive oil**

1 cup **sugar**

4 large **lemons**

2 (3-inch) **cinnamon stick**s

1 tablespoon **fennel seeds**

½ cup **red wine vinegar**

1 Preheat the oven to 500°F.

2 Cook the chicken and garlic: Season the outside of the chicken with salt. Use a fine-mesh strainer to sprinkle an even layer of the paprika and mustard over the whole chicken and cover the bird with aluminum foil. Transfer the chicken to a shallow baking pan fitted with a roasting rack, and roast for 15 minutes. Then lower the oven temperature to 350°F. In a small bowl, toss the garlic cloves with the olive oil and season with salt. Remove the foil and arrange the garlic cloves around the chicken. Roast uncovered until the juices run clear or the internal temperature reaches 160°F, 40 to 50 minutes.

Remove the chicken from the oven and allow it to rest for 15 minutes before carving.

3 While the chicken is roasting, cook the lemons: In a medium saucepan, combine the sugar, 2 teaspoons salt, and the lemons with 3 cups water. Bring to a simmer over medium heat. Add the cinnamon sticks and fennel seeds. Simmer until the sauce becomes slightly syrupy, 10 to 12 minutes. Add the red wine vinegar and cook over medium heat until the lemons become tender when pierced with the tip of a knife, 30 to 35 minutes. Allow the lemons to sit in the hot liquid for 15 minutes; then remove them with a slotted spoon. On a flat surface, cut each lemon into ½-inch-thick rounds. Remove the pits (if any). Set the slices aside in some of the cooking liquid to keep them moist until ready to serve.

4 Finish the dish: Arrange the chicken on a serving platter with the garlic cloves around it. Put the baking pan on a burner and simmer any chicken cooking juices over medium heat. Remove from the heat and stir in the drained lemon slices. Taste for seasoning and simmer for 2 to 3 minutes to allow the flavors to come together. Pour the sauce over the chicken. Serve with the roasted garlic.

CHICKEN BREASTS
WITH TARRAGON BUTTER

Tarragon is one of those ingredients that takes me straight to a French bistro. I imagine myself with a glass of super-dry white wine, the bustle of people around me, and this chicken dish in front of me. I never thought about how much a little butter could add to chicken until I tasted a dish as simple and tasty as this. When the thyme links up with the tarragon butter as it comes out of the oven, the combination is simply herbaceous. The Maldon salt also adds more texture. For an even deeper flavor, make the tarragon butter and let it sit in the fridge overnight.

2 tablespoons **canola oil**

2 (8-ounce) skin-on, bone-in **chicken breasts**

Kosher salt and freshly ground **black pepper**

1 tablespoon fresh **thyme leaves**

4 tablespoons **unsalted butter**, softened

Grated zest and some juice from 2 **lemons**

Leaves from 4 sprigs **fresh tarragon**, coarsely chopped (about 1 tablespoon)

Maldon sea salt

1 Preheat the oven to 350°F.

2 Cook the chicken breasts: In a medium ovenproof sauté pan, heat the canola oil over medium heat. Season the chicken breasts with salt and pepper. Sprinkle with the thyme leaves. When the oil begins to smoke lightly, remove the pan from the heat and add the chicken breasts, skin side down. Return the pan to the heat and brown the skin for 5 to 7 minutes.

Turn the chicken pieces over and put the pan in the center of the oven. Cook the chicken until the skin is golden brown and the juice runs clear when you pierce the flesh gently with the tip of a knife, 20 to 25 minutes. (Alternatively, a meat thermometer should register 160°F when inserted into the thickest part of the breast meat.)

3 Meanwhile, make the tarragon butter: In a small bowl, whisk the butter with the lemon zest and a couple squeezes of lemon juice. Stir the tarragon into the butter and season it with Maldon salt.

4 Finish the dish: When the chicken is cooked, remove the pan from the oven and squeeze any remaining lemon juice over the meat. Before removing the chicken from the pan, smear some of the tarragon butter on the flesh side of the chicken. Arrange the chicken breasts, skin side up, on a serving platter and top with the remaining butter. Serve immediately.

MY DAD'S LEMON CHICKEN

While my mother dabbled in French pâtés, Indian food, and American cakes of all kinds, my father found his true passion in Chinese food. He still has a special kitchen cabinet filled with various soy sauces, vinegars, and spices. When he cooks, every inch of the kitchen is covered in small bowls with all the prep. This dish remains, by far, my favorite—and requires the fewest bowls. The cornstarch creates a great crispy layer on the chicken, and the tang of the lemon and ginger makes it addictive.

2 large **eggs**

6 tablespoons **cornstarch**

1 pound boneless, skinless **chicken thighs**, cut into 1-inch cubes

Kosher salt

2 tablespoons **dark soy sauce**

Juice of 2 **lemons**

1 tablespoon **distilled white vinegar**

2 teaspoons **sugar**

1 tablespoon grated fresh **ginger**

2 medium **garlic cloves**, grated

6 cups **peanut oil**

1 **lemon**, cut into ¼-inch-thick rounds

½ small **Thai (bird's-eye) chile**

1 **Marinate the chicken:** In a large bowl, whisk the eggs with 3 tablespoons of the cornstarch until smooth. Season the chicken on all sides with salt, and submerge it in the egg mixture. Cover with plastic wrap and refrigerate for at least 4 hours and up to 6 hours.

2 **Make the lemon sauce:** In a medium saucepan, combine the soy sauce, lemon juice, white vinegar, and sugar. Simmer over medium heat until the flavors come together and the sugar has dissolved, 3 to 5 minutes. Add the ginger and garlic, and simmer for 1 additional minute. Remove from the heat and keep the sauce warm.

3 **Fry the chicken:** Pour the peanut oil into a large heavy-bottomed pot (or wok) and bring it to 350°F over medium-low heat. (Use a deep-frying thermometer to monitor the temperature as it heats.) Remove the chicken from any liquid in the bowl and spread it in an even layer on a baking sheet. Use a fine-mesh sieve to sprinkle the remaining 3 tablespoons cornstarch in an even layer over all sides of the chicken pieces. Drop some of the lemon slices carefully into the oil and fry until light brown with crisped edges, just 1 to 2 minutes. Remove with a slotted spoon to a baking sheet lined with a kitchen towel. In batches, add the chicken to the hot oil and cook until crispy and browned, 3 to 5 minutes. Use a slotted spoon to transfer the chicken to the baking sheet. Season with salt.

4 **Finish the dish:** Stir the lemon slices and fresh chile into the sauce. Arrange the fried chicken pieces on a platter, and pour the sauce over them. Serve immediately.

SPATCHCOCKED! ROASTED CHICKEN

This is a really cool technique that will impress friends and family. Far more important, it's a great way to roast poultry and get every inch of that skin exposed to heat and browned. The skin forms a sheet over the whole chicken, which is opened up through the back and spread out on a baking sheet. We want low sides on the roasting pan to encourage browning. This is high-heat cooking, so watch carefully to make sure the chicken doesn't burn.

1 (4-pound) **whole chicken**
Kosher salt

1 Preheat the oven to 500°F.

2 **Butterfly the chicken:** Remove any innards from the chicken. Put the whole chicken, breast side down, on a flat surface. (I like to put a kitchen towel underneath the bird to prevent the chicken from sliding around as I work.) Find the backbone running down the center. Use a pair of sharp poultry shears or scissors to cut up along the backbone on one side and then cut up on the other side. Remove the backbone and save it to add to chicken stock. Flip the bird over, breast side up. Gently press down on the breast meat to open the chicken up and flatten it. The breastbone will break as you press. The chicken should now sit almost flat.

3 **Cook the chicken:** Season the chicken on all sides with salt. Put the chicken on a baking sheet, put the sheet in the center of the hot oven, and cook undisturbed for 20 minutes. Then lower the oven temperature to 450°F and cook for an additional 30 to 35 minutes. The chicken is ready when an instant-read thermometer inserted in the thickest part of the bird registers 155° to 160°F.

4 **Serve the chicken:** Remove the chicken from the oven and allow it to rest for at least 10 to 15 minutes before transferring it to a cutting board for carving. I like to cut the pieces with clean poultry shears or scissors.

YOGURT-MARINATED CHICKEN THIGHS

WITH PICKLED MUSTARD SEEDS

My mother went through a big Indian cooking phase, and as a hungry and curious kid, I couldn't understand the effect yogurt was going to have on chicken. And then I tasted this dish. The yogurt tenderizes, it enriches the flavor, and it even adds a slight tang to the meat. The mustard seeds and grapes give freshness and a slight heat. Mustard seeds are a different ingredient once they're plumped in liquid.

½ cup **whole-milk yogurt**

1 tablespoon grated fresh **ginger**

1 teaspoon ground **cumin**

1 teaspoon crushed **red pepper flakes**

3 to 3½ pounds skin-on, bone-in **chicken thighs**

½ cup **cider vinegar**

2 tablespoons **honey**

2 tablespoons **yellow mustard seeds**

2 tablespoons **grainy mustard**

Kosher salt

1 cup seedless **red grapes**

Juice of 1 large **lemon**

1 Marinate the chicken: In a large bowl, combine the yogurt, ginger, cumin, and red pepper flakes. Whisk until smooth. Slather the chicken thighs with the yogurt mix, cover with plastic wrap, and refrigerate for at least 4 hours or, ideally, overnight.

2 Make the pickled mustard seeds: In a small saucepan, combine the cider vinegar, honey, and mustard seeds with ½ cup water. Bring to a simmer over medium heat and cook until almost all of the liquid has evaporated, 20 to 25 minutes. Remove from the heat and let stand for 5 minutes. Then stir in the grainy mustard.

3 Preheat the oven to 400°F.

4 Cook the chicken: Remove the chicken pieces from the marinade, season them with salt, and arrange them on a baking sheet lined with foil. For better browning, arrange the thighs as far apart as possible. Roast for 10 minutes. Then open the oven and toss the grapes onto the baking sheet. Continue cooking until the chicken is cooked through and the juices run clear, 25 to 30 minutes.

5 Finish the dish: Let the chicken rest for 10 to 15 minutes. Arrange the chicken and grapes on a serving platter. Squeeze the lemon juice over it and drizzle with the mustard sauce. Serve immediately.

CHICKEN UNDER A BRICK

WITH SOY AND SESAME

This is the kind of dish where you can cook one breast for yourself or eight breasts for a group of friends. The soy has a strong flavor, so having the sesame seeds and butter along for the ride tempers that saltiness. Flattening the chicken as it cooks also creates a wonderful skin without deep-frying or adding any more fat to the equation. More than anything, this dish is delicious and simple.

2 tablespoons **canola oil**

2 skin-on, bone-in **chicken breasts** (about 10 ounces each), small wing bone intact

Kosher salt and freshly ground **black pepper**

1 tablespoon **sesame seeds**

2 tablespoons **unsalted butter**, softened

2 teaspoons **dark soy sauce**

1 medium **shallot**, minced

1 **lemon**

Leaves from 2 sprigs fresh **mint**

1 Preheat the oven to 350°F.

2 Cook the chicken: Heat an ovenproof skillet that is large enough to hold the chicken breasts over medium heat and add the oil. Season the chicken breasts on both sides with salt and pepper. When the oil begins to smoke lightly, remove the skillet from the heat and put the breasts, skin side down, in the pan. Return the pan to the heat, put a small piece of foil over the breasts, and top that with a smaller pan (or pans) and something heavy in the center to weight the meat down as it cooks. Cook over medium heat, undisturbed, for 15 to 20 minutes. When the skin is crisped and browned, remove the weights, turn the pieces over, and continue cooking until the chicken is cooked through, 8 to 10 minutes.

3 Meanwhile, toast the sesame seeds: Spread the sesame seeds in a thin layer on a rimmed baking sheet and toast in the oven until light brown, 3 to 5 minutes. Remove the baking sheet from the oven.

4 Make the seasoned butter: In a medium bowl, whisk the butter and soy sauce together. Stir in the shallot, sesame seeds, and a few grates of lemon zest.

5 Finish the dish: When the chicken is cooked, squeeze the juice from the lemon over the meat. Before removing the chicken from the pan, smear some of the seasoned butter over the flesh side of the chicken. Arrange the chicken breasts, skin side up, on a serving platter, and top with the mint leaves. Serve immediately.

STAND-ALONE
MAIN
COURSES

LAMB TAGINE

I love the Moroccan flavors in this dish—somehow they seem as if they have mingled for days instead of just hours. Lamb has a powerful flavor on its own, and I find that with the right blend of spices, it tastes like an even better version of itself. I use lamb shoulder or leg meat for this recipe. The grated onions cooked with the lamb add natural body to the sauce. Because the lamb itself is hearty, I try to keep the rest of the ingredients light enough to allow the meat to take center stage.

FOR THE MARINADE
2 teaspoons **cumin seeds**
2 teaspoons **coriander seeds**, lightly crushed
2 teaspoons **caraway seeds**
1 teaspoon crushed **red pepper flakes**
2 teaspoons **garlic powder**
½ teaspoon ground **cloves**
½ teaspoon ground **ginger**
2 tablespoons **extra-virgin olive oil**
6 medium **garlic cloves**, grated
1 tablespoon **honey**
Juice of 1 **lemon**
¼ cup **golden raisins**, coarsely chopped

2 pounds **lamb meat**, preferably shoulder, cut into 1½- to 2-inch cubes
Kosher salt

VINAIGRETTE
1 tablespoon **yellow mustard seeds**
2 tablespoons **red wine vinegar**
Juice of 1 small **orange**
Juice of 1 **lemon**
¼ cup **extra-virgin olive oil**

2 tablespoons **canola oil**
3 medium **yellow onions**, grated
1 quart **beef stock**

1 Marinate the meat: In a medium bowl, combine the cumin, coriander, and caraway seeds with the red pepper flakes, garlic powder, cloves, and ginger. Whisk in the olive oil, grated garlic, honey, lemon juice, and golden raisins. Season the meat cubes on all sides with salt, and then toss them in the marinade to coat. Cover and refrigerate for 8 to 12 hours.

2 Make the vinaigrette: In a small saucepan, combine the mustard seeds and red wine vinegar with ½ cup water and the orange juice, and simmer until the liquid is reduced by a little more than half and the mustard seeds are tender, 5 to 8 minutes. Pour into a small bowl, whisk in the lemon juice and olive oil, and taste for seasoning. Set aside to serve with the lamb.

3 Preheat the oven to 350°F.

4 Cook the lamb: Remove the lamb from the marinade, reserving any marinade in the bowl. Scrape off any excess spices and raisins so they don't burn while browning the meat. Heat the canola oil in a large ovenproof skillet over medium heat. When the oil begins to smoke lightly, remove the pan from the heat and add the lamb pieces in a single layer. Return the pan to the heat and brown the lamb on all sides, 12 to 15 minutes. Stir in the grated onions and cook for 2 to 3 minutes. Add the beef stock and the reserved marinade, and bring to a simmer over medium heat. Put the skillet in the center of the oven and cook, uncovered, until the meat is practically falling apart. Check the meat after 1½ hours, though note it could take 2 to 3 hours total to become fully tender. Taste for seasoning. Allow the stew to sit on the stove and rest off the heat for 10 to 15 minutes before serving.

NOTE: The tagine can be made ahead, cooled, covered, and refrigerated for up to 2 days. Reheat completely before serving.

ROASTED SHRIMP
WITH CHILE AND ALMONDS

I really can't get enough shrimp—poached in a court bouillon with some coriander and bay leaves, grilled with lots of lemon, and like this: roasted with some heat from chile and some richness from almonds. I like to use a dried chile for this because that slow-burning spice unfolds more with each bite. While guajillo is my favorite, ancho or a few small árbol chiles would also do. The key is that balance of sweet briny shrimp, nutty rich almonds, and heat from a chile. Addictive.

1 dried **guajillo chile**, stemmed, most seeds removed

2 tablespoons **canola oil**

12 extra-large **shrimp** (10 per pound), peeled and deveined

Kosher salt

½ cup slivered blanched **almonds**

Juice of 1 **lemon**

1 Preheat the oven to 350°F.

2 **Grind the chile:** Put the guajillo in a spice or coffee grinder, or in a food processor, and pulse until it forms a coarse powder. Remove any large pieces.

3 **Cook the shrimp:** Heat a large ovenproof skillet over medium heat and add the oil. Season the shrimp on both sides with salt and the chile powder. When the oil begins to smoke lightly, add the shrimp in a single layer and sear on the first side, 30 seconds. Quickly flip the shrimp over and put the skillet in the oven. Roast until the shrimp are cooked through and no longer translucent, 3 to 4 minutes.

4 **Finish the dish:** Remove the skillet from the oven and transfer the shrimp to a serving bowl. Heat the skillet over medium heat and add the almonds. Cook, stirring, until the almonds brown, 3 to 5 minutes. Sprinkle the shrimp with the lemon juice and scatter the almonds over them. Serve immediately.

ROASTED BLUEFISH IN FOIL

I love sardines, mackerel, and bluefish. They have such great flavor that it doesn't take much to make a complete dish, maybe just a little dill and lemon to add freshness and acidity. Here mayonnaise adds richness and tempers the strong taste of the bluefish with an almost creamy note. Wrap the fish in foil in advance and just pop it on the grill when you are ready to eat.

2 **lemons**: 1 cut into ½-inch-thick slices, 1 cut into wedges

6 sprigs fresh **dill**

1 whole (5-pound) **bluefish**, scaled and gutted

Maldon sea salt

Freshly cracked **black pepper**

¼ cup **mayonnaise**, preferably Hellmann's or Best Foods

1 Preheat a grill.

2 Prepare the fish: On a flat surface, spread out a double layer of foil that is large enough to amply wrap around the whole fish. Put the lemon slices and dill sprigs inside the cavity of the fish. Season the outside of the fish on both sides with Maldon salt and cracked black pepper. Spread the mayonnaise over both sides. Wrap the foil all around the fish, taking care that the foil is sealed on all sides. Put the fish on a hot (but not the hottest) spot on the grill.

3 Cook the fish: Cook the fish for 5 to 8 minutes on the first side, and then turn it over onto the other side and cook for an additional 3 to 5 minutes. The goal is to cook until the flesh is no longer translucent and the fish flakes easily on the tines of a fork. Remove the packet from the grill. Open the foil and allow the fish to rest for 5 to 10 minutes. Then use a large spatula to transfer the bluefish to a serving platter. Season with salt. Serve with the lemon wedges on the side.

CEDAR-PLANKED SALMON

This was one of the first dishes that stopped me in my tracks at Larry Forgione's restaurant, An American Place. The smell of the cedar plank burning under the broiler while rich portions of salmon roasted on top was intoxicating. I remember thinking that I would likely never be able to cook something like that. In reality, this recipe couldn't be easier; the wood does all the work.

Kosher salt

½ teaspoon freshly ground **black pepper**

½ teaspoon ground **ginger**

½ teaspoon **dry mustard**

6 (6-ounce) portions **wild salmon**, skin and pin bones removed

2 tablespoons **unsalted butter**, softened

Juice of 1 **lemon**

1 Preheat the broiler. Soak two 12-inch cedar planks in cold water for 10 to 15 minutes.

2 Prepare the salmon: In a small bowl, combine 1½ teaspoons salt with the pepper, ginger, and mustard. Sprinkle an even layer of this mixture over both sides of each piece of salmon.

3 Prepare the planks: Drain the planks and set them under the broiler, at least a few inches from direct heat, to let the wood brown, 1 to 2 minutes. Then remove the planks from the broiler.

4 Cook the salmon: Put 3 portions of salmon on the browned side of each plank and return the planks to the broiler. Cook for 4 to 5 minutes for medium-rare to medium, and a few minutes longer for medium and medium-well (the thickness of your particular pieces of salmon will dictate the exact cooking time). Spread some of the butter on each piece of salmon and drizzle with the lemon juice. Season with salt and serve immediately.

ROASTED SALMON
WITH APPLE AND CELERY ROOT SLAW

The fresh texture of raw apples and celery root against rich, supple salmon makes this dish special. With the creamy mayonnaise, crunch of poppy seeds, and bright flavor of the lemon, the slaw is a well-rounded companion to the salmon.

2 **lemons**

½ cup **mayonnaise**, preferably Hellmann's or Best Foods

¼ cup **skim milk**

1 tablespoon **poppy seeds**

1 teaspoon crushed **red pepper flakes**

1 medium **celery root**, peeled and julienned

2 small **Empire apples**, cored and thinly sliced

½ cup chopped fresh **flat-leaf parsley leaves**

Kosher salt

2 tablespoons **extra-virgin olive oil**

6 (8-ounce) portions skin-on **salmon fillet**, pin bones removed

1 tablespoon **unsalted butter**

Freshly ground **white pepper**

1 Preheat the oven to 500°F.

2 **Section the lemons:** Use a sharp paring knife to slice off the top and bottom of each lemon and then set them upright on the cutting board. Cut down the length of each lemon all around, in essence peeling it, removing both the layer of skin and the white pith underneath. Cut the lemon flesh into sections, slicing between the membranes to remove the wedges of lemon, leaving any fibrous pieces and pits behind. Squeeze any juice from the empty membranes into a bowl with the sections and discard the membranes.

3 **Make the slaw:** In a large bowl, whisk together the mayonnaise, skim milk, poppy seeds, and red pepper flakes. Stir in the celery root, apples, lemon sections, and parsley. Season with salt. Cover with plastic wrap and refrigerate.

4 **Prepare the salmon:** Use half of the olive oil to grease the bottom of a roasting pan. Arrange the salmon fillets, skin side down, in the pan. Dot them with the butter and drizzle with the rest of the oil. Season with salt and white pepper.

5 **Cook the salmon:** Roast the salmon in the center of the oven, undisturbed, until medium-rare, 8 minutes. (For well-done fish, leave it in the oven for an additional 5 minutes.) Remove the pan from the oven and transfer the salmon to a serving platter. Set the salmon aside to rest for 5 to 10 minutes. When ready to serve, arrange the slaw on top of the salmon. Serve immediately.

ROASTED STRIPED BASS

WITH BARLEY, PECAN, AND SCALLION STUFFING

Pan-searing striped bass to get a good crispy skin and then finishing it in the oven is an easy and fast way to create an elegant main course. Striped bass has a hearty texture that becomes very tender when cooked. Make sure the fish is cooked through before serving it. Cooking barley and tossing it with vinegar and scallions creates both a companion dish and a sauce for the fish.

½ cup **pearl barley**

Kosher salt

2 tablespoons **unsalted butter**

½ cup **pecans**, finely chopped

6 **scallions** (green and white parts), thinly sliced

2 tablespoons **sherry vinegar**

2 tablespoons **dark soy sauce**

6 (6-ounce) skin-on **striped bass fillets**, pin bones removed

2 tablespoons **canola oil**

1 **Cook the barley:** In a medium saucepan, bring 2½ cups water to a simmer. Stir in the barley, season it with a generous pinch of salt, and reduce the heat to low. Simmer gently until the barley is tender and all of the liquid has evaporated, 40 to 45 minutes. Transfer the barley to a bowl and season again with salt.

2 **Make the vinaigrette:** Heat a medium skillet over medium heat and melt the butter in it. Add the pecans and season with salt. Cook, stirring constantly, until they brown slightly, 2 to 3 minutes. Then stir in the scallions, sherry vinegar, and soy sauce. Mix the barley into the vinaigrette. Taste for seasoning, and set aside.

3 Preheat the oven to 350°F.

4 **Cook the fish:** Season both sides of the fish liberally with salt. Heat half the canola oil in each of two large ovenproof sauté pans over medium heat. Put 3 fillets in each pan, skin side down. Use a spatula to gently press the fillets flat, making sure the skin is cooked evenly and becomes perfectly crisp. Cook for 3 to 4 minutes, and then transfer the pans to the center of the oven. Roast the fish until it is cooked through, 8 to 10 minutes.

5 **Finish the dish:** Arrange the barley on a serving platter and top it with the fish fillets, skin side up.

CURRIED BLACK BASS

WITH SPICY BLACK BEANS

One of the great culinary blessings of my childhood was my father's accidental love affair with Chinese food. He took a few classes at the China Institute with greats like Florence Lin, and he was off to the races. These spicy black beans are a taste memory I hold on to dearly. Salty, fermented, yeasty—they are a delicious way to bring out the sweet and briny notes in many fish, especially black bass. This dish is meant to be messy and enjoyed communally, with people picking pieces of the fish from a platter in the center of the table. I have also served it in bowls, with pieces of the fish and a drizzle of sauce arranged on top of steamed rice.

4 tablespoons **canola oil**

8 ounces fresh **shiitake mushrooms**, stemmed and halved

1 tablespoon **hot curry powder**

Kosher salt

4 medium **garlic cloves**, grated

¼ cup **black bean garlic sauce**

¼ cup **dark soy sauce**

2 tablespoons **rice vinegar**

2 tablespoons **sesame oil**

1 tablespoon **sesame seeds**

2 **whole black sea bass** (1½ to 2 pounds each), scaled and gutted

Juice of 2 **limes**

Maldon sea salt

1 Preheat the oven to 450°F. Line a baking sheet with foil and put it in the oven to preheat.

2 Make the sauce: In a medium skillet, heat 3 tablespoons of the canola oil over medium heat. When it begins to get hot, add the shiitake mushrooms and curry powder and season with kosher salt. Cook, stirring from time to time, until the mushrooms become tender and start to give up their liquid, 3 to 5 minutes. Stir in the garlic and cook for an additional 1 to 2 minutes. Stir in the black beans, soy sauce, rice vinegar, sesame oil, and sesame seeds. Remove the skillet from the heat but keep the sauce on the stove.

3 Cook the fish: Rub the remaining 1 tablespoon canola oil over the two fish and season both sides with kosher salt. Open the oven door and put the fish, spaced apart from each other, on the hot baking sheet without removing it from the oven. Close the door and cook the fish until it is tender and flakes slightly at the meatiest part closest to the head, 15 to 20 minutes.

4 Finish the dish: Use a metal spatula to transfer the fish to a large serving platter. Squeeze the lime juice and sprinkle a little Maldon salt over the fish. Reheat the sauce over medium heat and spoon it directly over the fish. Serve immediately.

BROILED CAULIFLOWER STEAKS

WITH PARSLEY AND LEMON

This is such a great dish because you can marinate the cauliflower ahead of time and then cook it just before you're ready to eat. I have been known to marinate this cauliflower for up to two days before cooking! The richness of the coconut and the slight heat from the red pepper flakes give the earthy vegetable just what it needs.

2 large heads **cauliflower** (2 to 2½ pounds each)
Kosher salt
2 (13.5-ounce) cans **unsweetened coconut** milk
2 tablespoons **coriander seeds**, lightly crushed
2 teaspoons crushed **red pepper flakes**
2 tablespoons fresh **lemon juice**
2 tablespoons **red wine vinegar**
⅔ cup **extra-virgin olive oil**
1 cup fresh **flat-leaf parsley leaves**

1 **Prepare the cauliflower:** Put one head of cauliflower upright on a cutting board. Using a large knife and picturing that you will be creating 2 large steaks, trim a little off each side so that when you split the cauliflower down the middle, each half will lie flat. Now cut the cauliflower in half to make 2 steaks, each weighing just shy of a pound. Repeat with the other head of cauliflower.

2 **Blanch the cauliflower:** In a pot that is large enough to hold the cauliflower steaks, bring 6 quarts water to a rolling boil and add 2 tablespoons salt. The water should taste like mild seawater. Line a baking sheet with a kitchen towel. Add the cauliflower steaks to the boiling water and cook until they are slightly tender when pierced with the tip of a knife, 6 to 8 minutes. Use a large slotted spoon or spatula to carefully remove them from the water, transferring them immediately to the baking sheet.

3 **Marinate the cauliflower:** In a container that is large enough to snugly contain the cauliflower in a single layer, whisk the coconut milk with the coriander seeds and red pepper flakes, and season with salt. Submerge the steaks in the marinade, cover with plastic wrap, and refrigerate for 4 hours or up to 48 hours.

4 **Make the vinaigrette:** In a medium bowl, whisk together the lemon juice, red wine vinegar, and olive oil.

5 Preheat the oven to 375°F.

6 **Cook the cauliflower:** Remove the cauliflower from the coconut milk and arrange the steaks in a single layer on a baking sheet. Season with salt. Roast until tender, 10 to 15 minutes. Then heat the broiler and put the baking sheet under the broiler until the top of the cauliflower chars, 3 to 5 minutes. Transfer the steaks to a serving platter (or individual plates) and drizzle liberally with the vinaigrette. Top with the parsley and serve immediately.

ONE-POT & SLOW-COOKED MEALS

CLASSIC POT ROAST

A classic pot roast honestly makes its own case. I like chuck or rump roast. My daughter always requests this on the first chilly fall night as the ultimate comfort food. It also makes tasty sandwiches. While I certainly never want to overcook meat, it's also important the vegetables retain some texture (and taste) as well to round this dish out.

2 tablespoons **canola oil**

1 boneless **beef chuck** roast (4 to 5 pounds)

Kosher salt and freshly ground **black pepper**

½ cup **cognac**

3 medium **red onions**, halved and cut into 1-inch-thick slices

1 medium **carrot**, cut into 1-inch pieces

2 **celery stalks**, cut into 1-inch pieces

2 cups **dry red wine**

8 cups **beef stock**

2 tablespoons **Dijon mustard**

½ cup coarsely chopped fresh **flat-leaf parsley leaves**

1 Preheat the oven to 375°F.

2 **Brown the pot roast:** Heat a large Dutch oven over medium heat and add the canola oil. Season the roast generously on all sides with salt and pepper. When the oil begins to smoke lightly, add the roast carefully to the pan and brown it on all sides over medium heat, 18 to 20 minutes. Do not rush this step. Browning the beef creates a ton of flavor for this dish. Add the cognac and reduce it over medium heat until no liquid remains, 5 to 8 minutes. Transfer the meat to a medium bowl.

3 **Build the braise:** Add the onions, carrot, and celery to the Dutch oven. Season the vegetables with salt and cook until they are translucent and slightly tender, 5 to 8 minutes. Add the red wine and simmer to reduce the liquid by about half, 10 to 12 minutes. Add the meat and the beef stock, cover the Dutch oven, and put it in the center of the oven. Check the meat after 1½ hours. The pot roast will likely need 2 to 2½ hours to become completely tender.

4 **Finish the dish:** Put the Dutch oven on top of the stove. Remove the meat and put it on a cutting board to rest. Season the meat with salt. Stir the mustard into the cooking liquid. Pour half of the cooking liquid and vegetables into a blender and puree until smooth. Stir the puree back into the sauce. Taste for seasoning. Stir in the parsley. Slice the meat or break it into pieces and return it to the Dutch oven.

BEEF AND CARROT STEW

This is a recipe my mom would pull out every once in a while. It is also one of the first dishes I ever made. There is something magical about the combination of sweet carrots, red wine, and beef. It is a classic for a reason. While many recipes call for covering a braise, I like that the exposed meat browns and roasts slightly when uncovered, enriching the dish. Just take care that there is enough liquid at all times to keep the meat moist as it cooks.

¼ cup **canola oil**

2 pounds boneless **beef short ribs**, cut into 2-inch pieces

Kosher salt

1 teaspoon crushed **red pepper flakes**

2 medium **yellow onions**, thinly sliced

6 medium **garlic cloves**

4 medium **carrots**, cut into 1½-inch pieces

2 cups **dry red wine**

4 cups **beef stock**

2 **bay leaves**

10 small **Red Bliss potatoes**, halved

1 tablespoon **red wine vinegar**

1 Preheat the oven to 350°F.

2 **Brown the beef:** Heat two large ovenproof skillets over medium heat and add half of the canola oil to each. Arrange the short ribs in a single layer on a baking sheet and season them on all sides with salt and the red pepper flakes. When the oil begins to smoke lightly, remove the skillets from the heat and add the short ribs in a single layer. Return the skillets to the heat and brown the short ribs on all sides, turning them periodically, 15 to 18 minutes total. Transfer the meat to the baking sheet and set aside. Add half the onions, garlic, and carrots to each skillet and cook until slightly tender, 5 to 8 minutes. Add half the red wine to each skillet and simmer until the liquid is reduced to about ½ cup, 8 to 10 minutes.

3 **Braise the beef:** Return the short ribs to the skillets, add half the beef stock and 1 cup water to each. Bring the liquid to a simmer over medium heat and skim any impurities from the surface. Add a bay leaf and half the potatoes to each skillet. Put the skillets in the center of the oven and cook until the meat is tender, 2 to 2½ hours.

4 **Finish the stew:** When the meat is cooked, remove the skillets from the oven. Combine the stew into one serving vessel, removing the bay leaves, and stir in the red wine vinegar. Taste for seasoning. Allow the meat to rest for 15 minutes before serving.

BRAISED CHICKEN
WITH PRUNES

This is a dish that is traditionally made with rabbit and prunes. I like rabbit, but I like chicken so much more: the rich flavor from chicken fat and skin really emerges when combined with the deep flavor of the sweet prunes and acidity of the red wine vinegar. The allspice and mustard offer a boost of flavor to chicken that is falling-off-the-bone tender. This tastes even better when served the next day.

2 tablespoons **canola oil**

1 **whole chicken** (3½ to 4 pounds), cut into 10 pieces

Kosher salt

½ teaspoon **cayenne pepper**

1 cup **pearl onions**, peeled

1 medium **carrot**, thinly sliced

6 medium **garlic cloves**

½ teaspoon ground **allspice**

¼ teaspoon ground **cloves**

½ cup **red wine vinegar**

2 cups **chicken stock**

16 **prunes**, pitted

1 tablespoon **Dijon mustard**

1 **Brown the chicken:** Heat a large ovenproof skillet over high heat, and add the canola oil. Arrange the chicken in a single layer on a baking sheet, and season the pieces with salt and cayenne on both sides. When the oil begins to smoke lightly, carefully add the chicken to the skillet. Do not overcrowd the pan. Resist the temptation to move or turn the pieces. Allow them to brown on the first side, 5 to 8 minutes. Then use metal tongs to turn the chicken pieces over, and brown the other side, 5 to 8 minutes. Transfer the chicken pieces to a baking sheet.

2 **Cook the vegetables:** In the same skillet, combine the onions, carrot, garlic, allspice, and cloves. Cook over medium heat until the vegetables are tender when pierced with the tip of a knife, 15 to 20 minutes. Add the red wine vinegar. Bring it to a simmer and reduce it over medium heat until there is almost no liquid remaining, 5 to 8 minutes.

3 Preheat the oven to 350°F.

4 **Braise the chicken:** Return the chicken to the skillet, and pour in the stock so the pieces are almost fully submerged in liquid. Add the prunes and put the skillet in the center of the oven. Braise until the chicken pieces are tender and the meat is falling off the bone, 15 to 20 minutes. Remove the skillet from the oven and allow the chicken to rest for 15 minutes before serving.

5 **Finish the dish:** Gently stir in the mustard. Taste for seasoning, and serve.

VEAL OSSO BUCO

I have a memory of our neighborhood butcher (yes, we had one in Manhattan) who would come over and sit in my mother's kitchen while she cooked. He drank coffee and talked beef shanks while my mother braised and sautéed and baked. One cut he would often bring over was veal shanks. They are marrow bones that impart richness as the meat cooks. Add the tang of tomatoes and you have a winner. I serve this with simple spaghetti tossed with a drop of olive oil or with a crunchy escarole salad tossed with lemon and olive oil.

4 tablespoons **canola oil**

8 pieces **veal shank**, each 1½ to 2 inches thick

Kosher salt and freshly ground **black pepper**

2 medium **yellow onions**, cut into 1-inch-thick slices

2 medium **carrots**, cut into 1-inch pieces

10 medium **garlic cloves**

6 sprigs fresh **thyme**

2 cups **dry white wine**

6 to 8 cups **beef stock**

1 (28-ounce) can whole peeled **San Marzano tomatoes**

Grated zest and juice of ½ **lemon**

½ cup fresh **flat-leaf parsley leaves**

1   Brown the veal shanks: In a large Dutch oven, heat 2 tablespoons of the canola oil over high heat. Arrange the veal shanks on a flat surface and season them generously on all sides with salt and pepper. Brown the first 4 shanks on all sides in the hot oil, 5 to 8 minutes per side. Remove them and set them aside to rest on a baking sheet. Add the remaining 2 tablespoons oil, let it heat up, and then brown the remaining 4 shanks. Don't rush the browning—it is the most important part in building a deep flavor for this dish. Remove the second batch of shanks from the Dutch oven to the baking sheet.

2   Preheat the oven to 375°F.

3   Brown the vegetables and braise the veal: Add the onions, carrots, garlic, thyme sprigs, and white wine to the Dutch oven. Simmer over medium heat until the wine is reduced by half, 10 to 12 minutes. Return the shanks to the pan and cover them with 6 cups of the beef stock, the tomatoes and their juices, and a little water if needed. Bring the liquid to a simmer over medium heat and skim any impurities from the surface. Cover the Dutch oven and put it in the center of the oven. Braise until the shanks are completely tender, 1½ to 2 hours. If the liquid reduces so that less than half of the meat is covered, add the remaining 2 cups stock and continue cooking the meat. If after 1½ hours or so, the meat is not completely tender, don't be afraid to add some water and cook it longer.

4   Finish the dish: Remove the shanks and arrange them in a large shallow bowl or serving platter. Season the meat with salt. Reduce the liquid in the Dutch oven slightly over medium heat. Taste it for seasoning, and stir in the lemon zest and juice and the parsley. Pour the sauce over the meat. Serve immediately.

BRAISED SPRING LAMB
WITH PEAS

The peas are barely cooked in this recipe while the lamb is cooked for hours. The result is meat with rich browned notes and peas that are almost raw and grassy. Lamb is definitely a sign of springtime, but it is rarely light. The red wine vinegar and mustard definitely add lightness here. The parsnips and other vegetables that cook along with the meat provide a wonderful group of backup singers.

2 tablespoons **canola oil**

3 pounds boneless **lamb stew meat**, preferably shoulder, cut into 1- to 1½-inch cubes

Kosher salt and freshly ground **black pepper**

2 medium **yellow onions**, thinly sliced

12 medium **garlic cloves**

8 small **parsnips**, split lengthwise

12 small **carrots**, split lengthwise

1 tablespoon **dark brown sugar**

1 cup **dry vermouth**

¼ cup **grainy mustard**

8 cups **beef stock**

1 **bay leaf**

1 cup shelled **green peas**

1 cup **sugar snap peas**, stemmed and halved crosswise

1 tablespoon **red wine vinegar**

1 Preheat the oven to 350°F.

2 Brown the lamb: Heat a Dutch oven over high heat and add the oil. Season the pieces of lamb on all sides with salt and pepper. When the oil begins to smoke lightly, use a pair of metal tongs to arrange the lamb in a single layer in the Dutch oven. Brown the meat on all sides, 12 to 15 minutes. Transfer the meat to a medium bowl.

3 Cook the vegetables: Stir the onions into the Dutch oven, and season them lightly with salt. Cook until tender, 3 to 5 minutes. Then stir in the garlic, parsnips, and carrots. Season with salt and add the brown sugar. Reduce the heat to medium and cook until the vegetables become slightly tender, 8 to 10 minutes.

4 Braise the lamb: Add the vermouth to the vegetables, and simmer until all of the liquid evaporates, 5 to 8 minutes. Stir in the mustard, beef stock, and bay leaf. Return the lamb to the Dutch oven, cover it, and put it in the center of the oven. Braise until the meat is tender when pierced with the tip of a knife, 1 to 1½ hours.

5 Finish the stew: Remove the pot from the oven and use a large spoon to skim any excess fat or impurities from the surface of the stew. Remove and discard the bay leaf. Taste for seasoning. Stir in the peas, snap peas, and red wine vinegar. Allow it to rest for 15 minutes before serving.

AFTER THE BEACH BELLY-WARMING SUMMER VEGETABLE STEW

There's something about the ocean air that clears my head and often leaves me with a hearty appetite. When I make a dish like this one, deceptively cozy and yet light, it feels so satisfying. I feel even better making a dish that's so meaty from only vegetables. Sometimes I serve this spooned over slices of toasted Italian bread. I like to get all the ingredients ready and just cook everything when I get home from the beach.

3 **lemons**

6 medium **globe artichokes**

2 tablespoons **extra-virgin olive oil**

2 medium **shallots**, grated

1 cup **pearl onions**, peeled

Kosher salt

1 cup **dry white wine**

1 cup shelled **green peas**

Leaves from 4 sprigs fresh **tarragon**, coarsely chopped

½ cup finely grated **Parmigiano-Reggiano cheese**

1 Clean the artichokes: Prepare a bowl of cold water that is large enough to hold the 6 artichoke hearts. Cut 2 of the lemons in half and add the juice and the halves to the water. Use a paring knife to trim the dark green skin from the stem and the base of each artichoke, but do not cut off the stems; they're edible and make for a more beautiful presentation. Remove the outer leaves from the artichokes and slice about 2 inches off the top of each artichoke and remove the small (and sharp-tipped!) inner leaves. Use a small spoon to scoop out the fuzzy choke from the center of each artichoke. Split the artichokes in half lengthwise. Cut the remaining lemon in half and rub the cut side of one half over the artichokes to prevent them from discoloring. Submerge the artichokes in the lemon water.

2 Cook the artichokes and onions: Heat a large skillet over medium heat and add 2 tablespoons of the olive oil. Add the shallots and onions in a single layer, and season with salt. Cook for 3 to 5 minutes. Then add the artichokes and cook for 3 to 5 minutes. Add the wine and simmer until it is completely reduced, 5 to 8 minutes. Add about ½ cup water and cook over medium heat until the artichokes and onions are tender, 12 to 15 minutes.

3 Finish the dish: Stir in the peas and simmer until they soften, 2 minutes. Then stir in the tarragon and a generous squeeze of juice from the remaining lemon half. Sprinkle with the cheese. Serve immediately.

ROOT VEGETABLES

CRISPY POTATO CAKE

With a few ingredients and a little elbow grease, you can make something that seems fancy and exciting without breaking the bank. This giant potato cake is wonderful when cut into small pieces and topped with anything from caramelized onions to trout roe and sour cream. Cut it into larger wedges and you have a great companion to a piece of fish or a steak. This potato cake can be made a few hours ahead and reheated in a hot oven.

½ pound (2 sticks) **unsalted butter**
6 large **Idaho potatoes**, peeled
Kosher salt
Leaves from 6 sprigs fresh **thyme**

1 **Clarify the butter:** In a small saucepan, melt the butter over low heat and bring it to a gentle simmer. Remove the pan from the heat and allow the butter to sit for a minute. The milk solids should start to sink to the bottom. Slowly pour the clear butter into a bowl, keeping as much of the white milky liquid as possible in the saucepan. Discard the milk solids, which are prone to burning. Keep the clarified butter warm near the stove.

2 **Prepare the potatoes:** Using a mandoline slicer or a sharp knife, cut all of the potatoes into thin (⅛-inch-thick) slices. Transfer them to a bowl and cover them with three-fourths of the clarified butter. Season with 1 tablespoon salt, sprinkle in the thyme leaves, and toss to coat the potatoes with the butter. Pour the remaining clarified butter into a 9-inch cast-iron skillet and swirl it around to coat the bottom and sides.

3 Preheat the oven to 350°F.

4 **Assemble the potato cake:** Remember that the bottom layer with be the top when you unmold this cake, so this assembling should be done with extra care. Arrange a circle of potato slices around the edge of the skillet, letting them overlap halfway, one over the other. Then make a second circle, inside the first one, of overlapping potato slices. There will likely be a third, smaller circle that makes the center of the bottom layer. Continue to layer overlapping circles until the entire bottom of the skillet is filled with potato rounds in smaller and smaller circles. Sprinkle with salt, and then repeat the circles to make a total of 5 or 6 layers. Press down gently on the potatoes to make sure they are starting to stick together and form a cake.

5 **Roast the potato cake:** Set the skillet over high heat and cook until the liquid starts to release from the potatoes and you can see the edges browning, 5 to 8 minutes. Transfer the skillet to the oven and roast until the potatoes feel tender in the center when pierced with the tip of a knife, 20 to 25 minutes.

6 **Finish the potato cake:** Remove the skillet from the oven and carefully pour any excess liquid into a bowl. Invert a platter over the skillet, and carefully holding them together (use oven mitts—the skillet will be hot), turn the platter and skillet over in one deft motion. Lift off the skillet and use a large metal spatula to slide the potato cake back into the skillet so it can brown on the second side. Pour the reserved liquid back into the skillet, put it in the oven, and cook for 5 to 8 minutes. Touch the top of the potatoes: they should feel hard and crispy, and the top should be golden brown. If not, return the skillet to the oven for a few more minutes of cooking. Remove the skillet from the oven, pour off any liquid, and season the potato cake with salt. Cut it into wedges like a pie, right in the skillet, and serve piping hot.

SWEET POTATO PUREE
WITH BROWN BUTTER

Sweet potatoes have a lot of flavor on their own, which is only enhanced by the subtle additions of citrus and fresh and ground ginger in this puree. Butter definitely belongs with this vegetable almost more than any other tuber. The puree has a slightly rustic chunky texture, perfect for a pork chop or chicken breast with any sauce.

4½ to 5 pounds medium **sweet potatoes**

8 tablespoons (1 stick) **unsalted butter**

½ cup packed **dark brown sugar**

1 tablespoon **blackstrap molasses**

Kosher salt and freshly ground **black pepper**

1 teaspoon **ground ginger**

2 tablespoons grated **fresh ginger**

½ teaspoon ground **cinnamon**

Juice of 1 **orange**

1 Preheat the oven to 450°F.

2 Roast the sweet potatoes: Put the sweet potatoes in a single layer on a baking sheet. Bake until the sweet potatoes are completely yielding when pierced in the center with the tip of a knife, 1 to 1¼ hours. Set them aside to cool slightly.

3 Make the brown butter: In a small saucepan, melt the butter over medium heat. Cook until it starts to turn a light brown color. Then immediately remove the pan from the heat and stir in the brown sugar and molasses.

4 Puree the potatoes: Cut the sweet potatoes in half, and use a large spoon to scoop out the flesh. Discard the skins and transfer the flesh to a medium bowl. Whisk vigorously to remove any large lumps (but not for too long or it will make the puree gummy), and then season with salt and pepper. Whisk in the ground ginger, fresh ginger, and cinnamon. Finish by stirring in the brown butter mixture and the orange juice. Taste for seasoning. Serve hot.

WARM POTATO AND SCALLION SALAD

The aroma of hot cooked potatoes tossed in a super-bright vinaigrette is intoxicating. You can literally watch the potatoes soak up the flavors like a sponge. Chopped cornichons and scallions punctuate the mustardy dressing here. I use some olive oil in the vinaigrette for flavor and then canola oil to balance it. Roasting the potatoes, instead of more traditionally boiling them, leaves you with a pure potato taste instead of waterlogged potatoes. If I'm feeling fancy, I drop some thinly sliced fried onions over the top. This salad is also great when made in advance and left out at room temperature until it's time to eat.

2 pounds small **Red Bliss potatoes**

6 tablespoons **sherry vinegar**

2 tablespoons **Dijon mustard**

1 tablespoon **grainy mustard**

6 **cornichons**, cut into ¼-inch pieces, plus 1 tablespoon cornichon liquid

¼ cup **extra-virgin olive oil**

3 tablespoons **canola oil**

Kosher salt and freshly ground **black pepper**

6 **scallions** (green and white parts), minced

1 Preheat the oven to 400°F.

2 Cook the potatoes: Arrange the potatoes in a single layer on a baking sheet and roast them in the oven until tender when pierced with a knife, 30 to 45 minutes, depending upon their size.

3 Meanwhile, make the vinaigrette: In a bowl that is large enough to hold the potatoes, whisk together the sherry vinegar, both mustards, and the cornichons and liquid. Whisk in the olive and canola oils. Season with salt and pepper. Stir the scallions into the dressing.

4 Make the salad: Remove the potatoes from the oven and allow them to cool for a few minutes. Peel about half of them, if desired. (I like to leave some potato skin for flavor.) Add the potatoes to the dressing and stir to break the potatoes up a little, but do not overmix. Season with salt and pepper. Serve warm or at room temperature.

SWEET POTATO PUREE
WITH BROWN BUTTER

WARM POTATO AND
SCALLION SALAD

CRISPY POTATO CAKE

MASHED TURNIPS
WITH NUTMEG

Turnips have a natural sweetness and the earthy qualities of cabbage as well. Once relieved of their thick, inedible skin, turnips cook quickly, and they pair nicely with strong flavors like salmon, duck, and lamb. The clean flavor of turnips leaves a lot of room for the olive oil, butter, and nutmeg to shine in this chunky puree. I always go for the purple-top turnips you commonly see at the supermarket. They are juicy, with a pleasant mustardy heat.

4 pounds medium **turnips**, peeled and cut into 1-inch-thick slices
Kosher salt
¼ cup **extra-virgin olive oil**
2 tablespoons **unsalted butter**
½ teaspoon coarsely ground **black pepper**
¼ teaspoon grated **nutmeg**
1 tablespoon **honey**
Juice of 1 medium **lemon**

1 Cook the turnips: Put the turnips in a large pot and cover them amply with cold water. Bring the water to a boil and then reduce the heat to a simmer. Add 2 tablespoons salt to the water and cook the turnips until they are tender when pierced with the tip of a knife, 15 to 20 minutes. Pour the water and turnips into a colander sitting in the sink to drain off all of the water.

2 Mash the turnips: Put a food mill fitted with a fine disk over a large bowl, and add the turnips. Turn the handle of the mill back and forth until all of the turnips are mashed. In a medium saucepan, combine the olive oil, butter, pepper, nutmeg, and honey. Whisk over low heat until you can smell the nutmeg, 2 to 3 minutes. Pour this mixture over the turnips, season with 2 teaspoons salt, and stir well. Taste for seasoning. Top with the lemon juice and serve hot.

ROASTED CARROTS
WITH CUMIN AND CORIANDER

I was always taught to peel carrots, but this recipe came about one night when I had some beautiful carrots and was just a little too tired to peel them before cooking. The cumin focuses on the pleasantly bitter taste of the carrot skins as they roast, and the coriander harnesses the sweetness of the carrot flesh itself. The honey and salt complete this balancing act of flavors. Carrots are naturally sweet, but I love the floral note of honey to amplify the sweetness. Surprisingly complex and yet so easy to make, this is my favorite kind of dish! When I can, I buy the carrots with tops—they are always the sweetest. When you get a bite of carrot with the vinegar, honey, and cumin, it's tasty!

12 medium **carrots** (about 2 pounds), ends trimmed
1 tablespoon **extra-virgin olive oil**
2 tablespoons **honey**
½ teaspoon freshly ground **black pepper**
2 teaspoons **coriander seeds**, lightly crushed
1 teaspoon **cumin seeds**
Kosher salt
2 teaspoons **red wine vinegar**

1 Preheat the oven to 375°F.

2 Make the carrots: In a large bowl, toss the carrots with the olive oil, honey, pepper, coriander seeds, cumin seeds, and 2 teaspoons salt. Arrange them in a single layer on a baking sheet lined with foil. Roast in the oven until the carrots are tender when pierced with the tip of a sharp knife, 20 to 25 minutes. Drizzle the vinegar over the carrots and taste a tiny piece for seasoning. Serve immediately.

SUMMER BEET CARPACCIO

I am a big fan of beets because they are so beautiful. If you have a mandoline slicer, put it on a narrow setting and gently slice the beets. If cutting by hand, use a sharp knife to cut slices as thin as you can manage. The thin raw slices are what make this dish so refreshing.

1 tablespoon **cider vinegar**

1 tablespoon **balsamic vinegar**

2 teaspoons **dark brown sugar**

Kosher salt and freshly ground **black pepper**

¼ cup **extra-virgin olive oil**

2 tablespoons grated fresh **ginger**

2 pounds medium to small **beets**, peeled and very thinly sliced

1 cup **arugula leaves**

1 small bunch fresh **chives**

Maldon sea salt

1 Make the vinaigrette: In a large bowl, whisk together the cider vinegar, balsamic vinegar, brown sugar, and kosher salt and black pepper to taste. Whisk in the olive oil and ginger.

2 Arrange the salad: Toss the beet slices in the bowl of vinaigrette. Then remove them with a slotted spoon and arrange them, overlapping slightly, on a platter, covering the entire surface of the platter (or do this on individual serving plates). Arrange the arugula around the edge of the platter and snip some chives over the top so the beets are still front and center. Top the arugula with the remaining vinaigrette, and season with Maldon salt.

SUPERMARKET
MUSHROOMS
MADE SEXY

RAW WHITE MUSHROOM SALAD

I give my daughter whole raw white mushrooms in her lunch box and she eats them with gusto. They have a delicious light and clean flavor with an almost nutty note. I like them sliced and tossed with a really punchy vinaigrette. Grated shallot and poppy seeds give a great subtle texture.

Juice of 2 **lemons**
2 teaspoons **honey**
1 small **shallot**, grated
1 teaspoon **poppy seeds**
8 tablespoons **extra-virgin olive oil**
Kosher salt
12 ounces large **white button mushrooms**, stems trimmed, halved and thinly sliced

In a medium bowl, whisk together the lemon juice, honey, shallots, and poppy seeds. Whisk in the oil and season with salt. Stir in the mushrooms and taste for seasoning.

ROASTED CREMINI MUSHROOMS
WITH SPICY THAI DRESSING

I think of mushrooms as sponges that already have a distinct, lovely flavor but are waiting to absorb stronger flavors. This is a dish where you have to be patient about cooking the mushrooms thoroughly, but then you just pour the dressing over them and dig in. The soy from the dressing connects with the butter coating the mushrooms. Tasty.

¼ cup fresh lime juice (from 2 large **limes**)
2 teaspoons **Sriracha hot sauce**
½ teaspoon crushed **red pepper flakes**
2 teaspoons **fish sauce** (nam pla)
1 tablespoon **dark soy sauce**
2 teaspoons **honey**
2 tablespoons **unsalted butter**
1 tablespoon **extra-virgin olive oil**
12 ounces **cremini mushrooms**, stems trimmed, halved
Kosher salt

1 Make the dressing: In a medium bowl, whisk together the lime juice, Sriracha, red pepper flakes, fish sauce, soy sauce, and honey until smooth.

2 Cook the mushrooms: In a medium skillet, melt the butter over medium heat and add the olive oil and mushrooms. Season with salt and cook until the mushrooms give up their liquid and it all evaporates, 10 to 12 minutes. Remove the pan from the heat and top with the dressing. Allow the pan to sit for a few minutes on the stove, and then serve the mushrooms and dressing on a platter or in a bowl.

STUFFED WHITE MUSHROOMS

This is make-ahead heaven to me. I often prepare these mushrooms a day or two in advance and then bake and broil them when we're ready to eat. I learned about the great combination of white mushrooms and dry vermouth from watching my mom cook a Julia Child recipe when I was a kid. The vermouth intensifies the earthy notes and meaty texture. Adding the sour cream rounds out the picture with richness.

¼ cup **extra-virgin olive oil**

1 medium **yellow onion**, minced

2 medium **garlic cloves**, minced

4 sprigs fresh **thyme**

Kosher salt and freshly ground **white pepper**

2½ pounds large **white mushrooms**, stems on

¾ cup **dry vermouth**

½ cup **full-fat sour cream**

Grated zest and juice of 1 **lemon**

Leaves from 6 sprigs fresh **tarragon**, coarsely chopped

2 tablespoons **unsalted butter**

½ cup freshly grated **Parmigiano-Reggiano cheese**

¼ cup **panko bread crumbs**, toasted

1 Make the stuffing: Heat a large skillet over medium heat. Add the olive oil, onion, garlic, and thyme sprigs, and season with salt and pepper. Cook until the onion is tender, 3 to 5 minutes. Meanwhile, trim the stems of about ¾ pound of the mushrooms and slice them thinly. Add the sliced mushrooms and cook for 2 to 3 minutes. Add ¼ cup of the vermouth and cook until the mushrooms are tender and a lot of their liquid has evaporated, 8 to 10 minutes. Remove the thyme sprigs. Add the sour cream and allow it to melt over the mushrooms. Then add the lemon zest, half of the lemon juice, and the tarragon. Taste for seasoning and transfer the stuffing to a bowl.

2 Cook the whole mushrooms: Rinse and wipe out the skillet and return it to medium heat. Add the butter and all of the remaining mushrooms, and season with salt and pepper. Add the remaining ½ cup vermouth and cook until the mushrooms are tender, 10 to 12 minutes. Taste for seasoning. Transfer the mushrooms to a baking sheet to cool.

3 Preheat the oven to 350°F.

4 Stuff and bake the mushrooms: Remove the mushroom stems, set the caps aside, and coarsely chop the stems. Toss the chopped stems and ¼ cup of the Parmigiano-Reggiano with the stuffing. Fill each mushroom cap with stuffing, packing it in firmly. Arrange the mushrooms in a single layer on a large baking sheet. Mix the bread crumbs with the remaining ¼ cup Parmigiano-Reggiano and use it to top the mushrooms. Bake in the oven until they are hot inside and lightly browned on the top, 5 to 8 minutes. Then run the mushrooms under the broiler for 1 to 2 minutes as a finishing touch. Sprinkle the remaining lemon juice over them, and serve immediately.

DUXELLES

This is one of my "sneak attack" recipes that make any number of dishes more delicious. A simple flavor bomb of sautéed white mushrooms and cream, duxelles can go in beef wrapped in puff pastry, in shepherd's pie, on a roasted chicken sandwich, or simply on grilled bread as a snack. Duxelles have such great flavor and texture that I have also been known to sneak a few spoonfuls into a mushroom or bean soup to add body and another layer of flavor.

4 tablespoons (½ stick) **unsalted butter**

2 medium **shallots**, minced

2 small **garlic cloves**, minced

½ teaspoon **sweet paprika**

Kosher salt and freshly ground **black pepper**

12 ounces **white mushrooms**, stems trimmed and coarsely chopped

½ cup **dry white wine**

1 cup **heavy cream**

Grated zest of ½ **lemon**, plus juice if needed

Leaves from 8 sprigs fresh **flat-leaf parsley**, chopped

Leaves from 8 sprigs fresh **tarragon**, chopped

1 Cook the mushrooms: Heat a large saucepan over medium heat. Add the butter, shallots, garlic, and paprika. Season with salt and pepper, and cook until the shallots are tender, 3 to 5 minutes. Add the mushrooms and cook until they give up some of their liquid, 2 to 3 minutes. Then add the wine. Cook until the mushrooms are tender and a lot of the liquid has evaporated, 8 to 10 minutes.

2 Finish the mushrooms: Add the heavy cream and allow it to melt over the mushrooms. Check the seasoning. Simmer over low heat to reduce the cream slightly, 3 to 5 minutes. Add the lemon zest, parsley, and tarragon. Taste for seasoning. If it needs some extra acidity, add a squirt of lemon juice. This keeps, covered, in the refrigerator for 2 to 3 days.

WHITE MUSHROOMS AND SPINACH

While the garlic and Marsala do some heavy lifting here, it's really about cooking the mushrooms until tender and stirring in the spinach at the very last minute. The pairing of earthy mushrooms with the barely cooked spinach is like introducing two great friends at a party. I love this next to a hearty steak or dish of baked pasta.

2 tablespoons **extra-virgin olive oil**

2 sprigs fresh **thyme**

1 pound **white button mushrooms**, stems trimmed

Kosher salt

2 small **garlic cloves**, minced

Freshly ground **black pepper**

½ cup **dry Marsala**

12 ounces **baby spinach leaves**

Grated zest of ½ **lemon**

Heat a large saucepan over medium heat. Add the olive oil, thyme sprigs, mushrooms, and 2 teaspoons salt. Cook until the mushrooms are tender and a lot of their liquid has evaporated, 3 to 5 minutes. Stir in the garlic and 1 teaspoon pepper and cook for an additional 3 to 5 minutes. Add the Marsala and continue cooking until most of the liquid has evaporated, 5 to 8 minutes. Remove and discard the thyme sprigs. Stir in the spinach leaves so they wilt slightly. Add the lemon zest and taste for seasoning. Serve immediately.

1984 PORTOBELLO SANDWICH

I remember it distinctly: sandwiches made using portobello mushrooms as a stand-in for the bread. Whether batter-dipped and deep-fried or tied together with a few long chives and grilled, they were all the rage. Wow, what an era! All I can say is that I survived it—and I miss it. Earthy portobellos, tangy cheese, and juicy tomatoes are bringing the '80s back!

4 large **portobello mushrooms**, stemmed, caps wiped clean

2 tablespoons **canola oil**

Kosher salt

½ teaspoon crushed **red pepper flakes**

6 ounces **goat cheese**, at room temperature

6 **cherry tomatoes**, halved

Juice of ½ **lemon**

1 Preheat the oven to 350°F.

2 Cook the mushrooms: Arrange the portobellos in a single layer on a baking sheet stem side up, and drizzle with the canola oil. Season with salt and the red pepper flakes. Bake the mushrooms until they release liquid from their centers, shrink slightly, and become tender, 22 to 25 minutes.

3 Assemble the sandwiches: Spread the goat cheese over two of the portobellos. Dot the cheese with the tomato halves, and season with salt and the lemon juice. Using the cheese as glue, stick the remaining two portobello tops on each sandwich. Cut the sandwiches in half and serve immediately.

OVEN-BAKED OYSTER MUSHROOMS

Oyster mushrooms have such a great meaty texture. With a hint of lemon and the crunch of some toasted hazelnuts, I don't think this mushroom could taste any better.

¾ cup (6 ounces) blanched **hazelnuts**, toasted and coarsely chopped

6 tablespoons **extra-virgin olive oil**

Grated zest and juice of 1 **lemon**

12 ounces **oyster mushrooms**, pulled apart

Kosher salt

¼ cup freshly grated **Parmigiano-Reggiano cheese**

1 Preheat the oven to 375°F.

2 Make the dressing: Spread the nuts out on a rimmed baking sheet and toast them in the oven until golden brown, 5 to 8 minutes. Let them cool for a few minutes. Then put the nuts, 4 tablespoons of the olive oil, and the lemon zest and juice in a small serving bowl.

3 Cook the mushrooms: In a medium bowl, toss the mushrooms with salt and the remaining 2 tablespoons olive oil. Arrange them on a baking sheet and roast until the mushrooms brown and give up their liquid, 12 to 15 minutes. Toss them with some of the dressing. Top with the Parmigiano-Reggiano, and serve immediately with the rest of the dressing on the side.

THE ONION FAMILY

GRANDPA GUARNASCHELLI'S SWEET-AND-SOUR ONIONS

Shaped like a flying saucer, the cipollini onion is sweet and delicious. The first time I ever saw cipollini was when I had turned thirteen and met my paternal grandfather for the first time. My father brought him a bag of these onions as a present, and you would have thought they were the finest white truffles from Alba. We peeled them and cooked them just like this, which I still think is the best way to prepare them. I serve these hot but I also enjoy them cold in a sandwich. And I have tossed a few in the blender when making a vinaigrette for a natural (and tasty) thickener!

2 tablespoons **extra-virgin olive oil**

3½ pounds **cippolini onions**, peeled

Kosher salt

½ teaspoon freshly ground **black pepper**

¼ cup **honey**

6 sprigs fresh **thyme**

½ cup **red wine vinegar**

2 teaspoons **soy sauce**

1 Cook the onions: Heat a skillet that is large enough to hold the onions in a single layer over high heat, and add the olive oil and the onions. Season them with 1 tablespoon salt and the pepper. Add 1 cup water and cook, stirring occasionally, until the onions are tender when pierced with the tip of a knife, 15 to 18 minutes. If the onions are not tender by the time the water evaporates, add a little more water and cook further. Transfer the onions to a bowl and cover with foil to keep them warm.

2 Make the sauce and finish the onions: In the same skillet, combine the honey and thyme sprigs. Simmer carefully over medium heat until the honey froths and starts to turn a darker shade of brown, 3 to 5 minutes. Remove the pan from the heat and wait for the foam to settle so you can see the color of the honey. If it has not darkened in color, cook for a couple minutes longer. Be very careful: this honey will be hot! Carefully pour in the vinegar and soy sauce, and simmer over medium heat so the vinegar cooks out a little and the flavors meld together, 3 to 5 minutes. Remove and discard the thyme sprigs. Carefully add the onions and continue to simmer until they are coated with the honey, 3 to 5 minutes. Taste for seasoning. Serve immediately.

WARM LEEKS "NIÇOISE"

Nice is one area of France that reveals its proximity to Italy in its traditional ingredients. In this dish, the tomatoes, olives, and basil in Nice's celebrated salad all pair brilliantly with the mustardy heat and light, crunchy texture of leeks. There are some cool touches here: the powdered sugar brings out the color and sweetness of the tomatoes as they roast, and the capers and olives provide natural sources of salt, making seasoning less challenging.

2 pints **cherry tomatoes**, halved

1 teaspoon **confectioners' sugar**

Kosher salt and freshly ground **black pepper**

10 tablespoons **extra-virgin olive oil**

4 tablespoons **red wine vinegar**

1 cup **black olives**, such as Gaeta, pitted and coarsely chopped

1 teaspoon **capers**, drained and roughly chopped

6 to 8 large **leeks** (3 to 3½ pounds)

½ cup tightly packed fresh **basil leaves**

1 Preheat the oven to 375°F.

2 Prepare the tomatoes: Put the tomato halves in a single layer on a baking sheet lined with parchment paper. In a bowl, whisk together the confectioners' sugar, salt and pepper to taste, and 2 tablespoons of the olive oil. Drizzle the mixture evenly over the tomato halves. Roast until the tomatoes are lightly browned, 20 to 25 minutes. Set them aside to cool.

3 Make the vinaigrette: In a medium bowl, whisk together the red wine vinegar and remaining 8 tablespoons olive oil. Gently stir in the olives and capers. Taste for seasoning, adding salt and pepper if needed. Set aside.

4 Prepare the leeks: Bring a large pot of water to a boil. Trim the root ends of the leeks, slice off the dark green tops, and peel off the outer layer of the trimmed leeks. Split the leeks in half lengthwise but do not slice all the way through the root end; the leeks should remain in one piece. Rinse the interior of each leek thoroughly under cold running water. (Leeks are very sandy. Take care to run the water through the various layers of each leek so there is no dirt remaining.) After each leek is washed, do your best to close them up as if they hadn't been cut.

5 Cook the leeks: Season the boiling water amply with salt; it should taste like seawater. Submerge the leeks in the boiling water and simmer until they are tender when pierced with the tip of a knife, 5 to 8 minutes. The leeks should still retain their shape and not feel mushy. Drain the leeks, cut them completely in half, and put them, cut side down, in a single layer on a kitchen towel. (This ensures that any excess cooking liquid drains out of the leeks.)

6 Assemble the dish: Put the warm leeks, cut side up, on a serving platter. Season them lightly with salt. Stir the basil into the vinaigrette and spoon the dressing over the leeks, taking care that it penetrates the inside layers of each leek half. The leeks will still be warm. Top with the roasted tomatoes. Serve immediately.

GRILLED ONION RINGS

I like to use red onions because they tend to cook more quickly than most yellow onions and have a little more bite. Grilling them before batter-dipping and frying adds extra flavor—as do a little sugar and paprika. The vodka and beer in the batter provide a great, reliable coating. These are delicious with a steak or on an iceberg wedge with blue cheese and tomatoes. They can make a vegetarian dish feel meaty. Note: The batter can be made in advance and kept covered in the refrigerator.

BATTER
12 ounces **beer** (Heineken is my favorite)

¼ cup **vodka**

¾ to 1 cup **seltzer**

1 tablespoon **hot paprika**

1 cup **all-purpose flour**, plus a little more if needed

ONIONS
8 large **red onions**, cut into 1½-inch-thick rounds

2 large **garlic cloves**, grated

1 tablespoon **extra-virgin olive oil**

2 tablespoons **sugar**

Kosher salt

4 cups **canola oil**

1 Heat a grill to high heat.

2 Prepare the batter: Pour the beer into a medium bowl and stir in the vodka and soda water. Slowly whisk in the paprika and flour. The batter should be fairly thick but also easy to stir. If it is a little loose, whisk in a little more flour. If a little thick, add more soda water. Set it aside in a warm place.

3 Grill the onions: Arrange the onion rounds on a baking sheet. In a small bowl, stir the garlic into the olive oil, and drizzle this over the onions. Season the onions with the sugar and 2 teaspoons salt. Put the onions in a single layer directly on the grill and cook undisturbed until lightly charred, 3 to 5 minutes (depending on the heat of the grill and the size of the onions). Use a pair of metal tongs to turn the onion rounds over onto the other side. The onions will not be fully cooked; the goal here is to put a nice grill mark and charred flavor on the onions. When the second side is charred, after 2 to 5 minutes, return the onions to the baking sheet.

4 Prepare the frying oil: Pour the canola oil into a heavy-bottomed pot (or, alternatively, a deep fryer). Heat the oil slowly to 375°F. (Use a deep-frying thermometer to monitor the temperature.) Line a baking sheet with a kitchen towel to drain the onion rings once they are cooked.

5 Fry the onion rings: Test the batter and the temperature of the oil at the same time by dropping a little batter into the hot oil. If it bubbles immediately and starts to brown, the oil is ready. Taste for seasoning. Working in batches, drop onion rounds into the batter, gently shake off the excess, and plunge them into the oil. Fry until crispy, 1 to 2 minutes, and then remove carefully with a slotted spoon. Drain the onions on the towel-lined baking sheet. Season with salt, and serve immediately.

BRAISED PEARL ONIONS

WITH PEAS AND BACON

This is a slight variation on the classic French combination of these three ingredients. There is something about this comforting side dish that begs for the childhood taste and texture of frozen peas. I don't cook the peas at all; I simply defrost them at room temperature and then toss them with the onions.

2 tablespoons **canola oil**

3½ pounds medium **pearl onions**, peeled

Kosher salt

½ teaspoon freshly ground **black pepper**

1 tablespoon **honey**

6 slices **bacon**, cut crosswise into ½-inch-wide pieces

10 ounces frozen **petite peas**

Splash of fresh **lemon juice**

1 Cook the onions: Heat a large skillet over medium heat and add the canola oil. When the oil begins to smoke lightly, remove the skillet from the heat and add the onions. Season them with 1 teaspoon salt and the pepper, and return the skillet to the heat. Add 1 cup water and cook over medium heat, stirring occasionally, until the onions are tender, 15 to 18 minutes. Note: If all of the water evaporates before the onions are tender, add a splash more to finish them. You do not want to end up with excess water when they are cooked because it would dilute the other flavors. Stir in the honey. Taste for seasoning.

2 Cook the bacon: Heat a large skillet over medium heat and add ½ inch of water. Bring the water to a boil and add the bacon. Cook over medium heat until all of the water evaporates and the bacon becomes crispy, 8 to 10 minutes. (Starting the bacon in water actually makes it cook crispier, even though it seems odd.) Drain the bacon on a kitchen towel, reserving the bacon fat.

3 Prepare the peas and finish the dish: In a medium bowl, toss the peas with 1 teaspoon salt. Reheat the onions over medium heat to make sure they are hot. Stir the peas, bacon, and a touch of the reserved bacon fat into the onions. Add the lemon juice. Taste for seasoning. Serve immediately.

SPICY WHITE ONION GRATIN

This is a bubbly, hearty gratin composed of wonderfully light onions. I like to use large and small onions in this dish so that while one bite may have a whole small onion, the next might be slivers of a larger one. It's texturally exciting. I cook them separately and then combine them with the cheese and cream to bake for a few minutes before serving. I like a little heat against the sweetness of the onions, but if you are more of a purist, simply omit the red pepper flakes.

4 tablespoons **canola oil**

2 teaspoons crushed **red pepper flakes**

Kosher salt

3½ pounds **cippolini onions**, peeled

6 large white **onions**, halved and thinly sliced

1 cup **whole milk**

2 cups **heavy cream**

2 tablespoons **Dijon mustard**

2½ cups grated **Gruyère cheese**

1 cup freshly grated **Parmigiano-Reggiano cheese**

1 cup grated **cheddar cheese**

1 tablespoon **Worcestershire sauce**, preferably Lea & Perrins brand

1 teaspoon **Tabasco**

1 Preheat the oven to 375°F.

2 **Cook the onions:** Heat two medium skillets over medium heat. To each add 2 tablespoons canola oil, 1 teaspoon red pepper flakes, and 1½ teaspoons salt. Add the cippolini onions to one and the sliced white onions to the other. Add ½ cup water to each and cook, stirring occasionally, until the onions are tender, 10 to 15 minutes. If the onions are not yet cooked by the time the water evaporates, add a little more water. The cippolini onions may take a little longer. Once the onions are tender when pierced with the tip of a knife, combine the two types of onions into one skillet and set aside.

3 **Make the gratin sauce:** In the empty skillet used to cook the onions, bring the milk and cream to a simmer over medium heat. Add the mustard, 1½ cups of the Gruyère, and 1 tablespoon salt. Simmer gently over low heat, stirring constantly, until the cheese is melted, 1 to 2 minutes. Add ½ cup of the Parmigiano-Reggiano, the cheddar, Worcestershire, and Tabasco. Stir with a wooden spoon and simmer again until smooth. Taste for seasoning.

4 **Finish the gratin:** Stir the sauce into the onions and transfer to a 14-inch gratin dish. Top with the remaining 1 cup Gruyère and ½ cup Parmigiano-Reggiano. Bake in the oven until golden brown, 15 to 18 minutes. Serve immediately.

DRY-ROASTED SCALLIONS
WITH ROMESCO SAUCE

One of my favorite sauces for all kinds of onions is romesco. The roasted tomatoes, the crunch of the toasted bread, and the nuts bring scallions, leeks, and their cousins to life. Scallions appear as a sidekick in many places, but we don't often think about making them the star of a dish. They are delicious when approached simply and roasted to bring out layers of flavor.

8 ripe **plum tomatoes**, halved lengthwise

Kosher salt

1 teaspoon **confectioners' sugar**

½ teaspoon **hot paprika**

10 tablespoons **extra-virgin olive oil**

2 medium **red bell pepper**s

2 medium **yellow onions**, cut into 1-inch pieces

5 medium **garlic cloves**, minced

2 teaspoons crushed **red pepper flakes**

½ cup (8 to 10) jarred **piquillo peppers**, drained

2 tablespoons **sherry vinegar**

1½ cups diced **sourdough bread**, toasted

¾ cup slivered blanched **almonds**, toasted

6 bunches **scallions**

1 Preheat the oven to 375°F.

2 Roast the tomatoes: Put the tomato halves in a single layer on a baking sheet lined with foil or parchment. Sprinkle with 2 teaspoons salt. In a bowl, whisk together the confectioners' sugar, paprika, and 2 tablespoons of the olive oil. Drizzle the mixture evenly over the tomato halves. Roast in the oven until the tomatoes are tender and browned, 30 minutes. Set them aside to cool. Leave the oven on.

3 Roast the bell peppers: Put each pepper directly on a gas burner and roast it over a high flame, turning as needed, until the skin is charred all over. (Alternatively, the peppers can be broiled to char the skin.) Transfer them to a medium bowl and cover the bowl tightly with plastic wrap.

4 Make the romesco sauce: In a medium skillet, heat 2 tablespoons of the olive oil over medium heat and add the onions. Season with salt. Add the garlic and red pepper flakes, and cook until the onions become tender, 5 to 8 minutes. Meanwhile, peel the skin from the bell peppers; it should come off fairly easily. (I sometimes use a kitchen towel to wipe off the charred skin.) Discard the stems and seeds. Combine the red pepper flesh with the onions, and add the piquillo peppers and sherry vinegar. Transfer the onion-pepper mixture to a food processor, add the roasted tomatoes, and pulse to combine. Add the remaining 6 tablespoons olive oil and the toasted bread and pulse to blend, but keep the mixture chunky. Transfer the sauce to a bowl and taste for seasoning. Stir in the almonds.

5 Roast the scallions: Arrange the scallions in a single layer on two baking sheets. Season with salt and roast in the oven until tender, 12 to 15 minutes.

6 Finish the dish: Spoon the romesco sauce over the bottom of a platter and arrange the scallions on top. (Alternatively, serve a pile of the scallions with the romesco in a bowl alongside them.)

BROILED CHINESE FIVE-SPICE ONIONS

I love cooking onions under the broiler because it chars them slightly and brings their natural sweetness to the forefront. In this case, the salt of soy, the richness of butter, the sharpness of five-spice powder, and the brightness of lime are waiting for them. This is a flavorful little dish that could easily be paired with chicken, pork, or salmon.

3½ pounds **cippolini onions**, peeled
2 tablespoons **extra-virgin olive oil**
2 tablespoons **dark soy sauce**
2 teaspoons **five-spice powder**
2 tablespoons **unsalted butter**
Grated zest and juice of ½ **lime**

1 Preheat the broiler.

2 Cook the onions: Arrange the onions in a single layer in a large ovenproof skillet and add the olive oil, soy sauce, five-spice powder, and 1 cup water. Add the butter and simmer gently over medium heat, stirring from time to time, until the onions are tender when pierced with the tip of a knife, 10 to 15 minutes.

3 Broil the onions: Put the skillet under the broiler and broil until the onions brown further on the top, 2 to 3 minutes. Sprinkle the lime zest and juice over the onions. Serve immediately.

PICKLED RED ONIONS

I like to keep these pickled onions on hand in the fridge. Sometimes I pickle them and eat a few only hours later, when the onions are still really fresh and pleasantly faintly pickled. Sometimes I make a batch and forget them for a while; then I puree them with some of the pickling liquid and some olive oil for a great vinaigrette. I might tuck them into homemade tacos and omelets, or serve them on top of any roasted meat or fish.

1⅓ cups **raspberry vinegar**
2 medium **bay leaves**
2 **star anise pods**
2 teaspoons crushed **red pepper flakes**
1 teaspoon whole **black peppercorns**
½ cup **sugar**
2 tablespoons **kosher salt**
2 small **garlic cloves**, lightly crushed
2 medium **red onions**, halved and thinly sliced

1 Make the pickling liquid: In a medium saucepan, combine the vinegar, bay leaves, star anise, red pepper flakes, black peppercorns, sugar, salt, and garlic. Add ½ cup water and bring the mixture to a simmer over medium heat until the sugar and salt dissolve.

2 Pickle the onions: Pack the onion slices into a clean quart container with a tight-fitting lid. Pour the hot pickling liquid over the onions, cover the container, and refrigerate for a few days before digging in. The onions will keep for at least a month in the refrigerator.

SAUCES & DRESSINGS

THE SHERRY VINAIGRETTE I USE ON EVERYTHING

I really have to resist the urge to put this on just about everything. There are very few dishes that I feel don't need a splash of sherry vinaigrette to brighten the flavors. I most frequently use this dressing over hard-boiled eggs, grilled vegetables, shrimp, and salads. Note: If the vinaigrette seems too thick, add a splash of water to loosen the texture.

1 large **egg yolk**
1 tablespoon plus 1 teaspoon **sherry vinegar**
1 teaspoon **kosher salt**
2 teaspoons **Worcestershire sauce**, preferably Lea & Perrins brand
⅛ teaspoon freshly ground **black pepper**
1 cup **canola oil**
¼ cup **extra-virgin olive oil**

In a blender, combine the egg yolk, vinegar, salt, Worcestershire sauce, and pepper on low speed. Turn the blender to medium speed and pour the canola oil, olive oil, and 1 tablespoon water through the top in a steady stream. Taste for seasoning. This dressing can be stored in a covered container in the refrigerator for several weeks.

LEMON VINAIGRETTE

This dressing is at home just about anywhere—especially on a house salad. This is a staple vinaigrette that I use particularly with bitter or flavorful greens or even when elements like cheese or olives come into play. Unlike a lot of other vinaigrettes, this one is best when made fresh and used right away so the lemon flavor is really bright.

½ cup fresh lemon juice (from about 4 medium **lemons**)
½ teaspoon **kosher salt**
⅛ teaspoon freshly ground **black pepper**
2 teaspoons **honey**
1 cup **extra-virgin olive oil**
¼ cup **canola oil**

In a medium bowl, whisk the lemon juice with the salt, pepper, and honey. Gradually whisk in the olive oil and canola oil. Taste for seasoning. This dressing can be stored in a covered container in the refrigerator for several weeks.

NOTE: If using the dressing at a later date, omit the salt and add it, if needed, when serving.

MUSTARD VINAIGRETTE

Mustard has a tingly heat and contains lecithin, a natural thickener. It gives great body to a dressing without being heavy. I love this on everything from tomatoes to chicken to watercress! Note: If the vinaigrette seems too thick, add a splash of water.

2 tablespoons **Dijon mustard**
1 tablespoon plus 2 teaspoons **grainy mustard**
½ teaspoon **kosher salt**
⅛ teaspoon freshly ground **black pepper**
2 tablespoons **sherry vinegar**
1 cup **canola oil**

In a small bowl, whisk the smooth and grainy mustards with the salt, pepper, and vinegar. Gradually whisk in the oil and 1 tablespoon cold water. Taste for seasoning. This dressing can be stored in a covered container in the refrigerator for several weeks.

CAESAR DRESSING

This classic dressing is forever delicious. I've tried it with many types of lettuce but find that crunchy romaine is the best. I also love it with a salad of shaved fennel and Parmesan. The natural saltiness of the anchovies, capers, and Worcestershire emerges as this dressing sits, so be judicious when seasoning it.

5 small canned **anchovy fillets**
2 teaspoons **capers**, drained, plus 1 teaspoon of their brine
1 medium **garlic clove**
1 large **egg yolk**
2 teaspoons **Dijon mustard**
¼ cup fresh lemon juice (from 2 medium **lemons**)
Splash of **Worcestershire sauce**, preferably Lea & Perrins brand
4 dashes **Tabasco**
1 cup **extra-virgin olive oil**
1 cup **canola oil**

In the bowl of a food processor, combine the anchovies, capers, caper brine, garlic, egg yolk, mustard, lemon juice, Worcestershire, Tabasco, and 2 tablespoons cold water. Pulse until smooth. With the machine running, slowly add both of the oils through the top.

BALSAMIC DRESSING

Balsamic vinegar has a great sweet note and the tang of a good glass of wine or cup of tea. To me, the fruity note of raspberry vinegar and the slight heat from Dijon mustard are the best ways to round out this dressing. The mustard also gives it great body, so a little can nicely coat any green and even stand up to heartier vegetables or meat.

2 tablespoons **Dijon mustard**

3 tablespoons **balsamic vinegar**

2 tablespoons **raspberry vinegar**

½ teaspoon **kosher salt**

⅛ teaspoon freshly ground **black pepper**

¾ cup **canola oil**

½ cup **extra-virgin olive oil**

In a small bowl, whisk together the mustard, balsamic vinegar, raspberry vinegar, salt, and pepper. Gradually whisk in both of the oils. Add a splash of water if needed to thin the dressing. This dressing can be stored in a covered container in the refrigerator for several weeks.

LEMON MINT VINAIGRETTE

This simple vinaigrette, enriched with mint, is wonderful on grilled or roasted pieces of fish, shrimp, or even shellfish.

Grated zest of 1 **lemon**

½ cup fresh lemon juice (from 4 medium **lemons**)

¾ teaspoon **kosher salt**

2½ teaspoons **sugar**

¾ cup **extra-virgin olive oil**

¼ cup **canola oil**

½ cup fresh **mint leaves**

1 **Make the vinaigrette:** In a medium bowl, whisk together the lemon zest and juice with the salt and the sugar. Gradually whisk in the olive oil and canola oil. Taste for seasoning.

2 **Finish the vinaigrette:** When ready to serve, use a large knife to coarsely chop and bruise the mint leaves on a flat surface. Stir them into the vinaigrette and serve immediately.

TARRAGON VINAIGRETTE
FOR SEAFOOD

LEMON MINT
VINAIGRETTE

PARSLEY, FRIED
CAPER, AND
CORNICHON
VINAIGRETTE

RAW BASIL PESTO

PARSLEY, FRIED CAPER, AND CORNICHON VINAIGRETTE

I really like capers more once they have been cooked. They are not so salty when tempered by a few moments of pan-frying. They also become crispy. The cornichon is a wonderful source of acidity and crunchy texture. I don't add any salt until I taste this at the end because the capers and pickles bring a nice amount of salt as it is. The parsley is there as a fresh, grassy component to round out this vinaigrette!

¼ cup fresh lemon juice (from 2 medium **lemons**)
1 small **shallot**, grated
1 tablespoon **Dijon mustard**
1 tablespoon **canola oil**
2 tablespoons **capers**, drained
½ cup **extra-virgin olive oil**
6 small **cornichons**, thinly sliced crosswise
1 cup tightly packed fresh **flat-leaf parsley leaves**
Kosher salt (optional)

1 Start the vinaigrette: In a medium bowl, whisk together the lemon juice, shallot, and mustard until smooth.

2 Cook the capers: In a small skillet, heat the canola oil over medium heat and add the capers. Cook until the capers bubble and become crispy, 3 minutes. Set aside to cool. Whisk the canola oil and capers into the lemon juice mixture, and then whisk in the olive oil and cornichons. Cut the parsley leaves with scissors and sprinkle them over the vinaigrette. Taste for seasoning, and add salt if needed.

RAW BASIL PESTO

I was always taught to blanch basil leaves and plunge them into an ice bath before blending them with some cold water and olive oil to make a lovely, smooth pesto. But after all these years, I miss the raw, grassy notes of raw basil. This pairs well with anything tomato and is great on flatbreads.

2 cups packed fresh **basil leaves**
1 medium **garlic clove**, grated
¼ teaspoon **kosher salt**
½ cup **extra-virgin olive oil**
½ cup freshly grated **Parmigiano-Reggiano cheese**

In the bowl of a food processor, combine the basil with the garlic and the salt, and pulse to blend. Slowly stream in the olive oil and 1 tablespoon cold water through the top of the machine, pulsing to combine, but do not overmix. Transfer the pesto to a bowl and stir in the Parmigiano-Reggiano. Taste for seasoning.

TARRAGON VINAIGRETTE FOR SEAFOOD

Tarragon is my favorite herb for lobster or shrimp and is equally wonderful on a fillet of grilled salmon, roasted pollock, or baked hake. There are hints of anise, grass, and sugar rolled into this herb—all the things needed to bring out even the subtlest notes in fish. The crisp, tart flavor from the apple complements the tarragon.

Leaves from 6 sprigs fresh **tarragon**, finely chopped
½ cup **extra-virgin olive oil**
1 teaspoon **kosher salt**
3 tablespoons **cider vinegar**
1 small **Macoun** or **McIntosh apple**, cored and cut into ½-inch cubes

In a food processor, blend the tarragon leaves, olive oil, and salt until smooth. Pour this into a small bowl. Stir in the cider vinegar and apples. Taste for seasoning.

LEMONGRASS DRESSING

I love lemongrass because it tastes like eating flowers, yet it is citrusy enough to stand up to other ingredients (even proteins) and add a real zingy accent. It almost lightens dishes, making it a good companion for cream or butter. This dressing is one of my favorite ways to enjoy it.

2 stalks **lemongrass**, the bulbs cut into thin rounds, upper stalks discarded
⅔ cup **rice vinegar**
1 tablespoon **honey**
1 tablespoon **sesame oil**
2 tablespoons **canola oil**
1 tablespoon **sesame seeds**
Kosher salt

1 Cook the lemongrass: In a medium saucepan, combine the lemongrass, rice vinegar, ⅔ cup water, and honey. Bring to a simmer over medium heat and cook until the liquid reduces by a little more than half and the lemongrass pieces become tender, 20 to 25 minutes. Set aside to cool.

2 Make the dressing: Strain the cooled lemongrass mixture through a fine-mesh sieve into a small bowl, pressing down on the solids to extract all the flavors and any lemongrass that gets through. Discard the solids. Whisk in the sesame oil, canola oil, and sesame seeds. Season with salt.

GINGER VINAIGRETTE

This dressing is a great vehicle for ginger, which can be a powerful ingredient. I love it on vegetable sides like grilled onions or sautéed peas. It's also beautiful on a bowl of arugula or escarole. I have drizzled this on dumplings and used it as a marinade for cabbage for slaw.

2 tablespoons grated fresh **ginger**

1 teaspoon **honey**

½ teaspoon **kosher salt**

1 medium **garlic clove**, grated

2 tablespoons **dark soy sauce**

Grated zest of 1 **lemon**

2 tablespoons **sherry vinegar**

2 tablespoons plus 2 teaspoons **extra-virgin olive oil**

In a medium bowl, whisk the ginger, honey, salt, and garlic with the soy sauce, lemon zest, vinegar, and olive oil. Taste for seasoning.

CREAMY SAUTÉED CHIVE DRESSING

Chives are often left raw as a finishing ingredient, but I love what happens to them when they are quickly cooked. Their texture softens and a more complex onion flavor emerges. This vinaigrette would be great for any fish dish or drizzled on a flatbread.

4 tablespoons **extra-virgin olive oil**

1 large bunch fresh **chives**, cut into ½-inch pieces (1 cup)

1 teaspoon **kosher salt**

3 tablespoons **full-fat sour cream**

Juice of 1 **lemon**

1 Cook the chives: Heat a medium sauté pan over medium heat and add 2 tablespoons of the olive oil. When it begins to get hot, add the chives and salt. Cook, stirring constantly, until the chives soften, 1 to 2 minutes. Set aside to cool for 5 to 10 minutes.

2 Make the dressing: Transfer the chives and oil to a medium bowl, and whisk in the remaining 2 tablespoons olive oil along with the sour cream and lemon juice. Taste for seasoning. Serve immediately.

HOMEMADE MAYONNAISE

You can definitely make mayonnaise by hand. In fact it's one of the fundamentals everyone has to accomplish, almost as a rite of passage, in culinary school. I like to make mayonnaise in a food processor, where the pouring of the oil can be more easily monitored than if I am whisking and watching the oil at the same time. This one can easily be made spicy by adding Sriracha and jalapeño (see Spicy Mayo, below).

3 large **egg yolks**
1 tablespoon **distilled white vinegar**
2 teaspoons **pickle juice**
2 teaspoons **Dijon mustard**
1 teaspoon **kosher salt**
1 cup **canola oil**

In a food processor, blend the egg yolks with the vinegar, pickle juice, mustard, and salt. With the machine running, pour the canola oil through the top in a slow but steady stream. After half of the oil has been successfully integrated, make the stream quicker and steadier. On the one hand, you want to add the oil gradually to avoid a separated mayonnaise; on the other, you want to avoid going so slowly that the machine heats up the eggs and ruins the mayonnaise. Transfer the mayonnaise to a serving bowl and taste for seasoning.

SPICY MAYO
Add 1 tablespoon Sriracha hot sauce when you add the vinegar, and stir in 1 minced seeded medium jalapeño at the end.

LOBSTER MAYONNAISE

I love lobster, and when I cook it, I like to use all of it. The coral (roe, or eggs) makes a wonderful sauce when it is finely chopped, sautéed, and blended with a little cream. This mayo is great with—surprise!—lobster, shrimp, or crab in particular. I also love to pair it with tomatoes, hard-boiled eggs, or a peppery green like arugula or watercress. The kimchi adds a bit of funk and a slight heat.

3 large **egg yolks**
1 tablespoon **sherry vinegar**
2 teaspoons **grainy mustard**
Grated zest and juice of 1 **lemon**
Coral from 3 **female lobsters**
1 teaspoon **cayenne pepper**
1 cup **canola oil**
1 heaping tablespoon coarsely chopped **kimchi**
6 **cornichons**, minced

In the bowl of a food processor, blend the egg yolks with the vinegar, mustard, lemon zest and juice, coral, and cayenne. With the machine running on medium speed, pour the canola oil through the top in a slow but steady stream. After half of the oil has been successfully integrated, make the stream quicker and steadier. On the one hand, you want to add the oil gradually to avoid a separated mayonnaise; on the other, you want to avoid going so slowly that the machine heats the eggs and ruins the mayonnaise. Transfer the mayonnaise to a medium bowl, and stir in the kimchi and cornichons. Taste for seasoning.

SPICED COCONUT MILK DRESSING

This is wonderfully creamy, a classic example of how the natural fat from coconut can provide such tremendous richness and body without feeling heavy. Resist the urge to add sugar to this dressing, and enjoy it with crudités or over broiled fish or steamed rice.

1 (13.5-ounce) can **unsweetened coconut milk**
1 teaspoon **kosher salt**
1 teaspoon **cayenne pepper**
1 teaspoon **hot paprika**
½ cup **canola oil**
¼ cup **rice vinegar**

1 Cook the coconut milk: Pour the entire contents of the can of coconut milk into a medium saucepan, and add the salt, cayenne, and paprika. Simmer over medium heat until reduced by half, 25 to 30 minutes. Set it aside to cool.

2 Make the dressing: Pour the cooled coconut milk mixture into a blender, and with the machine running on medium speed, slowly drizzle in the canola oil and vinegar through the top. Taste for seasoning.

INHUMANLY SPICY HOT SAUCE

Scotch bonnet chiles are so beautiful, but I sometimes think they are not meant to be eaten! A single slice of a fresh Scotch bonnet can render a dish inedible. However, I do find that when they are made into a hot sauce or fermented or mellowed, their flavor is wonderful. But spicy. Proceed with caution. It's best to wear gloves while handling these chiles. Otherwise, wash your hands and all surfaces very thoroughly afterward.

1 pound fresh **Scotch bonnet chiles**, stemmed
1 tablespoon grated fresh **ginger**
4 medium **garlic cloves**, minced
1 tablespoon **kosher salt**

In a food processor, pulse the chiles, ginger, garlic, and salt to blend—but don't make it completely smooth. Pack the mixture tightly into a pint jar with a tight-fitting lid. Make sure the liquid covers the solids in the jar. If you don't store it in a sealed jar, cover thoroughly with plastic wrap. Let it sit out at room temperature until you see some bubbles, evidence that the fermentation process has begun. It usually takes a day or two. When that happens, refrigerate for up to 6 weeks. The longer the hot sauce keeps, the better the flavor.

FRIED THYME VINAIGRETTE

I love lightly frying herbs to mellow their flavor. Sometimes I think they end up tasting even better than in their natural state. I often feel that way about thyme. I love this vinaigrette for grilled or roasted meats or hearty vegetables. I enjoy it most with beef, potatoes, and mushrooms. It has such an earthy, acidic flavor that it stands up to big ingredients!

½ cup **canola oil**
16 sprigs fresh **thyme**
½ teaspoon **kosher salt**
¼ cup **extra-virgin olive oil** (see Note)
1 small **shallot**, grated
Juice of 1 **orange**
Juice of 2 **lemons**

1 **Fry the thyme:** Heat the canola oil in a medium skillet over medium heat. When it gets warm, add the thyme sprigs. They should bubble and froth slightly. Allow the thyme to cook until the green color pales slightly and the leaves become crispy, 2 to 3 minutes. Use a slotted spoon to remove the sprigs carefully from the oil and put them on a kitchen towel to drain. Season the sprigs with the salt.

2 **Make the vinaigrette:** In a medium bowl, whisk together the olive oil, shallot, and orange and lemon juices. Flake the thyme leaves off the stems into the vinaigrette. Taste for seasoning.

NOTE: Since the oil does not get super-hot to crisp the thyme, you can reserve it for another use.

HOMEMADE GUAJILLO CHILE HOT SAUCE

I'd love to say I invented this recipe, but I really stole it shamelessly from Antonio Morales, one of the best chefs I have had the pleasure of working with. He makes this and stashes it in the fridge for whenever anyone wants a little tasty hot sauce. This sauce can be refrigerated for a long time and only gets better and better.

1½ cups **canola oil**

2 medium **yellow onions**, cut into 1-inch-thick slices

2 **plum tomatoes**, halved

Kosher salt

1 teaspoon crushed **red pepper flakes**

2 medium dried **guajillo chiles**, soaked in water until soft, drained (see Note)

2 tablespoons **red wine vinegar**

1 Cook the onions and tomatoes: In a large skillet, heat 2 tablespoons of the canola oil over medium heat. When it begins to smoke lightly, add the onion slices and tomato halves in a single layer. Season with salt and the red pepper flakes. Cook until the onions and tomatoes become tender, 15 to 18 minutes. If the onions are browning too quickly, lower the heat slightly and add a splash of water.

2 Make the hot sauce: In a blender, puree the guajillos with the vinegar. Then, with the machine running on medium speed, gradually blend in 1 cup of the oil. Add the onions and tomatoes and the remaining 6 tablespoons oil, and blend until just smooth. Taste for seasoning.

NOTE: If you want less spice, remove the seeds and ribs from the guajillo chiles once they are hydrated.

FRESH CHILE SALSA

You can adjust the heat level of this salsa according to how you intend to serve it. I add only two fresh chiles, my favorite combination of jalapeño and habanero, which gives this salsa quite a kick. When we make it at the restaurant, the spice level runs even higher. I love this on chicken, pork, fish, and even roasted vegetables. Try it on a baked Idaho or sweet potato. This salsa can be served immediately, but it's better when made a day ahead and left overnight in the fridge—this lets the flavors meld together. It's best to wear gloves while handling these chiles. Otherwise, wash your hands and all surfaces very thoroughly afterward.

½ cup chopped fresh **flat-leaf parsley**
¼ cup chopped fresh **cilantro**
3 tablespoons **capers**, drained and coarsely chopped
1 small **garlic clove**, grated
1 tablespoon **Dijon mustard**
2 tablespoons **grainy mustard**
1 tablespoon **red wine vinegar**
1 small **jalapeño**, thinly sliced
1 small **habanero chile**, thinly sliced
½ cup **extra-virgin olive oil**

In a large bowl, whisk together the parsley, cilantro, capers, garlic, and smooth and grainy mustards. Add the vinegar, jalapeño, habanero, and olive oil. Taste for seasoning.

MISO DRESSING

I believe in umami or that elusive "fifth taste" people speak of. It's where tastes and textures collude in a perfect way. I think umami resides in a small and choice number of ingredients. At the top of the list is blond miso paste (made from fermented soybeans). While this dressing is tasty on greens, I believe it is even better suited for crunchy vegetables—celery, cucumbers, and carrots—where these juicy vegetables thrive with the dressing. Toss your vegetables in some of this and let the mixture sit in the fridge for a few minutes. The neutral flavor of canola oil leaves room for the vinegars and miso to take center stage.

2 tablespoons **blond miso paste**
2 tablespoons **red wine vinegar**
2 tablespoons **rice vinegar**
1 teaspoon coarsely ground **black pepper**
½ teaspoon **kosher salt**
1 teaspoon **sugar**
1 medium **shallot**, minced
¾ cup **canola oil**

In a large bowl, whisk the miso and red wine vinegar together until smooth. Whisk in the rice vinegar, pepper, salt, sugar, and shallot. Whisking constantly, blend in the canola oil. Taste for seasoning.

TOMATO PULP VINAIGRETTE

The pulp of a tomato offers a wonderful combination of pectin (which works like gelatin) and little seeds. The texture is great. I like to make a vinaigrette by squeezing the seeds from overripe tomatoes and then tossing that dressing with the tomatoes themselves. Sometimes I make this dressing and then use the rest of the tomatoes to make a small batch of tomato sauce. You may have to play a little with the proportions because the juice and seed factor in tomatoes tends to vary.

About 6 large overripe **tomatoes**
2 teaspoons **kosher salt**
1 teaspoon **sugar**
½ teaspoon crushed **red pepper flakes**
2 tablespoons **red wine vinegar**
¼ cup **extra-virgin olive oil**

Slice the tomatoes in half crosswise, and squeeze the seeds and juices into a medium bowl. You want about ¾ cup liquid and seeds. Whisk in the salt, sugar, red pepper flakes, vinegar, and olive oil. Taste for seasoning.

COCKTAIL SAUCE

I am of the school of thought that if your nostrils tingle slightly when you eat a bite of cocktail sauce, then the sauce has done its job. The combination of the sweetness and tang of the ketchup with the bite of horseradish makes it an ideal sauce for seafood: particularly shrimp and oysters. I like rice vinegar for a mellower acid mixed with lemon juice. If you like heat, leave the seeds and ribs in the jalapeño.

1 cup **ketchup**, preferably Heinz brand
¼ cup freshly grated **horseradish**
1 teaspoon **kosher salt**
1 teaspoon coarsely ground **black pepper**
¼ cup **rice vinegar**
2 teaspoons **Worcestershire sauce**, preferably Lea & Perrins brand
Juice of 1 medium **lemon**
1 teaspoon **Tabasco**
1 small **jalapeño**, seeded and minced
1 small **garlic clove**, minced

In a large bowl, whisk together the ketchup, horseradish, salt, pepper, rice vinegar, Worcestershire, lemon juice, Tabasco, jalapeños, and garlic. Taste for seasoning.

MY DAD'S GARLIC AND RED WINE VINEGAR VINAIGRETTE

This is the kind of vinaigrette that makes your mouth pucker. It is best served with hearty greens like escarole, endive, or radicchio mixed with some mellower types like red oak-leaf or arugula. My father would disappear into the kitchen for a few minutes after the main course and toss the salad on the spot: ice-cold lettuce and this exact vinaigrette.

1 medium **garlic clove**, pressed or grated
1 teaspoon **kosher salt**
½ cup **red wine vinegar**
1½ cups **extra-virgin olive oil**

In a bowl that is large enough to hold your salad greens, whisk together the garlic, salt, and vinegar. Pour the olive oil into the vinegar, whisking constantly. If the vinaigrette doesn't come together, whisk in a splash of water.

SOY GINGER DRESSING

This is really a combination of three great ingredients: a little fiery fresh ginger, chunky peanut butter, and dark soy sauce. It's the kind of dressing that makes you want to lick the plate when you are done eating and then help yourself to seconds. I love it with roasted pork or ribs, it's great on naturally sweet vegetables like carrots, and it's wonderful on crisp cold lettuce, like romaine or iceberg.

1 tablespoon **canola oil**
3 medium **garlic cloves**, minced
½ teaspoon crushed **red pepper flakes**
1 teaspoon **kosher salt**
1 tablespoon grated fresh **ginger**
2 tablespoons **dark soy sauce**
Juice of 1 **lime**
2 tablespoons **chunky peanut butter**

1 Cook the garlic: Heat a small skillet over medium heat and add the canola oil. When it gets hot, add the garlic, red pepper flakes, and salt and cook, stirring constantly, until the garlic softens, 1 to 2 minutes. Pour the mixture into a salad bowl and set aside to cool for 5 to 10 minutes.

2 Make the dressing: Whisk the ginger, soy sauce, lime juice, and peanut butter into the garlic oil, and then stir in a couple tablespoons of water until the dressing reaches the desired consistency. Taste for seasoning.

SALADS
FOR EVERY SEASON

ENDIVE SALAD

WITH BLUE CHEESE AND SPICED WALNUTS

The bitterness of endive screams out for a creamy blue cheese dressing. This salad really has it all, from salty to sweet and crunchy to supple. It's hard to resist. A note about storing endive: it is grown in the absence of light, so keep it wrapped in foil or in a kitchen towel in the refrigerator so it stays underexposed to light until serving. My favorite blue cheeses for this salad are (Spanish) Cabrales, (French) Fourme d'Ambert, and (Italian) Gorgonzola. Spray the wooden spoon with non-stick cooking spray so it doesn't get coated with caramelized sugar. This is one of my favorite tricks.

Nonstick cooking spray

2 cups **sugar**

1½ cups **walnut halves**

½ teaspoon **hot paprika**

Kosher salt

¾ cup **mayonnaise**, preferable Hellmann's or Best Foods

1 cup **full-fat sour cream**

Juice of 1 **lemon**

2 tablespoons **red wine vinegar**

2 tablespoons **Worcestershire sauce**, preferably Lea & Perrins brand

2 teaspoons **Tabasco**

2 medium **garlic cloves**, grated

1 pound **blue cheese**, crumbled

4 large heads **Belgian endive**

1   Caramelize the nuts: Lightly grease a baking sheet with cooking spray. In a clean medium saucepan, combine the sugar with ¾ cup water and bring to a boil over medium heat. Lower the heat and simmer until the sugar dissolves and turns a medium brown color, 15 to 20 minutes. Don't touch or stir the sugar while it's cooking. Add the walnuts and paprika, and stir quickly with a clean wooden spoon to coat the nuts with the sugar syrup. Quickly turn them out onto the prepared baking sheet and spread them out to cool. Season with salt to taste. When the walnuts have cooled, break them apart.

2   Make the dressing: In a medium bowl, whisk together the mayonnaise, sour cream, lemon juice, red wine vinegar, Worcestershire sauce, Tabasco, and garlic. Season with salt to taste. Vigorously stir in half of the blue cheese so it breaks into small pieces. Gently add the remainder of the cheese. Taste for seasoning. Cover the dressing with plastic wrap and refrigerate for a few hours or even overnight.

3   Prepare the endive: Cut off the bottom of each endive and peel the leaves off, dropping them into a bowl. You will have to cut the bottom off again every few layers to loosen the leaves as they become smaller. Arrange the leaves in a single layer on a large serving platter.

4   Finish the salad: Top the endive with the dressing, taking care that each piece gets dressing. Top with the nuts. Serve immediately.

ROASTED ASPARAGUS SALAD
WITH CHOPPED EGG AND CAYENNE

Cooking asparagus on the stove in a little hot oil is easy and skips the need for boiling water and ice baths. Once you start cooking the asparagus, be ready to serve the salad; it is best warm, topped with the vinaigrette and chopped eggs, which are rich against the grassy notes of the asparagus. The sesame adds a toasted, nutty richness as well.

4 large **eggs**

6 tablespoons **extra-virgin olive oil**

2 tablespoons **sesame seeds**

Juice of 2 **lemons**

Kosher salt and freshly ground **black pepper**

2 tablespoons **canola oil**

1 pound **pencil asparagus**, ends trimmed

1 teaspoon **cayenne pepper**

1 Boil the eggs: Put the eggs in a medium saucepan and cover them with cold water. Bring the water to a boil and then reduce the heat so that the water simmers gently. Once it is simmering, cook for 11 minutes. Then drain the water from the eggs and run a steady stream of cold water over them to stop them from overcooking.

2 Make the vinaigrette: In a small bowl, whisk together the olive oil, sesame seeds, and lemon juice.

3 Marinate the eggs: Peel the eggs and rinse them under cold water to remove any remaining bits of shell. Roughly chop the eggs. Transfer them to a medium bowl, season lightly with salt and pepper, and drizzle a little of the vinaigrette over them.

4 Cook the asparagus and finish the salad: Heat a large skillet over medium heat and add the canola oil. When the oil begins to smoke lightly, remove the skillet from the heat and add the asparagus in a single layer. Season the spears with salt and dust them with the cayenne. Return the pan to high heat and cook the asparagus until they brown slightly and become tender, 3 to 5 minutes. Remove the skillet from the heat and arrange the asparagus on a serving platter. Spoon the remaining vinaigrette over them and top with the eggs. Serve immediately.

AVOCADO AND ORANGE SALAD

I used to make this salad on my day off when I lived in Paris. We never served avocado, bell peppers, or oranges at the restaurant, so I figure this was my ode to ingredients I missed. This salad is super-simple and super-juicy; serve it ice-cold or even spoon it onto a baguette. Why two kinds of salt? Kosher salt dissolves easily into the dressing. The flaky Maldon salt gives great flavor and crunch to the supple avocado.

¼ cup **balsamic vinegar**

1 teaspoon freshly ground **black pepper**

1 teaspoon **kosher salt**

2 teaspoons **sugar**

¾ cup **extra-virgin olive oil**

2 large **red bell pepper**s, quartered, seeded, and cut into 1-inch-wide slices

2 medium **avocados**, peeled, halved, pitted, and cut into 1-inch-wide slices

2 teaspoons **Maldon sea salt**

2 medium **navel oranges**, sectioned (see page 129)

1 Make the dressing: In a large salad bowl, whisk together the balsamic vinegar, black pepper, kosher salt, and sugar. Slowly drizzle in the olive oil, whisking constantly. Taste for seasoning.

2 Assemble the salad: In the bowl containing the dressing, toss the bell peppers and avocados with the Maldon salt. Add the orange sections and toss again. Serve immediately.

ICEBERG WEDGE
WITH RUSSIAN DRESSING

Ketchup and mayonnaise are two condiments that I don't make from scratch when whipping up Russian dressing. Hellmann's and Heinz have that covered. Maybe it's a childhood thing. The combination of these two with the right amount of kick and acidity is hard to improve upon. Spoon the dressing over a wedge of chilled iceberg and you are in Americana heaven. I like to ramp up the flavors with really good pickles and fresh horseradish when it's available.

1 cup **mayonnaise**, preferably Hellmann's or Best Foods

⅓ cup **ketchup**, preferably Heinz

2 medium **garlic cloves**, grated

1 medium **half-sour pickle**, finely chopped, plus 2 tablespoons pickle brine

1 tablespoon grated fresh or prepared **horseradish**

2 teaspoons **Worcestershire sauce**, preferably Lea & Perrins brand

1 teaspoon **Tabasco**

1 teaspoon **kosher salt**

2 large heads **iceberg lettuce**, outer leaves removed, cut in half or in thirds, and cored

1 small bunch fresh **chives**, cut into ½-inch pieces (½ cup)

1 Make the dressing: In a medium bowl, whisk together the mayonnaise, ketchup, garlic, chopped pickle and pickle juice, horseradish, Worcestershire, Tabasco, and salt. Taste for seasoning.

2 Assemble the salad: Put each wedge of lettuce on a plate. Drizzle with the dressing and top with the chives. Serve immediately.

ROASTED POTATO SALAD

WITH CRISPY ROSEMARY

Classic Red Bliss potatoes, often found in potato salads, are almost always boiled. They are also delicious and have a more pronounced flavor when roasted. In this salad I toss them, still warm, into the dressing and top them with rosemary. Frying the rosemary mellows its medicinal raw taste, making it a better version of itself.

2 pounds medium **Red Bliss potatoes**

6 tablespoons **sherry vinegar**

2 tablespoons **Dijon mustard**

1 tablespoon drained **capers**, chopped, plus 1 teaspoon caper brine

6 **cornichons**, cut into ¼-inch pieces, plus 1 tablespoon brine

¼ cup **extra-virgin olive oil** (see Note)

½ cup **canola oil**

3 sprigs fresh **rosemary**

3 teaspoons **kosher salt**

1 Preheat the oven to 400°F.

2 Cook the potatoes: Arrange the potatoes in a single layer on a baking sheet and roast them in the oven until tender when pierced with the tip of a knife, 35 to 40 minutes.

3 Meanwhile, make the vinaigrette: In a bowl that is large enough to hold the potatoes, whisk together the sherry vinegar, mustard, capers and brine, and cornichons and brine. Whisk in the olive oil. Taste for seasoning.

4 Fry the rosemary: Heat the canola oil in a medium skillet over medium heat. When it is hot, add the rosemary sprigs. They should bubble and froth slightly. Allow the rosemary to cook until its green color pales slightly and the needles become crispy, 2 to 3 minutes. Use a slotted spoon to remove them carefully from the oil and put them on a kitchen towel to drain. Season them with 1 teaspoon of the salt.

5 Assemble the salad: Halve the warm potatoes and add them to the bowl containing the dressing. As you mix, lightly crush them with the tines of a fork. Season with the remaining 2 teaspoons salt. Flake the crisp rosemary needles from the stems over the potatoes. Discard the stems. Serve immediately.

NOTE: Since the oil does not get super-hot to crisp the rosemary, you can reserve it for another use.

MIXED GREENS
LEAVE A TENDER MOMENT ALONE

One head of escarole, one piece of radicchio, one head of romaine: a single type of green in the right place with the right dressing can be better than ten types tossed carelessly with the wrong one! The first thing I look for is to choose lettuces that are bright green (or red, or yellow) and firm. Since most lettuces are water bombs, you should feel the weight of the head in your hand when buying it. Keep your greens dry and cool in a dark place, and don't wash them or mix them with anything acidic (lemon, vinegar) until right before eating.

I generally break greens into three categories: juicy, bitter, and peppery:

THE JUICY GREENS

BIBB OR BOSTON LETTUCE: I toss these with sherry or red wine dressing, sliced shallots, and parsley leaves.

ICEBERG: I love a good wedge with blue cheese. I also love chopping iceberg and mixing it with scallions, fresh chiles, or a really vibrant dressing. It has a great, juicy texture and natural sweetness. To me, it's nice to have a lettuce that leaves room for bold flavors. In the summertime, I also freeze wedges and serve them with lemon and olive oil.

ROMAINE: Romaine is juicy and also pleasantly grassy. It goes well with naturally salty flavors from capers, cornichons, anchovies, and grated cheese.

THE BITTER GREENS

DANDELION: These long spiky leaves are delicious both raw and when grilled quickly or roasted. Cut off the root end, wash the leaves thoroughly, lightly oil them, and drop them on the grill or in a hot sauté pan for a couple of minutes. A sprinkle of salt, pepper, and lemon juice and these greens can be the start of a great warm salad. Dandelion is intense, so if serving it raw, it's best to mix it with a more neutral green like romaine. Dandelion also takes the sweetness from fruit really well: apple or pear slices, even peaches . . .

ENDIVE: I love endive for its bitter flavor and also for its unique shape. We always talk about mixing flavors and staying seasonal, but a good mixed green salad also contains greens of varying sizes and shapes. That makes for better eating. A few endive spears tossed with some arugula and parsley leaves? Bitter, peppery, and grassy, all different sizes and shapes. Lemon dressing is great with this combination. Some tangy goat cheese or spiced walnuts would also round out the salad.

ESCAROLE: With wonderfully bitter juicy stems and a slight natural sweetness, these are sturdy greens that can handle any dressing.

FRISÉE: The curly, floppy-looking yellow and green head has great texture. It can fill in the gaps when tossed with a peppery leafy green like arugula. I love frisée with cheese or chopped hard-boiled egg. Bacon, too.

RADICCHIO: This is a wonderful bitter green. A little goes a long way, so while it may not look like much at the market, one head peeled of all its layers can really flesh out a salad that needs a pleasantly bitter note. It is wonderful paired with fruits, especially apples or raspberries. It can withstand the richness of toasted nuts or creamy goat cheese. For a charred note, I sometimes grill and cool the leaves before tossing them with blue cheese or toasted pumpkin seeds.

THE PEPPERY GREENS

ARUGULA: Arugula tastes like someone sprinkled it with cracked black pepper! It's a green I serve solo or with cherry tomatoes or strawberries.

COLLARD GREENS: When these are young, they are tasty raw. I finely slice smaller leaves for salads.

MUSTARD GREENS: At the stronger end of the intensity spectrum as far as green leafy vegetables go, mustard greens have an almost spicy heat. They sometimes taste to me like watercress mixed with a hit of fresh jalapeño.

WATERCRESS: Don't let the light, leafy look of watercress fool you. Despite its small stems and delicate leaves, watercress packs a sharp, peppery flavor. The juicy stems taste almost like mustard or ginger to me. Chop them and use them like an herb in a salsa or on grilled fish.

BUT HOW TO MAKE A GOOD MIXED GREENS SALAD?

I usually strike a balance between a juicy green (romaine), one sturdy bitter green (dandelion, escarole, endive), and a peppery green (mustard). I tend to mix delicate greens with herbs such as parsley, basil, and chives, for example. Cauliflower and broccoli florets can be peeled and minced into a "rice" and marinated in a bright dressing. You can also make a great pesto with the broccoli stems.

MY MIXED GREENS SALAD

SERVES 4

Juice of 1 **lemon**
3 tablespoons **extra-virgin olive oil**
2 cups roughly chopped **romaine leaves**
1 cup roughly chopped **radicchio leaves**
1 cup roughly chopped **mustard greens**
¼ cup **flat-leaf parsley leaves**
2 teaspoons **kosher salt**
½ teaspoon freshly ground **black pepper**

In a large salad bowl, whisk together the lemon juice and olive oil. Add the greens and toss lightly to coat them with the dressing. Season with the salt and pepper. Serve immediately.

FENNEL AND ORANGE SALAD
WITH WALNUT PESTO

When I was growing up, my dad used to make raw fennel salads with lemon and olive oil. When I first tasted roasted fennel in a Parisian bistro, I was hooked. This salad is meant to be served at room temperature with a great burst of juice from the orange and a peppery note from the arugula.

FENNEL
3 medium **fennel bulbs**
2 tablespoons **canola oil**
2 teaspoons **kosher salt**
½ teaspoon crushed **red pepper flakes**
1 cup **dry white wine**

WALNUT PESTO
½ cup **walnut halves**, toasted and coarsely chopped
Grated zest and juice of 1 **lemon**
2 teaspoons **kosher salt**
2 tablespoons **extra-virgin olive oil**

2 medium **navel oranges**, sectioned (see page 129)
1 cup **arugula leaves**

1 Prepare the fennel: If the outer layer of any of the bulbs is bruised or dried out, remove and discard that layer. Cut the bulbs in half lengthwise and then cut each half into 3 equal wedges so they look like sections of an orange.

2 Cook the fennel: Heat a large sauté pan over medium heat and add the canola oil. Remove the pan from the heat, arrange the fennel in a single layer in the pan, and season with the salt and red pepper flakes. Return the pan to the heat and cook, undisturbed, until the fennel turns light brown on the first side, 3 to 5 minutes. Use tongs to turn the fennel wedges over, and cook for another 3 to 5 minutes. When they have browned on the second side, remove the pan from the heat and add the white wine. Return the pan to low heat and simmer until all of the wine has reduced, 5 to 8 minutes. Insert a sharp knife into a few of the fennel pieces: They should be tender and yielding. If not, add ½ cup water and simmer again until the water evaporates. Ideally, there should be very little remaining liquid at the end of the process. Set the fennel aside to cool.

3 Make the pesto: In a small bowl, whisk together the walnuts, the lemon zest and juice, salt, and olive oil. Taste for seasoning.

4 Finish the salad: Transfer the fennel to a serving bowl and toss it with the walnut pesto. Gently mix in the orange sections and arugula. Taste for seasoning. Serve immediately.

FRESH AND FROZEN PEA SALAD

There are so many types of peas to turn to when making a pea salad. If you want, you can even top these with a hearty handful of pea shoots. This dressing has a way of making the peas, frozen and fresh, taste like an amplified, improved version of themselves. Every chef uses frozen peas—we just don't always admit it! They're tasty! In short, the salad takes peas from coach to business class and the dressing will take them all the way to first. The sugar in the cooking water and honey on the peas themselves also intensify the flavor.

DRESSING

2 tablespoons **Dijon mustard**

¼ cup fresh lemon juice (from about 2 medium **lemons**)

1 teaspoon drained **capers**, roughly chopped, plus 1 teaspoon of their brine

1 teaspoon **kosher salt**

Freshly ground **black pepper**

⅔ cup **extra-virgin olive oil**

Leaves from 6 sprigs fresh **tarragon**

PEAS

Kosher salt

1 tablespoon **sugar**

8 ounces **sugar snap peas**, stemmed

8 ounces **snow peas**, stemmed

1 cup frozen **peas**, defrosted

1 tablespoon **honey**

1 **Make the dressing:** In a medium bowl, whisk together the mustard, lemon juice, capers, caper brine, salt, and pepper. Gradually whisk in the olive oil and tarragon leaves. Taste for seasoning.

2 **Cook the peas:** Fill a large saucepan with water. Add salt until the water tastes like seawater. Add the sugar. Bring the water to a boil. Meanwhile, prepare an ice bath: Fill a large bowl halfway with ice cubes and add some cold water. Put a colander squarely inside the ice bath. (The colander will keep you from having to pick the peas out from among the ice cubes in the ice bath.) Add the sugar snap peas to the boiling water and cook for 1 minute. Add the snow peas and cook them together for 1 more minute. The peas should be bright green and retain a little crunch. Remove the peas from the water with a strainer and transfer them to the colander inside the ice bath. Let them cool completely.

3 **Drain the peas:** Pull the colander out of the ice bath and spread the peas out on a kitchen towel. Use another kitchen towel to gently pat them dry. (This step will prevent the water from diluting the flavor of the peas and the vinaigrette.)

4 **Assemble the salad:** When you are ready to serve the salad, put the cooked peas and defrosted frozen peas in a medium bowl and season with 1 tablespoon salt and the honey. Toss with the vinaigrette. Taste for seasoning. Serve immediately.

CRISPY BRUSSELS SPROUTS SALAD

One of my favorite ingredient combinations is Brussels sprouts and bacon. And I love using Brussels sprouts raw and cooked in the same dish. To me, fried Brussels sprouts taste like nori seaweed, full of umami. The soy sauce in the vinaigrette here adds a deep salty note alongside the bacon without taking away from our star veggie. Most of this can be prepared in advance and then tossed together at the last minute.

1 pound **Brussels sprouts**

6 ounces **bacon**, cut into 1-inch pieces

2 tablespoons **extra-virgin olive oil**

1 tablespoon **dark soy sauce**

Juice of 2 **lemons**

2 medium **shallots**, minced

3 cups **canola oil**

Kosher salt

¼ cup medium to small fresh **mint leaves**, roughly torn

½ cup fresh **flat-leaf parsley leaves**

1 **Prepare the Brussels sprouts:** Remove and discard any damaged outer leaves. Then peel away the outer layers from each Brussels sprout to yield a total of 2 cups. Set those leaves aside. Thinly slice the remaining core pieces of the Brussels sprouts, and set them aside separately.

2 **Cook the bacon:** Heat a medium skillet over medium-high heat, and add ½ cup water and the bacon slices. Cook until all of the water evaporates and the bacon becomes crispy, 12 to 15 minutes. Transfer the bacon to a kitchen towel to drain, reserving the fat in the pan.

3 **Make the vinaigrette:** In a large bowl, whisk 2 tablespoons of the reserved bacon fat with the olive oil, soy sauce, and lemon juice. Stir in the shallots. Taste for seasoning and set aside.

4 **Heat the oil:** Pour the canola oil into a medium heavy-bottomed pot and heat it slowly to 375°F. (Use a deep-frying thermometer to monitor the temperature.) Line a baking sheet with a kitchen towel and set it aside.

5 **Fry the Brussels sprouts:** Carefully drop the Brussels sprout leaves, in small batches, into the hot oil. They will hiss and splatter when you drop them in, so stand back! Fry the leaves, turning them over with a metal slotted spoon, until they are crispy, 2 to 3 minutes. Transfer the leaves to the lined baking sheet to drain, and season them immediately with salt.

6 **Assemble the salad:** In the large bowl holding the vinaigrette, toss the reserved thinly sliced Brussels sprout cores with the mint and parsley leaves. Season with salt. Stir in the bacon and the warm fried Brussels sprout leaves. Serve immediately.

GRILLED TOMATO SALAD
WITH OREGANO

It's in the details, not in any unusual ingredients, for this salad. By crisping the oregano in the oil for the dressing, by taking a moment to extract some of the pulp when you juice the limes, and by grilling the tomatoes, this simple list of ingredients becomes even more tasty with little added effort. This salad is downright refreshing for a summer patio meal or an early fall dinner. I make it whenever I get my hands on really good tomatoes.

4 tablespoons **extra-virgin olive oil**

8 sprigs **fresh oregano**, stemmed

½ teaspoon **dried oregano**

2 **limes**

7 large **heirloom tomatoes** (about 2½ pounds), cut into 1½-inch-thick slices

2 tablespoons **Maldon sea salt**

2 teaspoons freshly ground **black pepper**

1 tablespoon **sugar**

1 pint **cherry tomatoes**, halved

1 Preheat a grill to high heat.

2 Make the dressing: In a small sauté pan, warm 2 tablespoons of the olive oil over medium heat and add the fresh oregano. Cook the oregano in the warm oil until the green color fades and the leaves crisp up, 2 to 3 minutes. Pour the oil and oregano into a medium bowl. Add the remaining 2 tablespoons olive oil and the dried oregano. Cut the limes in half and squeeze all the juice into the bowl. Use a citrus reamer or a spoon to scrape the pulp from the limes as well, and add the pulp to the bowl. Whisk all together. Taste for seasoning.

3 Grill the heirloom tomatoes: Arrange the tomato slices in a single layer on two baking sheets. Season them on both sides with some of the Maldon salt, black pepper, and sugar. Put the cherry tomatoes on a separate baking sheet and season them, too. Use a pair of tongs to transfer the large tomato slices to the grill, arranging them in a single layer. Let them sit until they get a nice grill mark on the bottom (and a great charred flavor), 2 to 3 minutes. Turn them over and let them cook for a few minutes longer. Transfer the grilled tomatoes to a serving platter. Top with the cherry tomato halves.

4 Finish the salad: Drizzle the tomatoes with the dressing and sprinkle with any remaining sea salt. Taste a piece of tomato to check the seasoning. If it lacks sweetness, a sprinkle of sugar on the tomatoes can make all the difference. Serve immediately.

CREAMY FETA PANZANELLA
WITH OREGANO DRESSING

French feta is creamy and salty without being too much. It leaves room for other ingredients to shine as well. If it's not available, classic Greek feta is also fine. The bread in this salad plays against the cheese, and the greens are the fresh bridge tying them together. When you make the dressing, it won't really come together cohesively, but in this case, that's part of what makes each bite of this salad different from the next.

1 pound **sourdough bread**, cut into 1½-inch cubes (4½ cups)

8 tablespoons **extra-virgin olive oil**

2 teaspoons **kosher salt**

1 cup (4 ounces) crumbled **French feta cheese**

2 tablespoons **red wine vinegar**

2 teaspoons dried **oregano**

½ teaspoon crushed **red pepper flakes**

1 pint **cherry tomatoes**, halved

1 medium head **escarole**, leaves torn into bite-size pieces

Leaves from 4 sprigs fresh **dill**

1 Preheat the oven to 350°F.

2 Toast the bread: In a medium bowl, toss the bread cubes with 3 tablespoons of the olive oil and 1 teaspoon of the salt. Arrange them in a single layer on a baking sheet and bake until golden brown, 8 to 10 minutes.

3 Meanwhile, make the dressing: In a large bowl, stir together the cheese, red wine vinegar, oregano, red pepper flakes, and remaining 5 tablespoons olive oil. Season the tomatoes with the remaining 1 teaspoon salt and toss them in the dressing so they can start to soak up the flavors.

4 Assemble the salad: When the bread is toasted, toss the warm cubes, the escarole, and the dill leaves with the dressing and tomatoes. Taste for seasoning. Serve immediately.

TASTY TOMATO SALAD
WITH FRESH RASPBERRIES

This is a quick summer salad that needs only good tomatoes and raspberries. The raspberry jam provides a deep almost underground jammy and sweet flavor while the fresh raspberries are pleasantly seedy and tart. As you sprinkle the flaky sea salt, crush it lightly between your fingers so the larger pieces become smaller and are distributed more evenly.

2 tablespoons **balsamic vinegar**

1 tablespoon **raspberry jam**

1 tablespoon fresh **lemon juice**

¼ cup **extra-virgin olive oil**

1 pint fresh **raspberries**

3 pints **cherry tomatoes**, halved

1 tablespoon **Maldon sea salt**

1 teaspoon freshly ground **black pepper**

2 teaspoons **sugar**

1 Make the dressing: In a medium bowl, whisk together the balsamic vinegar, raspberry jam, and lemon juice. Whisk in the olive oil. Taste. Stir in the raspberries, leaving about half of them whole and lightly crushing the rest. Set aside.

2 Assemble the salad: Put the tomatoes on a platter and season them evenly with the salt, black pepper, and sugar. Drizzle the dressing over the tomatoes and toss gently. Serve immediately.

ROASTED RADISHES

CUCUMBER AND MINT SALAD

I like to serve this ice-cold because the chill adds to the refreshing, juicy aspect of the salad. It's a great companion to anything spicy when your mouth looks for a cooling element.

2 **hothouse cucumbers**, peeled and cut into 1-inch cubes
2 medium **Kirby cucumbers**, peeled and thinly sliced
1 tablespoon **kosher salt**
¼ cup **rice vinegar**
1 teaspoon **dry mustard**, preferably Colman's
2 tablespoons **extra-virgin olive oil**
¼ cup fresh **mint leaves**
1 tablespoon **honey**

1 Marinate the cucumbers: Arrange both types of cucumber in a single layer on a baking sheet. Season them on both sides with the salt. Combine the rice vinegar and dry mustard in a medium bowl, add the cucumbers, and toss. Cover and refrigerate for at least 1 hour and up to 4 hours.

2 Assemble the salad: Add the olive oil, mint, and honey to the cucumbers, and toss. Taste for seasoning. Serve immediately.

SPRING HERB SALAD

WITH SHERRY VINAIGRETTE

I really learned the value of a pure herb salad during the years when I worked for Daniel Boulud. He has always made an herb ravioli that has a flavor that continues to unfold as you eat. First there is basil, then parsley, and then hints of dill and tarragon. These flavors work equally well in a fresh salad. I love to eat this as is or to park it atop a piece of fish or a few thick slices of beefsteak tomato. While I love herb stems in pestos and many other places, I keep them out of this salad.

½ cup fresh **flat-leaf parsley leaves**
1 cup fresh **pea shoots** or **watercress leaves**
¼ cup fresh **tarragon leaves**
1 tablespoon fresh **dill leaves**
¼ cup fresh **basil leaves**
¼ cup (yellow) **celery leaves** from the heart of the celery
1 small bunch fresh **chives**, cut into 1-inch lengths (¼ cup)
2 tablespoons **sherry vinegar**
¼ cup **extra-virgin olive oil**
2 teaspoons **kosher salt**

In a large serving bowl, toss together all of the herbs and greens: parsley, pea shoots, tarragon, dill, basil, celery leaves, and chives. Make sure they are fully blended; in an ideal world, each bite will contain a little bit of everything. In a small bowl, whisk together the sherry vinegar and olive oil. Sprinkle with the salt. Toss the herb mixture with the vinaigrette, and serve immediately.

SALAD
FOR DINNER

MY MEMORY OF LARRY FORGIONE'S TASTY COBB SALAD

This is the first American salad I made in my first restaurant job, in Larry Forgione's kitchen. It's all about timing.

4 large **eggs**

2 tablespoons **canola oil**

2 (8-ounce) skin-on, bone-in **chicken breasts**

Kosher salt

8 slices **bacon**, cut crosswise into 1-inch pieces

3 tablespoons **red wine vinegar**

1 tablespoon **Dijon mustard**

8 tablespoons **extra-virgin olive oil**

1 teaspoon dried **oregano**

2 medium heads **iceberg lettuce**, cored, split in half

1 pint **cherry tomatoes**, halved and chilled

1 large **avocado**, peeled, halved, pitted, and cut into ½-inch cubes

4 ounces **blue cheese**, such as Cabrales or Danish blue, crumbled

1 Preheat the oven to 350°F.

2 Boil the eggs: Put the eggs in a medium saucepan and cover them with cold water. Bring the water to a boil and then reduce the heat so that the water simmers gently. Once it is simmering, cook the eggs for 11 minutes. Drain the water from the eggs and run a steady stream of cold water over them to stop them from overcooking. When they have cooled, peel and chop the eggs. Set aside.

3 Cook the chicken breasts and bacon: Heat a medium ovenproof skillet over medium heat and add the canola oil. When the oil begins to smoke lightly, season the chicken breasts on both sides with salt and add them, skin side down, to the skillet. Transfer the skillet to the oven. Roast until the chicken breasts are cooked through but still juicy, 18 to 20 minutes. Remove from the oven and allow the chicken breasts to rest on a cutting board. Pour off and reserve all the liquid from the skillet, and add the bacon to the skillet. Cook the bacon over medium heat until crispy, 8 to 10 minutes. Keep warm.

4 Make the dressing and assemble the salad: In a medium bowl, whisk together the red wine vinegar, mustard, olive oil, oregano, and reserved chicken juices. Taste for seasoning. Put an iceberg half on each of four plates. Season each one with ¼ teaspoon salt and a spoonful of the dressing. In a small bowl, toss the tomatoes with ¼ teaspoon salt and some of the dressing, and make a row of tomatoes on each iceberg wedge. Arrange a row of avocado cubes and chopped egg on each wedge, and top with a drizzle of dressing and a sprinkling of salt. Add the warm bacon and sprinkle with the blue cheese. Slice the chicken and arrange a few slices in a row on top of each. Finish with any remaining dressing. Serve immediately.

BEEFSTEAK TOMATO, BACON, AND RED ONION SALAD

When using raw onion in a salad, I like to slice it and crisp it up by soaking it in ice water with some vinegar (this also removes some of that assertive raw onion flavor). It's a simple step that makes a big difference. While many American steakhouses leave their tomatoes out and serve them at room temperature for optimal flavor, I like this refreshing tomato salad to be very cold, topped at the last minute with the warm bacon.

2 tablespoons **red wine vinegar**

1 medium **red onion**, thinly sliced

2 tablespoons **balsamic vinegar**

2 teaspoons **pomegranate molasses**

6 tablespoons **extra-virgin olive oil**

6 ounces sliced **bacon**, cut lengthwise into 1-inch-wide strips and then sliced crosswise into ½-inch pieces

3 large **beefsteak tomatoes**, cut into 1-inch-thick slices

1 pint **heirloom cherry tomatoes**, halved

2 teaspoons **sugar**

2 teaspoons **Maldon sea salt**

1 teaspoon freshly ground **black pepper**

Leaves from 6 sprigs fresh **tarragon**

1 Quickly pickle the red onion: In a small bowl, combine 1 cup water with a few ice cubes, and stir in the red wine vinegar and the onion slices. Set aside.

2 Make the dressing: In a small bowl, whisk together the balsamic vinegar, pomegranate molasses, and olive oil. Taste for seasoning, and set aside.

3 Cook the bacon: Heat a medium skillet over medium heat, and add the bacon pieces and ½ cup water. (The water will "blanch" the bacon as it cooks and you will end up with crispier, less greasy bacon.) Simmer until the water evaporates and the bacon is crispy, 8 to 10 minutes. Use a slotted spoon to transfer the bacon pieces to a kitchen towel to drain.

4 Assemble the salad: Arrange the beefsteak tomato slices, flesh side up, in a single layer on a platter or on individual plates. Scatter the cherry tomatoes over them. Season them evenly with the sugar, Maldon salt, and black pepper. Drain the onions, pat them dry with a kitchen towel, and sprinkle them over the tomatoes. Drizzle with the dressing and sprinkle with the tarragon. Finish with the warm bacon. Serve immediately.

PANCETTA, ARUGULA, AND ROASTED TOMATO SALAD

This is so simple yet tastes like so much. The combination of the naturally salty pancetta with the sweet tomatoes is super tasty. The peppery arugula strikes an even tastier balance with this salad. You could also add some slices of hard-boiled or a poached egg on top of each. Powdered sugar on tomatoes not only sweetens them but also brightens the color as the tomatoes roast.

1 pint **cherry tomatoes**, halved

1 teaspoon **confectioners' sugar**

1 teaspoon **Maldon sea salt**

4 tablespoons **extra-virgin olive oil**

1 teaspoon **canola oil**

4 ounces thinly sliced **pancetta**

1 small **red onion**, grated

2 medium **garlic cloves**, grated

Kosher salt

¼ cup **balsamic vinegar**

12 ounces **arugula leaves**

1 Preheat the oven to 375°F.

2 Roast the tomatoes: Arrange the tomatoes, cut side up, in a single layer on a rimmed baking sheet. In a bowl, whisk together the sugar, Maldon salt, and 3 tablespoons of the olive oil. Drizzle the mixture evenly over the tomato halves. Roast in the oven until the tomatoes are tender, 15 to 20 minutes. Set them aside to cool on the baking sheet.

3 Cook the pancetta and make the dressing: In a medium skillet, heat the canola oil over medium heat. In batches, cook the pancetta slices in a single layer until crispy, 10 to 12 minutes. Drain on a kitchen towel. Add the onion, garlic, and remaining 1 tablespoon olive oil to the skillet and cook, stirring gently, for 2 minutes. Season lightly with salt and pour the mixture into a large bowl. Add any oil or liquid from the roasted tomatoes. Whisk in the balsamic vinegar. Taste for seasoning.

4 Assemble the salad: Toss the arugula with the vinaigrette. Gently top with the tomatoes and pancetta. Serve immediately.

POACHED SALMON

WITH PAPRIKA AND DILL

This is such a simple way to take a naturally rich piece of fish and lighten it with great flavor. Chefs often talk about eating "clean" food—food that makes you feel great after you've eaten it. This is one of the dishes that is top of mind for me when I want to feel satisfied and good. I serve the salmon warm right out of the poaching liquid, or sometimes I chill it to serve cold.

¼ cup **dry white wine**

3 **lemons**, 1 juiced, 2 cut into ½-inch-thick slices

½ teaspoon whole **black peppercorns**

4 **bay leaves**

1 tablespoon **Tabasco**

Kosher salt

6 (8-ounce) portions **wild salmon**, skin on, pin bones removed

2 tablespoons **extra-virgin olive oil**

1½ teaspoons **hot paprika**

6 sprigs fresh **dill**, stemmed

½ teaspoon freshly cracked **black pepper**

12 ounces **arugula leaves**

Maldon sea salt

1   Poach the salmon: In a large wide saucepan, combine 2 quarts water with the white wine, lemon slices, peppercorns, bay leaves, Tabasco, and 1 tablespoon kosher salt. Stir to blend and bring to a simmer. Remove the pan from the heat and allow the liquid to cool for a few minutes. Then add the pieces of salmon in a single layer and allow them to sit in the liquid, off the heat, until they are cooked to medium rare in the middle, 10 to 12 minutes. (If you like the salmon cooked through, simply let it sit for 5 to 8 additional minutes, simmering the liquid again if it cools too much to cook the salmon.) Use a slotted spatula to transfer the salmon pieces to a flat surface. Gently remove and discard the skin from the salmon. Pat each portion dry with a kitchen towel and arrange the salmon on a serving platter.

2   Finish the salmon: In a medium bowl, whisk together the olive oil, paprika, dill, lemon juice, ½ teaspoon kosher salt, and the black pepper. Add the arugula, toss to coat, and arrange it over the salmon. Top with a sprinkling of Maldon salt. Serve immediately.

NIÇOISE SALAD FROM THE SOUTH OF FRANCE

This has always been one of my favorite salads because canned tuna plays wonderfully against fresh vegetables, tomatoes, and olives. It's also a salad that is truly reflective of the area where it became a classic. A traditional Niçoise usually includes potatoes and all the elements are arranged in little piles on the plate, but I skip those parts. I know it's so much more chic to make this with freshly seared tuna, but it's the juices from the canned tuna that are a big part of what makes all the flavors come together.

6 large **eggs**

1 tablespoon **Dijon mustard**

2 tablespoons **sherry vinegar**

1 tablespoon drained **capers**, chopped, plus 1 tablespoon of the brine

Kosher salt

⅔ cup **extra-virgin olive oil**

½ cup **black olives**, such as Gaeta or Alfonso, pitted and roughly chopped

1 pound **green beans**, trimmed

1 pint **cherry tomatoes**, halved

Pinch of **sugar**

1 (6-ounce) can **oil-packed tuna**, drained

Leaves from 4 sprigs fresh **basil**

1 Boil the eggs: Put the eggs in a medium saucepan and cover them with cold water. Bring the water to a boil and then reduce the heat so that the water simmers gently. Once it is simmering, cook the eggs for 11 minutes. Drain the water from the eggs and run a steady stream of cold water over them to stop them from overcooking. When they have cooled, peel the eggs and quarter them lengthwise.

2 Make the vinaigrette: In a medium bowl, whisk together the mustard, vinegar, capers, caper brine, and ¼ teaspoon salt. Slowly whisk in the olive oil. Stir in the olives. Taste for seasoning.

3 Cook the green beans: Bring 2 quarts water to a boil in a medium pot, and season it generously with salt. Prepare a medium bowl of cold water with ice cubes. Drop the green beans into the boiling water and cook until tender, 2 to 3 minutes. Use a slotted spoon to transfer the beans to the ice bath to cool and stop the cooking. When they have cooled, drain the beans and spread them on a kitchen towel to drain further.

4 Assemble the salad: In a medium bowl, toss the tomatoes with some salt, the sugar, and a generous spoonful of the vinaigrette. Arrange them on a serving platter. In the same bowl, toss the green beans and tuna with some more dressing (do not overmix). Layer that over and around the tomatoes. Arrange the eggs around the edges of the platter. Stir the basil into the remaining dressing, and drizzle it over everything. Serve immediately.

BLACK PEPPER STEAK AND CAESAR SALAD

I love that bite of this salad where the creamy dressing and the flavors of anchovy and capers connect with the black pepper and beef. The crunch of the romaine completes the picture. I use hanger steak because it is relatively inexpensive and packs great flavor.

DRESSING

3 small canned **anchovy fillets**

1 teaspoon **capers**, drained

1 small **garlic clove**, thinly sliced

1 large **egg yolk**

1 teaspoon **Dijon mustard**

2 tablespoons fresh **lemon juice**

1 teaspoon **Worcestershire sauce**, preferably Lea & Perrins brand

Dash of **Tabasco**

½ cup **extra-virgin olive oil**

½ cup **canola oil**

½ teaspoon **kosher salt**

½ teaspoon freshly ground **black pepper**

CROUTONS

4 tablespoons (½ stick) **unsalted butter**

2 medium **garlic cloves**, grated

Kosher salt

6 (1-inch-thick) slices **sourdough bread**, cut into 1-inch cubes

STEAK AND SALAD

2 tablespoons **canola oil**

1 (2-pound) piece **hanger steak**, trimmed of any sinew

Kosher salt and freshly ground **black pepper**

6 medium **romaine hearts**, quartered lengthwise

1 cup (4 ounces) shaved **Parmigiano-Reggiano cheese**

1 **Make the dressing:** In the bowl of a food processor, combine the anchovies, capers, garlic, egg yolk, mustard, lemon juice, Worcestershire, and Tabasco. Pulse and then blend until smooth. With the machine running, slowly add the olive oil, canola oil, salt, and pepper through the top.

2 **Make the croutons:** In a medium sauté pan, melt 2 tablespoons of the butter over medium heat and add half of the garlic. Season with ¼ teaspoon salt and cook until the garlic softens, 2 minutes. Add half of the bread cubes and season with salt. Toss and cook over medium heat until they become golden brown, 3 to 5 minutes. Drain on a kitchen towel. Repeat with the remaining butter, garlic, and bread cubes.

3 **Cook the steak:** Heat a large cast-iron skillet over high heat and add the canola oil. When it begins to smoke lightly, season the steak on all sides with salt and a generous amount of black pepper. Use a pair of metal tongs to carefully put the steak in the skillet. Cook over high heat for 3 to 4 minutes on each side. Remove the steak and allow it to rest on a cutting board for 8 to 10 minutes for medium-rare, depending on the thickness of the meat. If you like your steak a little more cooked, leave it in the pan a few minutes longer on each side.

4 **Assemble the salad:** Arrange the romaine spears on a plate and season them liberally with the dressing. Sprinkle with the croutons and Parmigiano-Reggiano. Slice the steak against the grain of the meat and arrange it on a large serving platter. Top with the dressed romaine, croutons, and cheese. Serve immediately.

EGG SALAD

WITH CAPERS AND DILL WITH HOMEMADE BBQ CHIPS

This is all about the grassy dill and salty capers bringing the egg flavor of this salad to life. Peppery watercress and the BBQ chips round out this meal. I know burgers and sandwiches are often enhanced with a layer of potato chips. Why not a salad, too?

¼ cup **Dijon mustard**

¼ cup **mayonnaise**, preferably Hellmann's or Best Foods

2 tablespoons **red wine vinegar**

1 teaspoon drained **capers**, roughly chopped, plus 1 teaspoon of the brine

Freshly ground **white pepper**

¼ cup **extra-virgin olive oil**

8 large **eggs**

Kosher salt

3 sprigs fresh **dill**, stemmed

2 quarts **canola oil**

1 tablespoon **dark brown sugar**

1 tablespoon **hot paprika**

2 teaspoons **onion powder**

1 teaspoon **garlic powder**

1 teaspoon **chili powder**

1 pound medium **Idaho potatoes**, very thinly sliced

2 bunches (12 ounces) **watercress**, stemmed

1 Make the vinaigrette: In a medium bowl, whisk together the mustard, mayonnaise, red wine vinegar, capers, caper brine, and white pepper. Gradually whisk in the olive oil.

2 Boil the eggs: Put the eggs in a medium saucepan and cover them with cold water. Bring the water to a boil and then reduce the heat so that the water simmers gently. Once it is simmering, cook the eggs for 11 minutes. Drain the water from the eggs and run a steady stream of cold water over them to stop them from overcooking.

3 Assemble the salad: Peel and roughly chop the eggs. Toss the chopped eggs in the bowl containing the vinaigrette. Add a pinch of salt. Taste for seasoning. Stir in the dill.

4 Make the chips: Pour the canola oil into a heavy-bottomed pot (or, alternatively, a deep fryer). Heat the oil slowly to 300°F. (Use a deep-frying thermometer to monitor the temperature.) Line a baking sheet with a kitchen towel. In a small bowl, mix together the brown sugar, paprika, onion powder, garlic powder, and chili powder. In small batches, drop the potato slices into the hot oil and fry until golden brown, 2 to 3 minutes. Remove from the oil with a slotted spoon. Spread the chips in a single layer on the baking sheet and dust with the spice mix.

5 Finish the dish: Arrange the watercress on a serving platter and top it with the egg salad. Serve the chips on top or in a bowl alongside.

FRIED CHICKEN WALDORF SALAD

I have always known Waldorf as a salad packed with apples and crunchy walnuts held together with mayonnaise. I love adding blue cheese and roasted grapes as well as fried chicken to take this classic to main-course status. It's irresistible.

SALAD
1 cup seedless **red grapes**

1 tablespoon **extra-virgin olive oil**

½ cup **mayonnaise**, preferably Hellmann's or Best Foods

¾ cup **full-fat sour cream**

1 tablespoon **Dijon mustard**

Juice of 1 large **lemon**

2 teaspoons **red wine vinegar**

1 teaspoon **Worcestershire sauce**, preferably Lea & Perrins brand

¼ teaspoon **Tabasco**

Kosher salt

4 ounces **blue cheese**, such as Cabrales or Danish blue, crumbled

2 large heads **Belgian endive**, separated into individual leaves

WALNUTS AND CHICKEN
3 cups (1½ pounds) **solid vegetable shortening**

¾ cup **walnut halves**

Kosher salt

6 boneless, skinless **chicken thighs**

2 large **eggs**, lightly beaten

⅓ cup **whole milk**

2 cups **all-purpose flour**

¼ cup **cornstarch**

1 tablespoon freshly ground **black pepper**

1 Preheat the oven to 375°F.

2 Roast the grapes: In a small bowl, toss the grapes with the olive oil. Lay the grapes in a single layer on a baking sheet and roast in the oven until they brown slightly and shrink a little, 15 to 18 minutes. Let cool.

3 Make the dressing: In a medium bowl, whisk together the mayonnaise, sour cream, mustard, half of the lemon juice, vinegar, Worcestershire, Tabasco, and ½ teaspoon kosher salt. Stir in the blue cheese. Taste for seasoning.

4 Fry the walnuts: In a deep heavy-bottomed pot over low heat, heat the shortening to 350°F. Drop the walnuts into the shortening and fry until they are slightly darker, 1 to 2 minutes. Use a slotted spoon to transfer the nuts to a kitchen towel to drain. Season them with salt. Keep the shortening in the pot at 350°F.

5 Fry the chicken: Put a rack on a baking sheet to hold the fried chicken after it is cooked. Season the chicken thighs with salt on all sides. In a medium bowl, whisk together the eggs and milk. In another medium bowl, blend the flour, cornstarch, 1 tablespoon salt, and the pepper. Dip the chicken pieces, one by one, in the egg mixture and then in the flour mixture. Drop the chicken into the hot shortening. Fry the chicken pieces, turning them with a pair of metal tongs periodically until they brown on all sides, 15 to 20 minutes. Put them on the rack to drain, season with salt, and transfer the rack to the oven to finish cooking for a few more minutes while you assemble the salad.

6 Assemble the salad: Spread a few large spoonfuls of the dressing on a serving platter. Arrange the endive all over the platter, and squeeze the remaining lemon juice over the leaves. Sprinkle with the walnuts and the roasted grapes. Cut each piece of fried chicken in half and arrange them over the endive. Drizzle with the remaining dressing. Serve immediately.

THAI BEEF AND WATERCRESS SALAD

My favorite part of this refreshing, addictive salad lies in a small detail: the texture and tiny zing that grated radish gives to the dressing. It counters the salt from the fish sauce and soy and makes way for the actual heat of the paprika and red pepper flakes. There are a lot of big flavors here, and a lot of freshness from the greens to balance them.

¼ cup fresh lime juice (from 2 large **limes**)

2 large **red radishes**, grated

2 teaspoons **fish sauce** (nam pla)

1 tablespoon **dark soy sauce**

2 teaspoons **honey**

1 teaspoon crushed **red pepper flakes**

½ cup plus 1 tablespoon **canola oil**, plus more if needed

1½ pounds **beef sirloin** or **beef tips**, trimmed and cut into bite-size pieces

1 tablespoon **kosher salt**

2 teaspoons **hot paprika**

1 bunch (6 ounces) **watercress**, lightly stemmed

¼ cup fresh **mint leaves**

½ cup fresh **cilantro leaves**

6 **scallions** (green and white parts), minced

Grated zest of 1 **lemon**

1 **Make the dressing:** In a large serving bowl, whisk together the lime juice, radishes, fish sauce, soy sauce, honey, and red pepper flakes. Whisk in ½ cup of the canola oil. Taste for seasoning and set aside.

2 **Cook the beef:** Heat a large nonstick skillet or a wok over high heat and add the remaining 1 tablespoon oil. Put the beef in a large bowl and season it with the salt and paprika. Stir to coat the meat with the seasoning. When the oil begins to smoke, remove the pan from the heat, add half of the beef, and return the pan to the heat. Stir the meat so it spreads out in the pan and browns as it cooks. Cook until the meat is browned and cooked through, 3 to 5 minutes. Remove the meat from the pan and keep it warm in a bowl. Repeat with the remaining beef, adding more oil if needed.

3 **Assemble the salad:** In the serving bowl containing the dressing, toss the watercress, mint, cilantro, scallions, and lemon zest with the dressing. Stir in the warm beef. Serve immediately.

Warm Wild Rice Salad *237*

Quinoa Salad with Toasted Almonds and Honey-Lemon Dressing *240*

Wheat Berry and Parsley Salad *241*

Pasta Salad with Basil Pesto *241*

Spicy Kidney Bean Salad *242*

Spicy Rye Berry and Eggplant Salad *243*

Crisped Basmati Rice with Sichuan Pepper *245*

GRAIN & BEAN SIDE DISHES

Braised Buttered Lentils *246*

Tabbouleh *246*

Elbow Macaroni and Wild Rice Salad *247*

Quinoa Pilaf *248*

Steamed Brown Rice with Lemon *248*

Curried Basmati Rice *249*

Chickpea and Charred Onion Salad *250*

WARM WILD RICE SALAD

One of my favorite grains is wild rice. Actually a grass, wild rice has a distinctive nutty flavor and a great chewy texture. The grains are almost always dark brown or black and tend to be longer than regular rice grains. These long grains mean that when it's cooked, wild rice is nicely fluffy. When the rice is cooked, there should be next to no liquid remaining in the saucepan. I enjoy cooking wild rice—the rich aroma filling the kitchen makes me hungry. This recipe reflects my preferred balancing act between acidic (vinegar, dried cherries) and nutty (sesame seeds) for this rice.

Kosher salt

1 cup **wild rice**

2 tablespoons **red wine vinegar**

1 teaspoon **molasses**

1 tablespoon **sesame seeds**

6 tablespoons **extra-virgin olive oil**

½ cup dried **cherries**

6 **scallions** (green and white parts), minced

1 **Cook the rice:** In a medium saucepan, bring 5 cups water to a boil over medium heat. Add 2 teaspoons salt and submerge the rice in the boiling water. Lower the heat so the water simmers gently. Cook until most of the grains are cracked and the fluffy white interior of the rice reveals itself, 50 to 55 minutes. If the water evaporates too much before the rice is done, simply add small increments of water until the rice is chewy yet tender. Ideally, when the rice is finished cooking, there shouldn't be an excess of water in the bottom of the pot. (The good starches will be in that excess water instead of in the rice.)

2 **Meanwhile, make the dressing:** In a large bowl, whisk together the red wine vinegar, molasses, sesame seeds, and olive oil. Stir in the cherries and scallions.

3 **Assemble the salad:** Drain any liquid from the wild rice and toss it, still warm, into the bowl containing the dressing. Season with 1 tablespoon salt. Taste for seasoning. Serve immediately or cover and refrigerate overnight.

WHEAT BERRY AND
PARSLEY SALAD

QUINOA SALAD
WITH TOASTED
ALMONDS AND
HONEY-LEMON
DRESSING

QUINOA SALAD

WITH TOASTED ALMONDS AND HONEY-LEMON DRESSING

Pairing quinoa with the rich flavor of toasted almonds and a simple dressing of lemon, olive oil, and chives makes a dish I could eat almost every day. Crisping some of the quinoa adds interesting texture. I have enjoyed this topped with hard-boiled eggs for breakfast and alongside a piece of fish at dinner.

4 tablespoons (½ stick) **unsalted butter**

2 medium **shallots**, minced

1 medium **garlic clove**, minced

Kosher salt

1½ cups **red quinoa**

¼ cup fresh lemon juice (from 2 medium **lemons**)

1 teaspoon **honey**

½ cup **extra-virgin olive oil**

2 tablespoons **canola oil**

½ cup slivered blanched **almonds**

½ cup minced fresh **chives**

1 Cook the quinoa: Heat a medium sauté pan over medium heat, and add 2 tablespoons of the butter, the shallots, and the garlic. Season with 1 tablespoon salt and cook until the shallots become translucent but not brown, 3 to 5 minutes. Stir in the quinoa and cook until you hear it crackling, about 2 minutes. Add 5 cups water and stir gently. Season with 1 tablespoon salt and bring to a simmer. Then simmer over low heat until the quinoa is tender, 25 to 30 minutes. Remove the pan from the heat, transfer the quinoa to a bowl, and keep warm.

2 Make the vinaigrette: In a large bowl, whisk the lemon juice with 1 teaspoon salt and the honey. Gradually whisk in the olive oil and canola oil. Taste for seasoning.

3 Crisp the quinoa: Wipe out the sauté pan you used to cook the quinoa and add the remaining 2 tablespoons butter. Heat the butter over medium heat until it melts and starts to brown slightly. Add a few tablespoons of the cooked quinoa and the almonds and sauté until they brown and become crispy, 5 minutes. Season with 1 teaspoon salt.

4 Assemble the salad: In the bowl containing the vinaigrette, stir in the cooked quinoa, 1 teaspoon salt, and the chives. Top with the crisped quinoa and almonds. Taste for seasoning, and serve.

WHEAT BERRY AND PARSLEY SALAD

This is a wonderfully chewy, grassy salad that complements main courses with a supple texture, for example, roasted salmon or tofu. For the best flavor, make this ahead of time and let it marinate for a few hours in the refrigerator.

2 tablespoons **extra-virgin olive oil**
2 medium **shallots**, minced
Kosher salt
1 cup **wheat berries**
1 tablespoon **Dijon mustard**
2½ teaspoons **grainy mustard**
1 tablespoon **sherry vinegar**
1 cup **canola oil**
½ cup chopped fresh **curly parsley, leaves and stems**

1 Cook the wheat berries: In a large skillet, heat the olive oil over medium heat and add the shallots and 1 tablespoon salt. Cook until the shallots are translucent, 5 to 8 minutes. Stir in the wheat berries, cover with 5 cups water, and bring the water to a simmer. Cook, stirring from time to time, until the wheat berries are tender, 50 to 55 minutes. Taste the wheat berries for doneness: they should be tender but still slightly chewy. You may very well need to add water in small increments until the wheat berries finish cooking.

2 Make the vinaigrette and finish the salad: In a large bowl, whisk the Dijon and grainy mustards with the sherry vinegar. Whisk in the canola oil and a splash of cold water. Stir the warm wheat berries into the mustard vinaigrette, and then stir in the parsley and 2 teaspoons salt. Taste for seasoning, and serve.

PASTA SALAD
WITH BASIL PESTO

Almost nothing smells better than the aroma of hot pasta tossed with pesto and Parmigiano-Reggiano cheese. The Parmigiano-Reggiano offers both a salty note and body to the dish. While I prefer to eat this warm, it is also delicious cold.

Kosher salt
¾ pound **fusilli pasta**, preferably De Cecco brand
Raw Basil Pesto (page 189)
Freshly grated **Parmigiano-Reggiano cheese**

1 Cook the pasta: In a large pot, bring 6 quarts water to a rolling boil. Add ½ cup salt. The pasta water should taste like seawater. Add the pasta to the boiling water and stir so it doesn't stick to the bottom as it cooks. Cook the pasta until it is al dente (chewy but not hard or raw tasting), 8 to 10 minutes. Drain the pasta in a colander, reserving a little of the pasta water in case you need it to adjust the sauce.

2 Finish the salad: Toss the hot pasta with the pesto, adding a little of the reserved pasta water if needed to help the pesto coat the pasta. Taste for seasoning, sprinkle with Parmigiano-Reggiano cheese and salt, if needed, and serve.

SPICY KIDNEY BEAN SALAD

Kidney beans are underloved. Not only are they beautiful and surprisingly earthy, but they also have a great, almost creamy texture. Bacon, apple, and spicy red pepper flakes and chili powder make this a taste explosion.

1 cup dried **red kidney beans**, soaked overnight in cold water

4 ounces **slab bacon**, cut into ½-inch-thick slices and then into ½-inch cubes

¼ cup **cider vinegar**

2 tablespoons **balsamic vinegar**

2 teaspoons **dark brown sugar**

1 teaspoon crushed **red pepper flakes**

2 teaspoons **chili powder**

1 large **Granny Smith apple**, peeled and grated

1 tablespoon plus 1 teaspoon **kosher salt**

2 tablespoons **extra-virgin olive oil**

1 small bunch **watercress**, stemmed

1 Cook the kidney beans: In a medium saucepan, bring 3 cups water to a boil over medium heat. Stir in the kidney beans and cook, stirring from time to time, until they are tender when pierced with the tip of a knife, 45 minutes to 1 hour. Note: Add more water if it all cooks out before the beans are tender. Keep warm.

2 Make the bacon apple vinaigrette: In a medium skillet, cook the bacon over medium heat until all of the pieces are browned and somewhat crispy, 10 to 12 minutes. Use a slotted spoon to transfer the bacon to a kitchen towel to drain. In the skillet containing the bacon fat, stir in the cider vinegar, balsamic vinegar, brown sugar, red pepper flakes, and chili powder. Bring the mixture to a boil over medium heat, and cook until the liquid has reduced by one-third, 2 to 3 minutes. Stir in the grated apple.

3 Assemble the salad: Drain the beans and put them in a medium bowl. Season them with 1 tablespoon of the salt, and toss with the olive oil. Then toss the apple vinaigrette with the kidney beans. Stir in the watercress, remaining 1 teaspoon salt, and crisp bacon. Taste for seasoning, and serve.

SPICY RYE BERRY AND EGGPLANT SALAD

Rye berries have a more delicate flavor and texture than wheat berries—but if you can't find them, go ahead and make this salad with wheat berries; it will still be delicious. The eggplant, with its tremendous earthy, acidic flavor, really brings this salad to life.

½ cup plus 2 tablespoons **extra-virgin olive oil**

2 medium **shallots**, minced

1 teaspoon crushed **red pepper flakes**

¼ teaspoon **cayenne pepper**

Kosher salt

½ cup **rye berries**

1 large **globe eggplant**, halved lengthwise

2 medium **garlic cloves**, minced

2 teaspoons dried **oregano**

2 tablespoons **Dijon mustard**

3 tablespoons **balsamic vinegar**

¼ cup **raspberry vinegar**

¼ cup **canola oil**

1 Preheat the oven to 350°F.

2 **Cook the rye berries:** In a large skillet, heat the 2 tablespoons olive oil over medium heat and add the shallots, red pepper flakes, cayenne, and 1 tablespoon salt. Cook until the shallots are translucent, 5 to 8 minutes. Stir in the rye berries and cover with 4 cups water. Bring the water to a simmer and cook, stirring from time to time, until the rye berries are tender, 50 to 55 minutes. Note: While you don't want to end up with excess cooking liquid at the end, you do want enough liquid while the rye berries are cooking. If necessary, add water in small increments until the rye berries are tender but still slightly chewy.

3 While the rye berries are simmering, cook the eggplant: Arrange the eggplant halves, flesh side up, on a baking sheet and drizzle with ¼ cup of the olive oil, the garlic, and oregano. Season liberally on both sides with 2 teaspoons salt. Roast until the eggplant is tender when pierced with the tip of a knife, 20 to 25 minutes. If the eggplant has a lot of seeds, scoop some of them out.

4 **Make the vinaigrette:** In a large bowl, whisk the mustard with the balsamic and raspberry vinegars. Gradually whisk in the remaining ¼ cup olive oil and the canola oil. Add a splash of water if the flavors are too strong or unbalanced.

5 **Assemble the salad:** On a cutting board, cut the eggplant halves into bite-size pieces. Toss the rye berries and eggplant in the bowl containing the vinaigrette. Taste for seasoning, and serve.

CRISPED BASMATI RICE

WITH SICHUAN PEPPER

I have always loved cooking a classic rice pilaf and then taking some of the cooked rice one step further by crisping it in butter for a few minutes before stirring it into the pilaf. The textural variations and the deep buttery flavor of the crisped rice bring this ingredient to a whole other level. This is especially great with something lean like grilled clams, steamed mussels, or shrimp.

2 cups **basmati rice**

2 teaspoons **Sichuan peppercorns**

1 teaspoon **fennel seeds**

12 whole **black peppercorns**

4 tablespoons (½ stick) **unsalted butter**

2 medium **shallots**, minced

Kosher salt

1 **Prepare the rice:** In a large bowl, soak the rice in 4 cups cold water for 30 minutes.

2 Preheat the oven to 350°F.

3 **Make the spice mix:** In a small bowl, combine the Sichuan peppercorns, fennel seeds, and black peppercorns. Spread the mixture out on a baking sheet and toast in the oven until fragrant, 2 to 3 minutes. Set aside to cool.

4 **Cook the rice:** Heat a medium sauté pan over medium heat and add 2 tablespoons of the butter. Add the shallots, season them with 1 teaspoon salt, and cook until they become translucent but not brown, 3 to 5 minutes. Stir in the toasted spices. Drain the rice, reserving the soaking water. Stir the rice into the shallots and cook until you hear it crackling, about 2 minutes. Then add the reserved soaking water. Stir gently. Add 1 tablespoon salt and bring to a simmer over medium heat. Lower the heat to medium-low and cook the rice, uncovered and undisturbed, until tender, 12 to 15 minutes. Using a fork (so as not to damage the rice), flake a few grains off the top and taste for doneness. It may need another 2 to 4 minutes to be fully cooked. Remove the pan from the heat and gently spoon the rice into a bowl.

5 **Crisp the rice:** Heat a skillet over medium heat, add the remaining 2 tablespoons butter, and heat it until it starts to sizzle. Then add 1 cup of the cooked rice and cook until the rice crackles, turns light brown, and starts to get crispy, 3 to 5 minutes. Add salt, if needed. Stir the crispy rice back into the cooked rice. Serve immediately.

BRAISED BUTTERED LENTILS

My opinion of lentils changed when I started working at Guy Savoy in Paris. Chef Savoy braises lentils simply, whisks in a ton of butter at the end, and then shaves fresh black truffle over them. Wow. I also ate them in a Parisian bistro, chilled, with some tangy fresh goat cheese and bracingly acidic vinaigrette. You can make either of those dishes with these lentils as the foundation. They are great warm or cold. I cook them a little al dente so they're not mushy.

1 pound **green** or **brown lentils**, preferably French lentilles du Puy, rinsed and drained
2 tablespoons **extra-virgin olive oil**
3 medium **garlic cloves**
2 **bay leaves**
¼ cup **red wine vinegar**
2 tablespoons **unsalted butter**
2 teaspoons **kosher salt**
1 teaspoon freshly cracked **black pepper**

1 Cook the lentils: In a large pot, combine the lentils, olive oil, garlic, and bay leaves with 8 cups water. Bring to a simmer and then lower the heat. Simmer the lentils, uncovered, until they are tender, 25 to 30 minutes. Note: If you need to add more water for the lentils to finish cooking, add a little at a time.

2 Season the lentils: Once they are cooked but still somewhat al dente, remove from the heat, drain any excess liquid, and discard the garlic cloves and bay leaves. Stir in the red wine vinegar, butter, salt, and pepper. Serve warm.

TABBOULEH

I love the texture of bulgur combined with the punch of garlic and mint. I like to prepare this ahead of time and fully chill it so the ingredients have time to come together.

½ teaspoon ground **allspice**
2 **bay leaves**
Kosher salt
1 cup coarse **bulgur**
¼ cup **extra-virgin olive oil**
4 medium **garlic cloves**, minced
⅓ cup fresh lemon juice (from 2 large **lemons**)
1 pint **cherry tomatoes**, halved
1 cup roughly chopped fresh **flat-leaf parsley leaves**
½ cup small fresh **mint leaves**
6 **scallions** (green and white parts), minced

1 Cook the bulgur: In a medium saucepan with a tight-fitting lid, combine 2 cups water with the allspice, bay leaves, and 2 teaspoons salt. Bring to a boil over medium heat and then stir in the bulgur. Remove the pan from the heat, cover it, and let the bulgur sit, undisturbed, for 25 to 30 minutes. Then flake it with a fork to test for doneness. It should be tender. If it is not, cook over low heat until it is tender, 15 to 20 minutes. Discard the bay leaves, and drain the bulgur thoroughly.

2 Make the vinaigrette: In a small sauté pan, warm the olive oil over medium heat. Stir in the garlic and 1 teaspoon salt, and simmer gently for 1 to 2 minutes to remove the raw flavor of the garlic. Transfer the garlic oil to a serving bowl and whisk in the lemon juice.

3 Finish the tabbouleh: Add the bulgur to the bowl containing the lemon vinaigrette. Stir in the tomatoes, parsley, mint, scallions, and 2 teaspoons salt. Taste for seasoning and serve.

ELBOW MACARONI AND WILD RICE SALAD

This is the kind of salad that you crave at a family reunion or beach picnic. There's something so nostalgic and gloriously American about the mayonnaise, bell peppers, and elbow macaroni. Adding the wild rice for a pleasantly chewy texture and the fresh fennel for an anise note really spruces up this salad.

Kosher salt

1 teaspoon crushed **red pepper flakes**

½ cup **wild rice**

½ cup **mayonnaise**, preferably Hellmann's or Best Foods

1 small **garlic clove**, grated

2 teaspoons **red wine vinegar**

Pinch of **sugar**

1 medium **red bell pepper**, seeded and finely chopped

1 small **fennel bulb**, outer layers removed, bulb finely chopped

½ cup minced fresh **chives**

8 ounces **elbow macaroni**, preferably De Cecco brand

1 **Cook the rice:** In a medium saucepan, bring 1½ cups water to a boil over medium heat. Add 2 teaspoons salt and the red pepper flakes, and submerge the rice in the boiling water. Lower the heat so the water simmers gently. Cook until most of the grains are cracked and the fluffy white interior of the rice reveals itself, 50 to 55 minutes. Note: If the water evaporates too much before the rice is done, simply add small increments of water until the rice is chewy yet tender. Ideally, when the rice is finished cooking, there shouldn't be an excess of water in the bottom of the pot.

2 **Make the dressing:** In a large bowl, whisk together the mayonnaise, garlic, red wine vinegar, sugar, bell pepper, fennel, and chives. Taste for seasoning.

3 **Cook the pasta:** In a large pot, bring 6 quarts water to a rolling boil. Add ½ cup salt and bring the water back to a boil. It should taste like seawater. Add the macaroni and stir to ensure that the pasta does not stick to the bottom of the pot as it cooks. Cook until the macaroni is al dente (chewy but not hard or raw tasting), 8 to 10 minutes.

4 **Assemble the salad:** Drain the macaroni thoroughly. Toss the macaroni and the wild rice in the bowl containing the dressing. Season with 1 teaspoon salt. Let the salad sit for a few minutes, or even a few hours, and serve at room temperature or chilled.

QUINOA PILAF

Red quinoa has a great nutty flavor and texture. I love to cook it like a classic rice pilaf and serve it with fish or meat, or to toss a handful into a salad or over avocado slices. I also sprinkle a little cooked quinoa over my pancakes or sprinkle some into my waffle batter to add crunch.

2 tablespoons **extra-virgin olive oil**

2 medium **yellow onions**, minced

2 **bay leaves**

1 tablespoon plus 2 teaspoons **kosher salt**

1½ cups **red quinoa**

1 Preheat the oven to 350°F.

2 Cook the quinoa: Heat a large ovenproof sauté pan over medium heat and add the olive oil, onions, bay leaves, and the 1 tablespoon salt. Cook until the onions become translucent but not brown, 3 to 5 minutes. Stir in the quinoa and cook until you hear it crackling, about 2 minutes. Add 4½ cups water. Stir gently and bring to a simmer over medium heat. Put the sauté pan in the center of the oven and bake, undisturbed, until the grains are tender and fluff slightly, 15 to 20 minutes.

3 Finish the quinoa: Remove the pan from the oven and allow the quinoa to rest for 10 minutes. Remove the bay leaves. Season the quinoa with the remaining 2 teaspoons salt, and spoon it gently into a bowl. Taste for seasoning, and serve.

STEAMED BROWN RICE
WITH LEMON

This is the kind of dish I make when I need something simple and comforting. The steamed rice, cooked without any oil, spices, or salt, actually has tons of inherent flavor that is otherwise obscured when tricked out with aromatics from garlic to peppercorns.

1 cup **brown rice**

Juice of ½ **lemon**

In a medium saucepan with a tight-fitting lid, bring 3 cups water to a simmer over medium heat. Stir in the rice, cover the pan, and cook, undisturbed, over medium-low heat until the rice has absorbed all the water, 45 to 50 minutes. Flake the rice with a fork and spoon it gently into a serving bowl. Sprinkle with the lemon juice, and serve.

CURRIED BASMATI RICE

In the case of basmati, no matter how I am going to cook it, I always soak it first. Soaking cleans out any small particles and also rids the rice of any starch on the grain. Much like saving pasta water for adjusting the sauce, I use the soaking water from the rice (which has some starch) to cook the pilaf here. The curry powder and bay leaves create an aromatic pilaf loaded with addictive flavor. The butter is also an important touch because it heightens the flavors of the spices.

2 cups **basmati rice**

1 teaspoon **cumin seeds**

1 tablespoon **medium-hot curry powder**

2 **bay leaves**

12 whole **black peppercorns**

2 tablespoons **unsalted butter**

2 medium **shallots**, finely diced

Kosher salt

1 **Prepare the rice:** In a large bowl, soak the rice in 4 cups cold water for 30 minutes.

2 Preheat the oven to 350°F.

3 **Make the spice mix:** In a small bowl, combine the cumin seeds, curry powder, bay leaves, and peppercorns. Spread the mixture out on a baking sheet and toast in the oven until fragrant, 2 to 3 minutes. Set aside to cool.

4 Cook the rice: Heat a medium sauté pan over medium heat and add the butter. Add the shallots, season them with 1 teaspoon salt, and cook until they become translucent but not brown, 3 to 5 minutes. Stir in the toasted spices. Drain the rice, reserving the soaking water. Stir the rice into the shallots and cook until you hear it crackling, about 2 minutes. Add the reserved soaking water and stir gently. Add 1 tablespoon salt and bring to a simmer over medium heat. Then lower the heat to medium-low and cook the rice, uncovered and undisturbed, until tender, 12 to 15 minutes. Using a fork (so as not to damage the rice), flake a few grains off the top and taste for doneness. It may need another 2 to 4 minutes until fully cooked.

5 Finish the rice: Remove the pan from the heat and allow the rice to rest for 10 minutes before transferring it gently to a serving bowl. Remove and discard the bay leaves. Taste for seasoning, and serve.

CHICKPEA AND CHARRED ONION SALAD

I love cooking chickpeas from scratch and then marinating them overnight in the refrigerator. There is something so therapeutic about waking up the next day to find something untouched and ready to eat, like a missed Christmas present hiding under the tree. While I do often use canned beans, canned chickpeas can taste so metallic and oversalted that I try to cook them from scratch whenever I get the chance. Soaking the chickpeas overnight makes a big difference; they cook more evenly and quickly.

2 cups dried **chickpeas**

4 tablespoons **canola oil**

1 medium **red onion**, thinly sliced and then chopped

Kosher salt

½ cup **tahini**

Juice of 1 **lemon**

1 tablespoon **red wine vinegar**

½ teaspoon ground **coriander**

6 **scallions** (green and white parts), thinly sliced

1 Soak the chickpeas: Put the chickpeas in a medium bowl and add water to cover generously. Soak overnight.

2 Cook the chickpeas: Drain the chickpeas. In a medium saucepan, heat 2 tablespoons of the canola oil over medium heat. Add the chickpeas and stir to coat them with the oil. Then cover with 5 cups water and bring it to a boil over medium heat. Lower the heat and simmer until the chickpeas are tender but still hold their shape, 45 minutes to 1 hour. You may need to add more water to finish cooking them. Drain.

3 Char the onion: Heat a medium skillet over medium heat and add the remaining 2 tablespoons oil. When the oil begins to smoke lightly, remove the skillet from the heat and add the onion and 1 teaspoon salt. Return the pan to high heat and cook, stirring from time to time, until the onion chars around the edges, 5 to 8 minutes. Remove the skillet from the heat.

4 Make the dressing and finish the salad: In a large bowl, whisk together the tahini, lemon juice, red wine vinegar, and coriander until smooth. If the dressing is too thick, stir in a little water. Stir in the onion, chickpeas, 1 tablespoon salt, and the scallions. Taste for seasoning, and serve.

ITALIAN AMERICAN
COOKIES

DARK CHOCOLATE PEPPERMINT BARK

Every year I tell myself that the holiday bark I scarfed down the previous year was an anomaly, that I don't really care about bark. So far, years into this ruse, I can tell you it has been ineffective. Chocolate bark is wonderful when it is made with toasted nuts or dried fruits. But my favorite version has crunchy, minty crushed candy canes atop slightly bitter dark chocolate. I like to use high-quality candy canes and chocolate—great ingredients always make a difference and especially in a recipe like this where there are so few. Don't be afraid of tempering chocolate. The worst thing that can happen is you get a tasty candy treat that isn't super-glossy. Still a winning situation in my book!

1 pound **dark chocolate**

4 ounces **semisweet chocolate**

Nonstick cooking spray

8 ounces **candy canes**, lightly crushed

1 **Temper the chocolate:** In the top of a double boiler set over simmering water, melt the dark chocolate, stirring it constantly with a wooden spoon, until it reaches 105° to 115°F on a candy thermometer. Remove the pan from the heat and immediately use a rubber spatula to transfer the chocolate to a medium bowl. (This will help drop the temperature of the chocolate.) Stir in the semisweet chocolate. Stir until the temperature reduces to between 88° and 90°F.

2 **Make the bark:** Lightly grease a baking sheet with cooking spray. Using a rubber spatula, stir half of the crushed candy canes into the chocolate, and spread an even layer of the chocolate on the prepared baking sheet. The thickness should be like that of a Hershey's bar. Immediately sprinkle an even layer of the remaining candy canes over the chocolate layer. Refrigerate the bark for about 20 minutes, and then leave it out at room temperature for at least an hour before breaking it into chunks.

DARK CHOCOLATE
PEPPERMINT BARK

CARAMEL
POPCORN

SESAME SEED
WAFER SANDWICH
COOKIES

SESAME SEED WAFER SANDWICH COOKIES

I love the texture and taste of sesame seeds, which add fabulous nuttiness and crunch to dishes such as roasted asparagus or a bowl of chilled Chinese noodles—and these rich cookies. The filling is pleasantly bitter from the marmalade and is brightened by a splash of red wine vinegar and Grand Marnier.

DOUGH

1 cup **sesame seeds**

8 tablespoons (1 stick) **unsalted butter**, softened

¾ cup packed **light brown sugar**

1½ cups **all-purpose flour**

1¼ teaspoons **baking powder**

½ teaspoon **baking soda**

1 teaspoon **kosher salt**

1 large **egg**

2 teaspoons **vanilla extract**

FILLING

¼ cup **honey**

1 tablespoon **Grand Marnier**

½ cup **orange marmalade**

2 teaspoons **red wine vinegar**

1 Preheat the oven to 375°F. Line two baking sheets with parchment paper.

2 Toast the sesame seeds: Spread the sesame seeds in a thin, even layer on a rimmed baking sheet. Toast the seeds in the oven until they are golden brown, 5 to 7 minutes. Set aside to cool.

3 Make the dough: In the bowl of a stand mixer fitted with the paddle attachment, beat the butter and brown sugar on medium speed until the butter becomes fluffy and doubles in volume, 5 to 8 minutes. Meanwhile, in a medium bowl, whisk together the flour, baking powder, baking soda, and salt. When the butter and brown sugar are fully integrated, add the egg and vanilla and mix until blended. Remove the bowl from the mixer, and use a rubber spatula to gently fold in the dry ingredients and ½ cup of the toasted sesame seeds. You want to combine without overmixing. The less you stir the flour, the more tender the cookie!

4 Roll and bake the cookies: Using your hands, roll the dough into balls about 1 inch in diameter. Roll each ball in the remaining sesame seeds to coat. Arrange the balls on the prepared baking sheets, spacing them 1½ to 2 inches apart (the cookies spread as they bake). Gently press down on each ball to flatten it slightly. Bake, rotating the baking sheets halfway through, until the cookies are browned on the edges, 8 to 10 minutes. Let the cookies cool for 5 to 8 minutes on the baking sheets. Transfer the cookies to a wire rack to cool completely.

5 Make the filling: In a small saucepan, bring the honey to a simmer over medium heat. When it begins to froth and turn light brown, after 2 to 3 minutes, remove the pan from the heat and carefully add the Grand Marnier. Return the pan to the heat—carefully, to avoid potentially flaming up the alcohol—and simmer for 2 to 3 minutes to allow the Grand Marnier to cook into the honey. Stir in the marmalade and red wine vinegar and simmer, whisking from time to time, until smooth, 2 to 3 minutes. Allow the filling to cool for 10 to 15 minutes.

6 Assemble the cookies: Spread out half of the cookies so they are flat side up, and spoon the filling on top. Top with the remaining cookies. Devour.

CARAMEL POPCORN

I fell in love with caramel corn as an adult. I first tasted it at the Santa Monica greenmarket when I should have been sampling thirty varieties of local heirloom tomatoes. I like the brown sugar in the caramel because it contrasts starkly with the savory popcorn and creates that addictive salt-sugar combo.

Nonstick cooking spray
1 tablespoon **canola oil**
2 tablespoons **popcorn kernels**
2 teaspoons **kosher salt**
2 tablespoons **unsalted butter**
1½ cups packed **light brown sugar**

1   Make the popcorn: Spray a baking sheet with a light layer of cooking spray. Heat a medium pot with a tight-fitting lid over medium heat. Add the oil and the popcorn kernels to the pot, cover the pot, and cook, shaking it from time to time, until the popcorn starts popping. Then lower the heat and allow the popcorn to continue popping until finished. Remove the pot from the heat and remove the lid. Spread the popcorn out on the prepared baking sheet, sprinkle it with the salt, and allow it to cool.

2   Make the caramel: In a medium saucepan, melt the butter over medium-low heat. Add the brown sugar and ⅓ cup water, and bring the mixture to a gentle simmer. Insert a candy thermometer into the caramel and take its temperature. Boil until the sugar turns brown and reaches 234°F, otherwise known as the soft ball stage.

3   Finish the popcorn: Remove the pan from the heat and carefully pour the caramel over the popcorn in an even layer. Allow the popcorn to cool for a couple of minutes before rolling it into balls or separating it into individual kernels, as desired.

CHEWY ALMOND COOKIES

I am a sucker for the texture of cookies like these. Loaded with almonds and almond extract, the taste will take you straight to that Italian bakery where those white boxes are tied up with seemingly invincible red and white string. How many times did I try to sneak my hand in through one of the side flaps only to end up with a handful of crushed cookie crumbs?

Nonstick cooking spray

1⅔ cups ground **almonds**

½ cup plus 1½ tablespoons **superfine sugar**

Grated zest of 1 **lemon**

½ teaspoon **almond extract**

½ teaspoon **kosher salt**

2 large **egg whites**

1 tablespoon **honey**

½ cup **confectioners' sugar**

1 Preheat the oven to 325°F. Grease two baking sheets with cooking spray.

2 **Make the batter:** In a large bowl, combine the ground almonds, superfine sugar, lemon zest, almond extract, and salt, and rub the mixture with your fingertips to disperse the zest and extract evenly.

3 **Whip the egg whites:** In the bowl of a stand mixer fitted with the whisk attachment, beat the egg whites and honey on medium speed until they reach a soft meringue consistency, 5 to 8 minutes. Remove the bowl from the mixer and use a rubber spatula to carefully fold the meringue into the almond mixture. The mixture will come together but remain fluffy. Mix it as little as possible in order to keep the maximum amount of air in the batter.

4 **Bake the cookies:** Put the confectioners' sugar in a shallow bowl. Use a tablespoon to scoop an even ball of the batter into the bowl of confectioners' sugar. Roll it around gently, coating all sides in the sugar, and put it on one of the prepared baking sheets. Repeat, allowing about 2 inches between cookies (they spread as they bake). Bake in the oven until the cookies are just light brown on the edges, 10 to 12 minutes. The center of each cookie should look slightly undercooked. (Cookies, like steak, have a little carry-over cooking!) Remove the baking sheets from the oven and allow the cookies to cool for a few minutes before using a spatula to transfer them to a wire rack to cool completely.

QUINOA ALLSPICE OATMEAL COOKIES

I love the texture and toasted notes of cooked quinoa. I don't eat it to be healthy; that's an incidental by-product of enjoying this cookie. I have actually never been a huge lover of oatmeal cookies—I always pass them by for the chocolate chip or dark chocolate ones. That's why this recipe is so special to me: it has just the right balance of spice and toasted grain flavors to make it an unusual and welcome addition to my cookie plate.

½ pound (2 sticks) cold **unsalted butter**, cut into small pieces

Grated zest of 1 **lemon**

1 cup packed **dark brown sugar**

1 cup **granulated sugar**

2 large **eggs**

2 tablespoons **unsulphured molasses** (not blackstrap)

2 teaspoons **vanilla extract**

2½ cups **all-purpose flour**

½ cup **quinoa flour**

2 teaspoons **kosher salt**

1½ teaspoons **baking powder**

1 teaspoon **baking soda**

½ teaspoon ground **cinnamon**

½ teaspoon ground **allspice**

½ teaspoon ground **ginger**

1½ cups **old-fashioned rolled oats**

1 cup **quinoa flakes**

1 Preheat the oven to 350°F. Line two baking sheets with parchment paper.

2 **Start the dough:** In the bowl of a stand mixer fitted with the paddle attachment, beat the butter, lemon zest, brown sugar, and granulated sugar on medium speed until fully integrated, 3 to 5 minutes. Add the eggs, one by one, mixing on high speed. Add the molasses and vanilla. Use a rubber spatula to scrape down the sides of the bowl to make sure all of the ingredients are mixed together.

3 **Finish the dough:** In a medium bowl, whisk together the all-purpose flour, quinoa flour, salt, baking powder, baking soda, cinnamon, allspice, ginger, oats, and quinoa flakes. Remove the bowl from the mixer and use a rubber spatula to stir in the dry ingredients. The dough will be slightly crumbly. Use a tablespoon to scoop up dough, and roll it into 1-inch balls. Arrange the dough balls about 2 inches apart on the prepared baking sheets (the cookies spread as they bake).

4 **Bake the cookies:** Bake, rotating the baking sheets about halfway through, until the cookies are browned, 12 to 15 minutes. Allow them to cool for 2 to 3 minutes before transferring them to a wire rack to cool for at least a few minutes more before devouring.

COCONUT ALMOND CLUSTERS

This cluster tastes the way I always imagine fresh coconut will taste. The cookie is slightly sweet, with added crunch from the almonds, and light because it's really just coconut and egg whites. The clusters are almost juicy when you bite into them. They have other wonderful qualities: they are flourless and satisfying.

4 large **egg whites**

1⅓ cups **sugar**

¾ cup **almonds**, toasted and finely chopped

1 cup shredded **sweetened coconut**

1 Preheat the oven to 350°F. Line two baking sheets with parchment paper.

2 Make the meringue: In the bowl of a stand mixer fitted with the whisk attachment, whip the egg whites on medium speed for a minute to break them up. Gradually add the sugar and continue to whip them until they start to form peaks, 3 to 5 minutes. You will see the trace left by the whisk in the whites as it spins. Using a rubber spatula, gently fold the almonds and coconut into the egg whites.

3 Bake the clusters: Drop large tablespoons of the meringue onto the prepared baking sheets, making sure to leave a decent amount of space between them. Bake the clusters until they are light brown, 15 to 18 minutes. Do not allow the cookies to get too dark. Remove the baking sheets from the oven and immediately use a flat metal spatula to transfer the clusters to a wire rack. Allow them to cool a little before eating.

DARK CHOCOLATE BROWNIES

This brownie is somewhere between fudgy and cakey. It stands wonderfully on its own and also makes a great friend for vanilla ice cream and hot fudge sauce. I have made the batter, poured it into the pan, wrapped it tightly, stored it in the freezer, and then baked the brownies at a later date with great results. It's never a bad idea to have some brownies on hand. I have a nine-year-old who likes an occasional surprise.

Nonstick cooking spray

4 ounces **unsweetened chocolate**, chopped

8 tablespoons (1 stick) **unsalted butter**

2 cups **sugar**

1 teaspoon **kosher salt**

1 tablespoon **vanilla extract**

4 large **eggs**

1 cup **all-purpose flour**

1 cup chopped **walnuts**

1 Preheat the oven to 350°F. Grease a 9 × 13-inch baking pan with cooking spray.

2 Melt the chocolate: In a small saucepan set over very low heat, melt the chocolate and butter together, stirring to avoid scorching. Set the mixture aside to cool, 5 to 10 minutes.

3 Mix the batter and bake the brownies: Stir the sugar, salt, and vanilla into the warm chocolate. Whisk in the eggs, one by one. Use a rubber spatula to gently stir in the flour and walnuts. When all of the ingredients are blended, pour the batter into the prepared baking pan. Bake until the center is almost firm, 20 to 25 minutes. Remove the pan from the oven and allow the brownie to cool in the pan for 10 to 15 minutes before cutting it into 2-inch squares.

BROWN SUGAR CHOCOLATE CHIP COOKIES

This chocolate chip cookie is a classic—improved, I think, by using slightly more salt and darker forms of sugar. I love bolstering the flavor of the sugars with a splash of molasses. The bitter note of chocolate up against that sweetness intensifies the flavor of the cookie.

Nonstick cooking spray

6 tablespoons (¾ stick) **unsalted butter**, softened

¼ cup **granulated sugar**

¼ cup packed **light brown sugar**

½ cup packed **dark brown sugar**

1 tablespoon **molasses**

1 large **egg**

1 teaspoon **kosher salt**

1½ teaspoons **vanilla extract**

1 cup plus 2 tablespoons **all-purpose flour**

½ teaspoon **baking soda**

1¼ cups **semisweet chocolate chips**

1 Preheat the oven to 375°F. Grease two baking sheets with cooking spray.

2 **Make the dough:** In the bowl of a stand mixer fitted with the paddle attachment, beat the butter with the granulated and brown sugars until smooth, 5 to 8 minutes. Make sure the butter and sugars are fully combined—it's the key to a great cookie! Add the molasses, egg, salt, and vanilla and beat until blended. In a small bowl, whisk together the flour and baking soda. Remove the bowl from the mixer and stir in the flour mixture and the chocolate chips.

3 **Bake the cookies:** Drop tablespoons of dough about 2 inches apart on the prepared baking sheets (the cookies will spread as they bake). Bake until the cookies are light brown on top and around the edges, 12 to 15 minutes. Remove the baking sheets from the oven and allow the cookies to firm up a little on the sheets, 5 to 10 minutes, before serving or transferring them to a wire rack to cool completely.

THIN CRIPSY GINGERBREAD COOKIES

BROWN SUGAR CHOCOLATE CHIP COOKIES

THIN CRISPY GINGERBREAD COOKIES

When I am not eating chocolate or fruit pies with wild abandon, gingerbread is my favorite. Desserts that celebrate spices are such great palate cleansers. I like my ginger cookies thin and crispy, which provides all sorts of opportunities to pair them with ice creams, puddings, or frosting.

12 tablespoons (1½ sticks) **lightly salted butter**, softened

1⅔ cups **sugar**

Grated zest of 1 **orange**

3½ cups **all-purpose flour**, plus more for rolling the dough

1½ teaspoons **baking powder**

½ teaspoon **baking soda**

1 tablespoon ground **ginger**

½ teaspoon grated **nutmeg**

½ teaspoon ground **allspice**

2 teaspoons ground **cinnamon**

¼ teaspoon ground **cloves**

½ teaspoon **kosher salt**

2 large **eggs**

½ cup **dark molasses**

Juice of 1 **lemon**

1 Preheat the oven to 350°F. Line two baking sheets with parchment paper.

2 **Start the dough:** In the bowl of a stand mixer fitted with the paddle attachment, beat the butter, sugar, and orange zest on high speed until smooth, 5 to 8 minutes.

3 **Meanwhile, combine the dry ingredients:** In a medium bowl, whisk together the flour, baking powder, baking soda, ginger, nutmeg, allspice, cinnamon, cloves, and salt.

4 **Combine the wet ingredients:** In another bowl, whisk together the eggs, molasses, and lemon juice.

5 **Finish the dough:** Lower the speed of the mixer and add the dry ingredients. Then add the wet ingredients and mix until just incorporated. When the dough is blended, wrap it in plastic wrap and allow it to rest in the fridge for 15 minutes.

6 **Cut and bake the cookies:** Use a rolling pin to roll the dough about ½ inch thick on a lightly floured surface. Cut the dough into similar-size shapes with cookie cutters, and arrange them on the prepared baking sheets. Bake the cookies in batches until they are brown around the edges, 10 to 12 minutes. Allow to cool for 2 to 3 minutes before transferring them to a wire rack to cool completely.

BERRIES & JUICY FRUITS

BAKED PLUMS
WITH DATES AND CINNAMON

I first made the connection between plums and hazelnuts working in the south of France. I roasted some local plums with sugar and ginger and was snacking on hazelnuts when I took the fruit from the oven. The smell of the plums and the taste of the hazelnuts in my mouth created the idea for this dessert. Serve it solo or with a scoop of lemon sorbet. Note: If you have very ripe plums, reduce the cooking time in step 3, so the fruit retains its texture and shape.

1 tablespoon **unsalted butter**

4 large, firm **black plums**, halved and pitted

½ cup **sugar**

1 tablespoon grated **fresh ginger**

¼ cup blanched **hazelnuts**, toasted and chopped

¼ cup pitted dried **dates**, coarsely chopped

Pinch of **kosher salt**

½ teaspoon ground **cinnamon**

½ teaspoon **ground ginger**

2 teaspoons **red wine vinegar**

2 cups **heavy cream**

1 Preheat the oven to 375°F.

2 Cook the plums: Heat an ovenproof skillet that is large enough to hold the plum halves in a single layer over medium-low heat, and add the butter. Arrange the plums, cut side down, in the skillet. Sprinkle them with ¼ cup of the sugar and cook until the plums start to become tender, 3 to 5 minutes. Flip the plums over so they are flesh side up, and dot them with the fresh ginger.

3 Season and finish the plums: In a small bowl, combine the hazelnuts and dates with the remaining ¼ cup sugar, and the salt, cinnamon, and ground ginger. Sprinkle the plums with the spice mixture and toss to blend. Cook over medium heat, stirring to combine the ingredients. Add ¼ cup water and the red wine vinegar and immediately put the skillet in the oven. Bake until the plums are tender but still holding their shape, 10 to 12 minutes.

4 Whip the cream and serve the plums: In the bowl of a stand mixer fitted with the whisk attachment (or a handheld electric mixer), whip the cream until it holds soft peaks. Spoon the plums and their juices into individual bowls, and top with the whipped cream.

PAVLOVA

WITH FRESH STRAWBERRIES

This dessert is decadent without being rich or heavy. The meringue is somewhat fluffy and reminiscent of marshmallows. Tangy strawberries fit in really well. Raspberries are a good tart alternative.

1 pound fresh **strawberries**, hulled and halved

1 tablespoon seedless **raspberry jam**

Grated zest and juice of 1 large **lemon**

1 teaspoon **red wine vinegar**

¼ cup packed **dark brown sugar**

1 tablespoon grated fresh **ginger**

1 **vanilla bean**, split lengthwise, seeds scraped out and reserved

Nonstick cooking spray

1 cup **granulated sugar**

2 teaspoons **cornstarch**

4 large **egg whites**

¼ teaspoon **cream of tartar**

1 cup **heavy cream**

1 Macerate the fruit: Put the strawberries and the raspberry jam in a medium bowl and sprinkle them with a light layer of lemon zest, the lemon juice, and the red wine vinegar. Add the brown sugar, ginger, and vanilla pod and toss gently to combine all of the flavors. Cover with plastic wrap and refrigerate for at least 30 minutes and up to 4 hours.

2 Position an oven rack as close to the top as you can. Preheat the oven to 250°F. Line a baking sheet with parchment paper, draw a 12-inch circle onto it, and turn the paper over. Spray it with cooking spray.

3 Make the meringue: In a medium bowl, thoroughly mix the granulated sugar with the cornstarch. In the bowl of a stand mixer fitted with the whisk attachment, blend the egg whites and cream of tartar on high speed until the whites hold their shape and the whisk leaves a trace in the whites. Lower the mixer speed to medium and start adding the sugar mixture, tablespoon by tablespoon, waiting until each spoonful is incorporated before adding more. The meringue should be firm and glossy.

4 Bake the meringue: Spoon the meringue onto the prepared baking sheet, spreading it out to fill the circle in an even layer. You can neaten the edges of the circle by wiping away any stray meringue with a kitchen towel. Bake, undisturbed, for 45 minutes. Then rotate the baking sheet in the oven and bake for an additional 20 minutes. The exterior of the meringue should be crusty when touched (ever so gently!), while the interior should still be moist (and somewhat goopy). If it isn't crunchy on the outside, bake it for an additional 10 to 15 minutes. Remove from the oven and set it aside to cool completely.

5 Whip the cream and serve the dessert: Thoroughly wash and dry the mixer bowl and the whisk attachment, and return them to the mixer. Combine the cream and the reserved vanilla seeds in the bowl, and beat with the whisk until it holds fairly stiff peaks. Top the meringue with the whipped cream and the strawberries. Serve immediately.

RASPBERRY CRÈME CARAMEL

This is a dessert my mother made on the regular. I love to eat crème caramel straight from the ramekin when it is a little warm, when the caramel is more liquefied and creeps up the sides of the luscious custard. It's also good at room temperature or chilled, making this a great make-ahead dessert. Raspberries are the ideal fruit here: they are tart and their seeds offer some texture.

1¾ cups **sugar**

5 large **eggs**, at room temperature

¼ teaspoon **kosher salt**

3 cups **whole milk**

1 teaspoon **vanilla extract**

1 pint fresh **raspberries**

1 Preheat the oven to 300°F. Arrange eight 6-ounce ramekins in a roasting pan or baking dish.

2 Make the caramel: In a medium stainless steel sauté pan, combine 1 cup of the sugar with ⅓ cup water, swirl to blend, and heat over medium heat until it forms a clear syrup, 5 to 8 minutes. Raise the heat and cook until the syrup forms an amber caramel. Remove the pan from the heat and immediately divide the caramel evenly among the ramekins, covering the bottom of each ramekin and not so much on the sides. Set aside until the caramel cools and then hardens, at least 30 minutes.

3 Make the custard: In a medium bowl, whisk together the eggs, the remaining ¾ cup sugar, and the salt. In a medium saucepan, bring the milk and vanilla to a gentle simmer. Pour the milk over the egg mixture, whisking to blend. Distribute the custard mixture evenly among the eight ramekins. Place the ramekins in a large roasting pan. Put the pan in the oven and pour 2 inches of water into the bottom of the roasting pan to make a water bath for the custards as they cook. Cover the pan tightly with aluminum foil and bake until the custards are firm in the center, 55 minutes to 1 hour. Allow the custards to cool for 30 minutes in the hot water, then remove them from the water bath. Let the custards cool at least 1 hour before serving. (The custards can be refrigerated and served chilled the next day as well.)

4 Serve the crème caramel: Run a knife around the edge of each ramekin. Divide the raspberries among 8 rimmed dessert plates, and unmold the custards on top of them.

CHERRIES IN RED WINE
WITH FROZEN YOGURT

The tannins in red wine contrast brilliantly against slightly sour cherries and tart yogurt, all of which make this dessert the ideal way to end a meal. The cherries discolor slightly once cooked, but the flavor is worth it. Warm cherries and red wine sauce poured over icy scoops of frozen yogurt are perfection.

1 (750-ml) bottle **rich red wine**, preferably Merlot or Zinfandel

2 (3-inch) **cinnamon stick**s

2 **star anise pods**

2 tablespoons **dark brown sugar**, plus more as needed

2 tablespoons **strawberry jam**

1 tablespoon **extra-virgin olive oil**

1 pound fresh **cherries**, halved and pitted

¼ cup **granulated sugar**

2 teaspoons **red wine vinegar**

1 pint **vanilla frozen yogurt**

1 Make the red wine sauce: In a medium saucepan, bring the wine, cinnamon sticks, star anise pods, and brown sugar to a boil over medium heat. Lower the heat and simmer until about 2 cups liquid remain, 15 to 20 minutes. Discard the cinnamon and star anise. Whisk in the jam. Taste for sweetness. If the sauce is not sweet enough, add another tablespoon or two of brown sugar, and stir it in until dissolved.

2 Cook the cherries: Heat a large sauté pan over medium heat. Add the olive oil, swirling it around until it gets good and hot. Quickly add the cherries in a single layer and turn the heat to high. Cook until the cherries are lightly seared and some of their liquid has emerged, 1 to 2 minutes. Sprinkle the granulated sugar and red wine vinegar over the cherries. Pour in the wine sauce and let the cherries bubble over high heat for a minute so the wine sauce can coat them. Remove from the heat.

3 Serve the cherries: Spoon the warm cherries into individual bowls, and top each serving with a scoop of frozen yogurt.

RASPBERRY-FILLED CHOCOLATE SHORTBREAD SANDWICHES

When I was a kid, I often had chocolate raspberry cake for my birthday. This combination of bitterness and fruity flavor is dynamite, and I love it as much today as I did then. The fruit doesn't have to be completely crushed for the filling here—it's nice when there are some larger pieces of raspberry still intact.

CHOCOLATE SHORTBREAD

½ pound (2 sticks) **lightly salted butter**, softened, plus more for the baking sheet

2 ounces **semisweet chocolate**, chopped

½ cup **sugar**

2 cups **all-purpose flour**, sifted

1 teaspoon **kosher salt**

FILLING

1 teaspoon **unsweetened dark cocoa powder**

2 tablespoons **clover honey**, plus more to taste

2 pints fresh **raspberries**

1 Preheat the oven to 325°F.

2 **Make the shortbread dough:** In a medium saucepan over very low heat (or in a double boiler), melt the butter and chocolate together, stirring constantly. Remove the pan from the heat and stir in the sugar. Then gently fold the flour and the salt into the chocolate mixture.

3 Bake the shortbread: Grease a 15-inch baking sheet with butter. Gently press the dough into an even 1-inch-thick layer on the baking sheet. Bake for 35 to 40 minutes. To test for doneness, insert the tip of a small knife into the shortbread; it should emerge clean. Remove the baking sheet from the oven and allow the shortbread to cool for 5 minutes. Then transfer the shortbread to a cutting board and cut it into 20 squares. Allow them to cool on a wire rack for at least 15 to 20 minutes.

4 Make the filling and assemble the sandwiches: In a medium bowl, whisk together the cocoa powder and honey until smooth. Mix in the raspberries, lightly crushing them. Taste, and add more honey if desired. Put half of the shortbread squares on a platter or on individual plates, and spoon the raspberry filling over them. Top with the remaining shortbread squares.

CHERRIES

WITH GINGER LEMON CURD

I am addicted to the flavor combination of raw cherries with the heat of ginger and the tartness of lemon curd. When cherries link up with citrus, they taste almost like a pomegranate or Concord grapes. Serve this as is or layered in a parfait glass. You can also pack the curd and cherries into a baked tart shell or spoon them over slices of a simple yellow cake.

3 large **eggs**

⅓ cup **sugar**

Grated zest of 1 large **lemon**

A few grates of the zest plus the juice of ½ large **orange**

½ cup fresh lemon juice (from about **4 lemons**)

4 tablespoons (½ stick) **unsalted butter**, cubed and chilled

1 teaspoon **ground ginger**

3 tablespoons grated **fresh ginger**

1 pound fresh **cherries**, halved and pitted

1 tablespoon **clover honey**

½ cup small to medium fresh **basil leaves**

1 Make the curd: In a large stainless steel saucepan, combine the eggs, sugar, lemon zest, and orange zest. Whisk until the mixture lightens in color, 2 to 3 minutes. Then whisk in the lemon juice and orange juice.

2 Cook the curd: Put the pan over low heat and cook, whisking constantly, until the mixture thickens, about 8 to 10 minutes. Start gradually whisking in the butter. When all of the butter has been integrated, remove the pan from the heat and whisk in the ground and fresh ginger. Transfer the curd to a bowl and cover it tightly with plastic wrap, pressing the plastic against the surface of the curd so it won't form a skin as it cools. Chill the curd in the refrigerator for at least 1 hour, until it cools and thickens.

3 Finish the dessert: In a medium bowl, toss together the cherries, honey, and basil, tearing the basil leaves slightly as you drop them into the bowl. Spoon the curd into individual bowls and layer the cherries on top.

PEACH LIME BARS

My mother never made fruit bars when I was growing up because lemons and limes were always reserved for pies and cakes. I was swimming in a sea of lemon curd at all times, it seemed. Now I make these fruit bars when I want a dessert that can go with any meal and also double as an indulgent breakfast treat. You would be surprised how well hot coffee and these fruit notes go together—like a sliver of lemon peel with an espresso.

Nonstick cooking spray

DOUGH
½ pound (2 sticks) **unsalted butter**, softened
½ cup **granulated sugar**
½ teaspoon **kosher salt**
½ teaspoon grated **nutmeg**
2 cups **all-purpose flour**, plus more for rolling the dough

FILLING
4 large **eggs**
⅔ cup **all-purpose flour**
2 cups **granulated sugar**
1 tablespoon grated **lime zest**
⅓ cup lime juice (from 2 to 4 **limes**)
⅓ cup lemon juice (from 2 **lemons**)
4 large **peaches**, halved, pitted, and cut into thin slices
2 tablespoons **dark brown sugar**

1　Preheat the oven to 350°F. Spray the bottom and sides of a 9 × 12-inch rimmed baking sheet with cooking spray.

2　**Make the dough:** In the bowl of a stand mixer fitted with the paddle attachment, combine the butter, granulated sugar, and salt and beat on medium speed until smooth, 5 to 8 minutes. If the batter sticks to the sides of the bowl, shut off the mixer and scrape down the sides with a rubber spatula. Remove the bowl from the mixer, and gently stir in the nutmeg and flour until just blended.

3　**Roll the dough:** Lightly flour a flat surface and spread the dough out on it with your hands. Roll it with a floured rolling pin until it is about ½ inch thick, 10 inches wide, and 13 to 14 inches long. Roll the dough up on the pin and then unroll it onto the prepared baking sheet. Press the dough into the bottom and sides of the pan, trimming away any overhang. Gently make holes in the dough with the tines of a fork. Bake until the crust is light brown, 20 to 25 minutes. Set it aside to cool.

4　**Make the filling and bake the bars:** In a medium bowl, whisk together the eggs, flour, and granulated sugar until smooth. Whisk in the lime zest, lime juice, and lemon juice. Pour the filling over the cooled crust. Layer the peach slices on top, and sprinkle with the brown sugar. Bake until the filling is set, 25 to 30 minutes. Let cool, and then slice into 16 to 20 bars.

WARM BLUEBERRY GINGER TURNOVERS

The combination of ginger's slight heat with juicy blueberries is sublime in these anytime pastries: great for breakfast, tea, or dessert. I like to roll the hot turnovers in a little granulated sugar for added texture.

CRUST

2 cups **all-purpose flour**, plus more for rolling the dough

¼ cup **granulated sugar**

½ teaspoon **kosher salt**

½ pound (2 sticks) **unsalted butter**, cut into small pieces and chilled

¼ cup **ice-cold water**

FILLING

1 tablespoon **unsalted butter**

3 cups fresh **blueberries**

¼ cup packed **light brown sugar**

1 tablespoon grated fresh **ginger**

2 teaspoons **red wine vinegar**

2 tablespoons **blueberry jam**

Nonstick cooking spray

2 large **egg yolks**

Granulated sugar (optional)

1 **Make the dough:** In a food processor, combine the flour, granulated sugar, and salt. Pulse to blend. Transfer the mixture to a bowl, add the pieces of butter, and toss to coat them with the mixture. Return the mixture to the food processor and pulse until it is crumbly. The butter should be almost thoroughly integrated with the dry ingredients. While pulsing to combine, pour the cold water through the feed tube. Remove the dough from the food processor and roll it into a ball. Flatten it slightly, cover it with plastic wrap, and refrigerate it for at least 30 minutes and up to 8 hours.

2 **Make the filling:** Heat a medium sauté pan over medium heat and add the butter. When it melts and is just starting to brown, lower the heat and stir in the blueberries and brown sugar. Then stir in the ginger, vinegar, and jam, and cook only until the jam melds with the fruit, 2 minutes. Transfer the filling to a shallow dish and let it cool. Cover with plastic wrap and refrigerate until cold.

3 On a flat floured surface, roll the dough until it is ¼ inch thick, making sure you lightly flour under and on top of the dough as you roll it. Cut the dough into eight 3-inch-diameter rounds. Put them in a single layer on a baking sheet and refrigerate them until firm, at least 30 minutes and up to 4 hours.

4 Preheat the oven to 350°F.

5 **Assemble and bake the turnovers:** Spray a 15-inch baking sheet with cooking spray. In a small bowl, beat the egg yolks with 2 teaspoons cool water. Scoop a spoonful of the blueberry filling onto the center of each round of dough and fold one side over to create a half-moon shape. Brush the edges with egg wash and seal them. Arrange the turnovers in a single layer on the prepared baking sheet, brush lightly with egg wash, and bake until they are golden brown, 18 to 22 minutes. Remove the baking sheet from the oven, and roll the turnovers in granulated sugar for added texture, if desired. Serve immediately.

STOVETOP PEACHES
WITH HONEY

Few things beat biting into a juicy peach and having the juice run down your arm, but somehow finding that perfect peach can be a challenge. Sautéing peaches is my favorite way to accentuate the positive: whether slightly underripe or over-ripe, they only benefit from time over heat with a little honey, butter, and lime. Choosing between yellow or white peaches? Whichever looks better, although I am partial to yellow ones.

4 tablespoons (½ stick) **unsalted butter**
8 large **yellow peaches**, halved and pitted
¼ cup **clover honey**
1 cup **raw sugar**
1 teaspoon **kosher salt**
A few grates of the zest plus the juice of 1 large **lime**

Heat a large skillet over medium heat and add the butter. When it begins to froth and turn light brown, after 3 to 5 minutes, add the peach halves, flesh side down, in a single layer. Drizzle with the honey, sprinkle with the sugar and salt, and cook over high heat until the peaches become tender, 10 to 12 minutes. Remove from the heat. Turn the peaches over and add the lime zest and juice. Baste the peaches with the juices, and serve.

STRAWBERRY SALAD
WITH CRUSHED BASIL LEAVES

This is such a simple combination. It can be served as is or paired with anything from scoops of vanilla ice cream to slices of pound cake.

1 large **lemon**
Pinch of **kosher salt**
½ cup **sugar**
1 tablespoon **Grand Marnier**
1 pound fresh **strawberries**, hulled and halved
½ cup medium to small fresh **basil leaves**

1 Macerate the fruit: Using a vegetable peeler and a light touch, remove the zest from one third of the lemon, leaving the pith (the white part) behind. Cut the lemon in half, juice both halves, and in a medium bowl, combine the juice with the zest, salt, sugar, Grand Marnier, and a generous half of the strawberries. Cover and refrigerate for at least 30 minutes and up to 4 hours. Cover and refrigerate the remaining strawberries separately.

2 Assemble the salad: Combine the macerated strawberries with the remaining berries. Stir in the basil leaves, and serve.

JAMES BEARD STRAWBERRY SHORTCAKE
WITH SORBET

This is a great cake that I made for the first time at Larry Forgione's restaurant, An American Place. The method behind using the hard-boiled egg yolk to add flavor and enhance the texture is all James Beard. I think raspberries bring out the flavor of strawberries—hence the sorbet here. Otherwise, this a classic strawberry shortcake.

BISCUITS

2 large **eggs**

2 cups **all-purpose flour**, plus more for kneading the dough

2 tablespoons **sugar**

1 tablespoon plus ½ teaspoon **baking powder**

1½ teaspoons **kosher salt**

6 tablespoons (¾ stick) **salted butter**, cut into small pieces and chilled

¾ cup **heavy cream**

CREAM AND FRUIT

1 cup **heavy cream**

2 pints fresh **strawberries**, hulled and quartered

2 teaspoons lemon zest and juice of 1 large **lemon**

1 pint **raspberry sorbet**

1 Boil the eggs: Put the eggs in a medium saucepan and cover them with cold water. Bring the water to a boil and then reduce the heat so that the water simmers gently. Once it is simmering, cook for 11 minutes. Then drain the water from the eggs and run a steady stream of cold water over them to stop them from overcooking. Peel the eggs, and separate the yolks from the whites. Save the whites for another use.

2 Preheat the oven to 375°F. Line a baking sheet with parchment paper.

3 Make the biscuits: In a medium bowl, whisk together the flour, sugar, baking powder, and salt. Add the butter, and using your hands, work the butter into the dry ingredients until the mixture resembles wet sand. On a floured work surface, knead the cooked yolks into the flour mixture, and then add the cream. Mix just to combine. (Overworking the flour will make the biscuits tough.) Flatten the dough to form a 1½- to 2-inch-thick rectangle. Cut the dough into roughly 2-inch squares. You may need to roll the scraps to make 8 squares. Arrange them (with some distance between them for even browning) on the prepared baking sheet. Bake until they are light brown, 10 to 12 minutes. Remove the baking sheet from the oven, transfer the biscuits to a wire rack, and let them cool completely.

4 Whip the cream and prepare the fruit: In the bowl of a stand mixer fitted with the whisk attachment, whip the cream until it holds soft peaks. In a medium bowl, toss the strawberries with the lemon zest and half of the lemon juice.

5 Assemble the dessert: Cut the shortcakes in half and open them up as if you were making sandwiches. Put the bottom halves on a platter or on individual plates. Cover them with a generous spoonful of the strawberries and any juice. Top with a small scoop of raspberry sorbet, some of the remaining lemon juice right on the sorbet, and a huge dollop of whipped cream. Put the tops on and serve immediately.

BLACKBERRY CLAFOUTIS

A claufoutis is such a simple, tasty dessert. It falls somewhere between a cake and a steamed pudding. It's also a great showcase for a single fruit—blackberries or raspberries in particular. It's best served warm (or even hot if you can't wait to dig in!), topped with whipped cream.

1 tablespoon **unsalted butter**

1 pound fresh large **blackberries**

Grated zest and juice of 1 **lemon**

2 large **eggs**

1 large **egg white**

⅓ cup **sugar**

1 cup **whole milk**

½ teaspoon **kosher salt**

⅔ cup **all-purpose flour**

1　Preheat the oven to 325°F. Grease the bottom and sides of a 9-inch pie pan with the butter.

2　Macerate the fruit: In a large bowl, combine the blackberries with the lemon zest and juice. Cover with plastic wrap and refrigerate for at least 1 hour and up to 4 hours.

3　Make the batter: In the bowl of a stand mixer fitted with the whisk attachment, beat together the eggs, egg white, and sugar on medium speed until the mixture turns pale yellow, 8 to 10 minutes. Remove the bowl from the mixer and stir in the milk, salt, and flour. Do not overmix.

4　Assemble and bake the clafoutis: Strain the blackberries, reserving any juices. Arrange the blackberries in an even layer in the prepared pie pan. Spoon the batter over the fruit, tapping the sides of the pan gently so the batter sits in an even layer. Bake until the top is puffed and light brown, 35 to 40 minutes. Serve warm, drizzled with the reserved blackberry juices.

CAKE

MY CANNOLI FILLING RUM CAKE

FROM CHILDHOOD

I love a cup of seriously strong coffee alongside a classic Sicilian cannoli from Caffe Dante on MacDougal Street in Manhattan. When I am making this cake at home, I am holding it up to that standard. While I generally have no patience and want to devour dessert as soon as I am finished making it, this cake really benefits from sitting for a few hours or even overnight to allow the flavors to meld together. A note about the filling: If your ricotta seems loose and liquidy, wrap it in cheesecloth and set it in a strainer over a bowl to drain for a few hours (and even overnight) in the refrigerator to remove excess moisture before using it.

FILLING

2 cups **ricotta cheese**, preferably whole-milk

¾ cup **confectioners' sugar**

1 teaspoon ground **cinnamon**

¼ teaspoon ground **allspice**

¼ cup **heavy cream**

¼ cup **semisweet chocolate chips**

Grated zest of 1 **lemon**

RUM GLAZE

1 cup **confectioners' sugar**

¼ cup **dark rum**

2 layers **Yellow Layer Cake** (page 291)

1 Make the filling: In a medium bowl, whisk the ricotta until smooth. Sift in the confectioners' sugar, cinnamon, and allspice, and whisk to blend. In a separate bowl (or in the bowl of a stand mixer fitted with the whisk attachment), beat the heavy cream until it holds fairly stiff peaks. Using a rubber spatula, gently fold the whipped cream into the ricotta mixture. Stir in the chocolate chips and lemon zest.

2 Make the rum glaze: In a medium saucepan, combine the confectioners' sugar with the rum and cook over low heat, whisking constantly, until smooth. Set aside to cool.

3 Assemble the cake: Set one cake layer, right side up, on a flat surface. Brush half of the rum glaze over the top and cover that with the ricotta filling. Put the second cake layer, right side up, squarely on top, and gently press the two layers together. Pour the remaining rum glaze over the cake. Cover and refrigerate for at least 4 hours or overnight before serving.

YELLOW LAYER
CAKE WITH
CHOCOLATE
FROSTING

DARK
CHOCOLATE
MAYONNAISE
LAYER CAKE
WITH VANILLA
FROSTING

MY CANNOLI
FILLING RUM
CAKE FROM
CHILDHOOD

DARK CHOCOLATE MAYONNAISE LAYER CAKE
WITH VANILLA FROSTING

For me, this is the classic childhood chocolate cake. Something about using mayonnaise, so rich, and then water, so lean, makes for a moist and flavorful cake. The coffee makes the chocolate taste like a better version of itself. The frosting is just the wonderful marshmallowy vanilla goo that chocolate cake needs.

CAKE
2 tablespoons **unsalted butter**

3 large **eggs**

1½ cups plus 1 tablespoon **sugar**

1¼ cups **mayonnaise**, preferably Hellmann's or Best Foods

¾ cup plus 1 tablespoon **unsweetened dark cocoa powder**

2 teaspoons **instant coffee granules** (optional)

¾ teaspoon **baking soda**

¼ teaspoon **baking powder**

½ teaspoon **kosher salt**

2¼ cups **all-purpose flour**

FROSTING
2 large **egg whites**

1⅓ cups **sugar**

¼ teaspoon **cream of tartar**

1 tablespoon **light corn syrup**

1 teaspoon **vanilla extract**

4 ounces **semisweet chocolate**, grated

1 Preheat the oven to 350°F. Thoroughly grease the bottoms and sides of two 9-inch round cake pans with the butter.

2 Make the cake batter: In the bowl of a stand mixer fitted with the whisk attachment, beat the eggs and sugar on high speed until light, fluffy, and lemon-colored, 5 to 8 minutes. In a medium bowl, whisk together the mayonnaise, cocoa powder, coffee granules, baking soda, baking powder, and salt. Remove the bowl from the mixer and whisk the mayonnaise mixture into the egg mixture until smooth. Stir in the flour. Then gently stir in 1½ cups hot water. Mix until all of the ingredients are thoroughly combined.

3 Bake the cake layers: Pour half of the batter into each of the prepared cake pans. Bake until a toothpick inserted in the center emerges clean, 20 to 25 minutes. Let the layers cool completely in the pans.

4 Make the frosting: Make a stovetop water bath by filling a large skillet halfway with water and heating the water until it simmers. In a clean medium-size heatproof bowl, whisk together the egg whites, sugar, cream of tartar, 1 tablespoon water, and the corn syrup. Set the bowl in the water bath and whisk the mixture constantly (with the heat off) until it fluffs up and reaches a temperature of 140°F. Remove the bowl from the water bath, stir in the vanilla extract, and whisk for another 1 to 2 minutes to cool it off a little. Cover the bowl with plastic wrap and refrigerate until you are ready to frost the cake.

5 Frost the cake: Gently turn the cake rounds out onto a flat surface. Spread about a third of the frosting on one layer, right side up, letting some of it spill over the sides. Set the other layer, right side down, squarely on top of the first, and use the remaining frosting to coat the top and sides of the cake. Sprinkle the top with the grated chocolate.

YELLOW LAYER CAKE
WITH CHOCOLATE FROSTING

I used to find myself thumbing through cookbooks to find a simple, reliable cake that belongs anywhere. I settled on this recipe a few years ago and have never looked back. It's truly one of my staple recipes. Who doesn't need a good yellow cake recipe as a go-with for an array of seasonal fruits? While I recommend topping this cake with brandied cherries (because I love them), this cake could go with anything from a goopy marshmallow frosting to a dark chocolate ganache or buttercream.

CAKE
½ pound (2 sticks) plus 2 tablespoons **unsalted butter**, softened
2 cups **all-purpose flour**
2 teaspoons **baking powder**
¾ teaspoon **kosher salt**
2 cups **sugar**
6 large **eggs**
Grated zest and juice of 1 large **lemon**

FROSTING
14 ounces **bittersweet chocolate**, chopped
1½ cups **sugar**
2 cups **heavy cream**
1 teaspoon **vanilla extract**
12 tablespoons (1½ sticks) **unsalted butter**, cubed

½ cup drained **brandied cherries**

1 Preheat the oven to 350°F. Grease the bottom and sides of two 9-inch round cake pans with the 2 tablespoons butter.

2 Make the cake batter: In a medium bowl, whisk together the flour, baking powder, and salt. In the bowl of a stand mixer fitted with the paddle attachment, beat the remaining 2 sticks butter and the sugar on medium speed until smooth, 5 to 8 minutes. Add the eggs, one by one, and then add the lemon zest and juice. Remove the bowl from the mixer and stir in the flour mixture.

3 Bake the cake: Fill each prepared cake pan with half of the batter. Bake until a toothpick inserted in the center of each cake emerges clean, 25 to 30 minutes. Unmold each cake onto a plate. Allow the cakes to cool for 30 minutes. Using a long serrated knife and a gentle sawing motion, split each cake in half horizontally to form 4 cake layers. Let cool completely.

4 Make the frosting: In a medium bowl, mix the chocolate and sugar. In a medium saucepan, bring the heavy cream and vanilla to a simmer. Pour the hot cream over the chocolate mixture and stir until all of the chocolate has melted. Gently whisk in the butter cubes. Set aside to cool.

5 Frost the cake: In the (clean) bowl of the stand mixer fitted with the whisk attachment, whip the frosting to lighten it, 1 to 2 minutes. Put one cake layer, right side up, on a cake plate and spread some of the frosting over it. Place the second layer, right side down, neatly stacking it on top of the first, and spread frosting over it. Repeat with the remaining two layers, and then frost the entire outside of the cake. Top with the brandied cherries.

TIRAMISU FOR TWO

While I always went for the cannoli or the *sfogliatella* when we hit an Italian bakery when I was a child, I now also appreciate a good tiramisu. Instead of the usual party-size creation, this smaller-scale recipe leaves you just enough to enjoy a little left over the next day. Tiramisu rides a perfect line between pudding and cake. I also think that chocolate and dark rum is one of life's great combinations.

12 **ladyfingers** (*savoiardi* in Italian)

3 large **egg yolks**

⅓ cup **sugar**

⅓ cup **sweet Marsala**

½ cup **heavy cream**

1 teaspoon **vanilla extract**

6 ounces **mascarpone cheese**, whisked slightly

1 cup **strong brewed coffee**, cooled

1 tablespoon **dark rum**

1 tablespoon **clover honey**

4 ounces **semisweet chocolate**, finely grated

2 teaspoons **unsweetened dark cocoa powder**

1 Preheat the oven to 350°F.

2 Dry the ladyfingers: Arrange the ladyfingers in a single layer on a baking sheet and bake in the oven for 10 minutes to dry them out. Set them aside to cool.

3 Start the filling: Create a makeshift double boiler by bringing 2 inches of water to a simmer in a medium saucepan. In the bowl of a stand mixer fitted with the whisk attachment, beat the egg yolks and sugar on high speed until pale and lemon-colored, 5 to 8 minutes. Lower the speed and add the Marsala and 1 tablespoon cold water. Remove the bowl from the mixer and set it over the pan of simmering water and whisk steadily until the eggs reach 160°F, 5 to 8 minutes. (Use a deep-frying or candy thermometer to monitor the temperature.) Remove from the heat and transfer to a cool bowl.

4 Make the mascarpone cream: In another bowl, beat the heavy cream until it forms soft peaks and then add the vanilla. Use a rubber spatula to mix the mascarpone into the whipped cream. Fold in the egg mixture.

5 Assemble the tiramisu: In a small bowl, stir together the coffee, rum, and honey. Quickly dip both sides of half of the ladyfingers into the coffee mixture and arrange them vertically around the edges of a small deep serving bowl. Spoon half of the mascarpone cream into the bowl, and sprinkle it with half of the grated chocolate. Dip and layer in the remaining ladyfingers, gently pressing down to pack the tiramisu into the bowl. Spread the remaining mascarpone cream over the ladyfingers and top with the remaining grated chocolate. Cover the bowl tightly with plastic wrap and refrigerate for at least 2 hours or overnight. Just before serving, sift the cocoa powder over the top of the tiramisu.

RICOTTA CHEESECAKE

FROM THE ITALIAN BAKERY

This is a cheesecake my mother would make periodically when I was a kid. She definitely took her inspiration from the Italian bakery we went to while I was growing up. Sometimes she would have a slice of their cheesecake. I could see the wheels turning in her head as she ate each bite carefully . . . I didn't fully appreciate cheesecake in the face of other higher-ticket items like chocolate layer cake and blueberry pie. Now I crave the wonderful subtle flavors of pine nuts and citrus meandering through the cheese, and the buttery note of the simple pat-in-the-pan crust.

CRUST

9 tablespoons (1 stick plus 1 tablespoon) **lightly salted butter**, cubed and chilled

1½ cups **all-purpose flour**

½ teaspoon **kosher salt**

1 large **egg yolk**, lightly beaten

FILLING

4 large **egg yolks**

1 cup **sugar**

2 teaspoons **vanilla extract**

1 tablespoon **all-purpose flour**

5 tablespoons **pine nuts**, toasted

2 tablespoons chopped **candied citron** or candied lemon peel

3 cups **whole-milk ricotta cheese**

1 Preheat the oven to 350°F. Grease a 9-inch springform pan with 1 tablespoon of the butter.

2 Make the crust: In a large bowl, combine the flour and salt. Using your fingers, work the remaining 8 tablespoons butter into the flour until the mixture resembles coarse crumbs. Gently pat the crust into the bottom and about 1½ inches up the sides of the prepared springform pan. Brush the egg yolk over the crust to form a protective coating. Line the crust with foil or parchment paper, and fill it with pie weights or dried beans. Bake until the crust is golden brown, 15 to 18 minutes. Remove the weights and foil and let the crust cool completely. Leave the oven on.

3 Make the filling: In the bowl of a stand mixer fitted with the whisk attachment, beat the egg yolks, sugar, and vanilla on high speed until pale and lemon-colored, 8 to 10 minutes. Remove the bowl from the mixer and use a rubber spatula to stir in the flour, pine nuts, citron, and ricotta.

4 Bake the cheesecake: Smooth the filling over the crust and bake the cheesecake for 30 minutes. Lower the oven temperature to 325°F and bake until a toothpick or small knife inserted in the center emerges clean, 25 to 30 minutes. Let the cheesecake cool completely in the springform pan before releasing and removing the sides. Then refrigerate it for at least 4 hours before serving.

ORANGE WALNUT BUNDT CAKE

I love assembling this cake: filling the pan with some of the batter, spooning in a hidden ring of marmalade, and covering it gingerly with the remaining batter. This cake can be served as is or with a simple glaze for a brunch. Or it can be topped with a buttercream or dark chocolate ganache and become dessert for a dinner party.

Nonstick cooking spray

1 cup **orange marmalade**

1½ cups **walnut halves**, toasted and chopped

¾ pound plus 2 tablespoons (3¼ sticks) **unsalted butter**, sliced, at room temperature

2½ cups **sugar**

¼ cup plus 2 tablespoons **whole milk**

4 large **eggs**

2 large **egg yolks**

2 teaspoons **vanilla extract**

3 cups **cake flour**

1½ teaspoons **baking powder**

1 teaspoon **kosher salt**

2 tablespoons grated **lemon zest**

1 Preheat the oven to 350°F. Grease a bundt pan with cooking spray.

2 **Prepare the filling:** In a medium bowl, stir together the marmalade with 1¼ cups of the nuts.

3 **Start the batter:** In the bowl of a stand mixer fitted with the paddle attachment, beat the butter and sugar until fluffy, 8 to 10 minutes. Meanwhile, in a medium bowl, whisk together the milk, eggs, egg yolks, and vanilla. In another bowl, whisk together the flour, baking powder, and salt.

4 **Finish the batter:** Add the lemon zest to the butter and mix to combine. Add half of the milk mixture and blend on low speed. Add half of the flour mixture and blend only until combined. Mix in the remaining milk and then the remaining flour. Do not overmix.

5 **Bake the cake:** Spoon about half of the batter into the prepared pan. Spoon about three-quarters of the marmalade mixture in a ring in the middle of the batter. Gently spoon the remaining batter over the top of the marmalade so it's hidden in the center. Bake in the center of the oven until a toothpick inserted in the middle comes out clean, 50 to 55 minutes. Let cool for 30 minutes. Unmold the cake onto a serving platter and top with the remaining marmalade and the remaining ¼ cup walnuts. Serve warm or at room temperature.

PINEAPPLE UPSIDE-DOWN CAKE
WITH PINK PEPPERCORN CARAMEL

This recipe pairs tangy pineapple with caramel and the tingly heat of pink peppercorns for an unusual twist on the classic. Upside-down cake is traditionally unmolded, cooled, and served. I like it piping hot with a scoop of vanilla ice cream or lemon sorbet.

CAKE
1 medium **pineapple**
8 tablespoons (1 stick) **unsalted butter**, softened
¾ cup packed **dark brown sugar**
2 large **eggs**, lightly beaten
½ cup **buttermilk**
1 teaspoon **vanilla extract**
1 cup **all-purpose flour**
¾ cup **granulated sugar**
¾ teaspoon **baking powder**
¼ teaspoon **baking soda**
1 teaspoon **kosher salt**

CARAMEL
1 cup **granulated sugar**
Juice of 1 large **lime**
2 tablespoons **light corn syrup**
2 teaspoons **pink peppercorns**, lightly crushed

1 Preheat the oven to 350°F.

2 **Prepare the pineapple:** Cut a slice off the bottom and top of the pineapple and stand the pineapple up on a cutting board. Using a large sharp knife, slice down along the sides of the pineapple, taking care to cut off all the brown spiny skin. Cut the pineapple into 6 or 7 (1-inch-thick) slices.

3 **Cook the pineapple:** Heat an ovenproof 12-inch skillet over medium heat and melt 2 tablespoons of the butter in it. Add the pineapple slices in a single layer and sprinkle the brown sugar over the fruit. Cook to allow the pineapple to brown slightly, 3 to 5 minutes. Turn the pineapple slices over and remove the skillet from the heat.

4 **Make the batter:** In a medium bowl, whisk the remaining 6 tablespoons butter with the eggs, buttermilk, and vanilla until smooth. Use a rubber spatula to stir in the flour, granulated sugar, baking powder, baking soda, and salt until completely smooth. The batter will be fairly stiff. Pour the batter over the pineapple.

5 **Bake the cake:** Put the skillet in the oven and bake until a toothpick inserted in the center of the cake emerges clean, 40 to 45 minutes. Let the cake cool for about 10 minutes before carefully unmolding it onto a serving platter.

6 **Make the caramel and finish the cake:** In a medium stainless steel saucepan, combine ¼ cup water with the granulated sugar, lime juice, and corn syrup. Bring to a gentle simmer over medium heat, and cook until the sugar dissolves and the mixture turns a light brown (amber) color, 8 to 10 minutes. Remove the pan from the heat and set it aside to let the caramel cool slightly. Then pour the caramel over the cake and sprinkle the top with the crushed pink peppercorns.

CHOCOLATE HAZELNUT CAKE

I love the combination of hazelnuts and chocolate. This cake tastes so much richer than the sum of its ingredients and is surprisingly light. I have served it as is, and I have covered it with dark chocolate frosting and toasted nuts. It's also tasty with a caramel sauce.

13 tablespoons (1½ sticks plus 1 tablespoon) **unsalted butter**, cubed

½ cup blanched **hazelnuts**, lightly toasted

⅓ cup **all-purpose flour**

9 ounces **semisweet chocolate**, chopped

6 large **egg yolks**

1 cup **sugar**

1 tablespoon **vanilla extract**

6 large **egg whites**

¼ teaspoon **cream of tartar**

1 Preheat the oven to 375°F. Line the bottom of a 9-inch springform pan with parchment paper. Grease the parchment and sides of the pan with 1 tablespoon of the butter.

2 Start the batter: Bring 2 inches of water to a simmer in a medium saucepan. In the bowl of a food processor, process the hazelnuts and flour until smooth; set the mixture aside. In a heatproof bowl, combine the chocolate and the remaining 12 tablespoons butter. Put the bowl over the simmering water (do not let the water touch the bowl), and heat the chocolate mixture until it is melted; remove the bowl from the heat. In the bowl of a stand mixer fitted with the whisk attachment, beat the egg yolks, ¾ cup of the sugar, and the vanilla on high speed until the mixture is pale yellow, 5 to 8 minutes. Using a rubber spatula, stir in the chocolate mixture and then the flour mixture. Do not overmix. Transfer to a large bowl.

3 Finish the batter: Wash and thoroughly dry the mixer bowl and whisk. Combine the egg whites and cream of tartar in the mixer bowl and whip on high speed until the whisk leaves visible paths in the egg whites and the mixture looks light and very fluffy, 3 to 5 minutes. Beat in the remaining ¼ cup sugar and continue whipping until stiff peaks form, 1 to 2 minutes. Use a rubber spatula to fold the egg whites into the chocolate mixture. Gently transfer the batter to the prepared springform pan.

4 Bake the cake: Put the pan in the oven and bake until a toothpick inserted in the center of the cake emerges clean, 35 to 40 minutes. Let the cake cool completely in the pan. The center will sink a little; don't worry. Run a paring knife around the edge of the pan to make sure the edges are free before releasing and removing the sides.

FLOURLESS CHOCOLATE SHEET CAKE

This is a basic sheet cake that I often use as a lighter form of brownies. I have also made a double recipe and stacked the two layers with some vanilla frosting (see page 290) in between to make a fluffy cake that is light on calories but heavy on flavor. You can use this cake to make a jelly or whipped cream roll, or cut it in half to make a smaller cake that has two layers. Or enjoy as is.

1 tablespoon **unsalted butter**

6 ounces **bittersweet chocolate**, roughly chopped

3 tablespoons **espresso** or strong brewed coffee, cooled

2 teaspoons **vanilla extract**

6 large **egg whites**

½ teaspoon **cream of tartar**

¾ cup **sugar**

6 large **egg yolks**

1 tablespoon **unsweetened dark cocoa powder**

1 Preheat the oven to 375°F. Line the bottom of an 11½ × 17½-inch rimmed baking sheet with parchment. Grease the parchment and the sides of the baking sheet with the butter.

2 Melt the chocolate: Bring 2 inches of water to a simmer in a medium saucepan. In a medium heatproof bowl, combine the chocolate with the coffee and vanilla. Put the bowl over the saucepan (do not let the bowl touch the water), and stir until the chocolate melts and the mixture is smooth. Transfer to a large bowl and set aside to cool slightly.

3 Make the batter: In the bowl of a stand mixer fixed with the whisk attachment, combine the egg whites and cream of tartar and beat on high speed until the whisk leaves visible paths in the egg whites and the mixture looks light and very fluffy, 3 to 5 minutes. Beat in the sugar and continue whipping until stiff peaks form, 1 to 2 minutes. In a small bowl, whisk the egg yolks until smooth. Gradually whisk the egg yolks into the melted chocolate, and then use a rubber spatula to fold the egg whites into the chocolate mixture just until combined. Gently transfer the batter to the prepared baking sheet.

4 Bake the cake: Put the baking sheet in the oven and bake for 10 minutes. Then lower the temperature to 325°F and bake until a toothpick inserted in the center emerges clean, 5 to 8 minutes. Let the cake cool on the baking sheet for about 10 minutes. Then run a paring knife around the edges of the baking sheet to make sure the cake hasn't stuck, and unmold it onto a wire rack. Use a fine-mesh sieve to sift a light, even layer of cocoa powder over the cake.

NO-BAKE CHEESECAKE

This is essentially a cheesecake with a no-bake filling that sets as it chills. The condensed milk in the filling adds a creamy note that sweetens and complements the tang of the cream cheese. Surprisingly, the added structure of store-bought orange juice (versus freshly squeezed) actually works better in this recipe. If you prefer, you can make a simpler crust by crushing shortbread cookies with some melted butter and confectioners' sugar and pressing that into the bottom and sides of the pan.

CRUST

9 tablespoons (1 stick plus 1 tablespoon) **lightly salted butter**, cubed and chilled

1½ cups **all-purpose flour**

½ teaspoon **kosher salt**

1 large **egg yolk**, lightly beaten

FILLING

2 (8-ounce) packages **cream cheese**, at room temperature

½ teaspoon ground **cinnamon**

¼ cup **orange juice**

1 (14-ounce) can **sweetened condensed milk**

1 cup slivered blanched **almonds**, toasted

1 Preheat the oven to 350°F. Grease the bottom and sides of a 9-inch springform pan with 1 tablespoon of the butter.

2 Make the crust: In a large bowl, combine the flour and salt. Using your fingers, work the remaining 8 tablespoons butter into the flour until the mixture resembles coarse crumbs. Gently pat the crust over the bottom and about 1½ inches up the sides of the prepared springform pan. Brush the egg yolk over the crust to form a protective coating. Line the crust with foil or parchment paper, and fill it with dried beans or pie weights. Bake until the crust is golden brown, 15 to 18 minutes. Remove the weights and foil. Set the crust aside to cool.

3 Make the filling: In the bowl of a stand mixer fitted with the whisk attachment, beat the cream cheese and cinnamon on medium speed until smooth, 3 to 5 minutes. Turn the mixer to low speed and slowly pour the orange juice and then the condensed milk into the cream cheese.

4 Finish the cheesecake: Spoon the filling over the crust, tapping the sides of the pan so the filling sits in an even layer over the crust. Refrigerate until firm, 2 to 3 hours or preferably overnight. Release and remove the springform sides, and coat the chilled cheesecake with the toasted almonds.

SUPER VANILLA ANGEL FOOD CAKE

I really didn't appreciate an angel food cake when I was growing up. I always wanted either a classic yellow cake covered in chocolate buttercream or a devil's food cake. It was only later on that I really fell in love with this light cake and understood all of the wonderful things that can be paired up with it, from fresh fruit to a white chocolate glaze.

Nonstick cooking spray
1 cup **cake flour**, sifted
¾ cup **sugar**
1 teaspoon **kosher salt**
12 large **egg whites**, chilled
1 teaspoon **cream of tartar**
Juice of 1 large **lemon**
1 teaspoon **vanilla extract**
1 **vanilla bean**, split lengthwise, seeds scraped out

1 Preheat the oven to 350°F. Grease the sides and bottom of a tube pan thoroughly with cooking spray.

2 Make the batter: In a medium bowl, combine the cake flour, sugar, and salt. In the bowl of a stand mixer fitted with the whisk attachment, whip the egg whites and cream of tartar on high speed until the whisk leaves visible paths in the egg whites and the mixture looks light and very fluffy, 3 to 5 minutes. Beat in 1 tablespoon cold water and the lemon juice, vanilla extract, and the vanilla seeds. Continue whipping until stiff peaks form, 3 to 5 minutes. Put the flour mixture into a sifter or a fine-mesh sieve, sprinkle a small amount over the whites, and use a rubber spatula to fold it into the egg whites. The less volume you lose here, the lighter and fluffier the cake! Repeat, sifting and folding the flour mixture into the egg whites in small increments. When all the flour has been folded in, gently transfer the batter to the prepared pan.

3 Bake the cake: Carefully put the pan in the oven and bake until a toothpick inserted in the center of the cake emerges clean, 30 to 35 minutes. Remove the pan from the oven and let the cake cool in the pan for 10 minutes. Then invert the pan onto a serving platter and leave it there until the cake has cooled completely. This will make it easier to unmold. Then, using a thin metal spatula to help release the cake, remove the pan from the cake.

PIES, TARTS & CRISPS

PEAR ALMOND CRISP

I love the crunch of nuts with pears. The season for finding a good pear is really pretty long. Don't be inhibited by the varieties of pear available: buy what you like. Firmer, less ripe pears are wonderful in this recipe; just take care to extend the cooking time if they need it to become tender.

TOPPING

9 tablespoons (1 stick plus 1 tablespoon) **unsalted butter**, cubed and chilled

¾ cup **all-purpose flour**

1 cup packed **dark brown sugar**

1 teaspoon **kosher salt**

½ teaspoon ground **cinnamon**

½ teaspoon ground **ginger**

⅛ teaspoon grated **nutmeg**

1 cup slivered blanched **almonds**, toasted

FILLING

About 3 pounds **Bosc** or **Anjou pears**

1 tablespoon **dark brown sugar**

Grated zest of 1 **lemon**, plus more for serving

Juice of 2 **lemons**

1 Preheat the oven to 350°F. Grease the bottom and sides of an 8-inch square baking dish with 1 tablespoon of the butter.

2 **Prepare the topping:** In a bowl, combine the flour, brown sugar, salt, cinnamon, ginger, and nutmeg. Add the remaining 8 tablespoons butter and the almonds, and break up the butter cubes with your fingers until the butter is the size of peas and the ingredients are mixed.

3 **Prepare the filling:** Peel, halve, and core the pears. Cut them into thin slices. Put the slices in a bowl and toss them with the brown sugar, lemon zest, and lemon juice.

4 **Assemble and bake the crisp:** Layer the pears in the prepared baking dish and cover them evenly with the almond topping. Bake until the pears are tender when pierced with the tip of a knife, 40 to 45 minutes. Let the crisp cool slightly. Then top it with additional lemon zest and serve warm.

FRENCH APPLE TART

This is really a simplified *tarte Tatin*. I like to bake the pastry separately so it gets puffy and browned on its own without being bogged down by the baked caramel-coated apples, and then combine and cook them together.

Nonstick cooking spray
1 (8-ounce) sheet frozen **puff pastry**, defrosted
3 pounds medium **Granny Smith apples**
1 cup **sugar**
Grated zest and juice of 1 large **lemon**
4 tablespoons (½ stick) **unsalted butter**, melted

1   Preheat the oven to 375°F. Grease a baking sheet with cooking spray.

2   Prepare the puff pastry: Lay the sheet of puff pastry on the prepared baking sheet, and bake until the pastry is golden brown, 25 to 30 minutes. Remove the baking sheet from the oven and turn the puff pastry over on it so it will deflate as it cools. Set it aside.

3   While the puff pastry is cooling, prepare the apples: Core and peel the apples. Cut them in half and then into ¼-inch-thick slices. In a large bowl, toss the apple slices with ¾ cup of the sugar and the lemon zest and juice.

4   Bake the tart: Arrange the apple slices in rows, slightly overlapping, on top of the puff pastry. Brush the apples liberally with the melted butter and sprinkle with the remaining ¼ cup sugar. Bake until the apples are golden brown, 20 to 25 minutes. As the tart bakes, if the apples are getting too brown, decrease the oven temperature to 350°F. Allow to cool slightly. Serve warm.

CRUSTLESS CARAMEL APPLE PIE

Caramel desserts benefit from a hit of vinegar. Cutting the sweetness actually amplifies the caramel flavor. You can dress up this simple fall apple bake with a scoop of vanilla ice cream and a splash of Calvados (apple brandy).

1 tablespoon **unsalted butter**
4 pounds medium **Granny Smith apples**
Grated zest and juice of 1 large **lemon**
1¼ cups **raw sugar**
2 tablespoons **blackstrap molasses**
1 teaspoon ground **cinnamon**
½ teaspoon grated **nutmeg**
2 tablespoons **all-purpose flour**
2 teaspoons **red wine vinegar**

1   Preheat the oven to 375°F. Grease a 10-inch glass or ceramic pie pan with the butter.

2   Make the filling: Core and peel the apples. Cut them in half and then into ¼-inch-thick slices. In a large bowl, toss the apple slices with the lemon zest and juice, ¼ cup of the sugar, and the molasses. Sift in the cinnamon, nutmeg, and flour and mix again.

3   Bake the pie: Pour the fruit mixture into the prepared pie pan. Put the pan on a rimmed baking sheet (in case the filling overflows). Bake until the filling is golden brown and bubbling, 45 to 50 minutes. Let cool completely.

4   Make the caramel and finish the pie: Warm the remaining 1 cup sugar in a heavy-bottomed saucepan over low heat until it dissolves completely, 5 to 8 minutes. Carefully stir in the vinegar until smooth. Pour the caramel over the apples. Serve immediately.

BLUEBERRY JAM CRISP

This is just an excuse to eat a lot of blueberry jam, one of my favorite flavors of summer. When I make toast in the morning, I tend to put 2 tablespoons of jam on half a slice of toast. This dessert fulfills that love of the fruit. While ice cream is always a great sidekick, I love raspberry sorbet with this.

1 tablespoon **unsalted butter**

FILLING
Grated zest and juice of 1 large **lemon**
2 tablespoons **cornstarch**
5 cups fresh **blueberries**
1 cup **granulated sugar**
2 tablespoons **all-purpose flour**
½ teaspoon **kosher salt**
12 ounces **blueberry jam**

TOPPING
1 cup **all-purpose flour**
1 cup packed **light brown sugar**
½ teaspoon ground **cinnamon**
½ teaspoon **kosher salt**
8 tablespoons (1 stick) **unsalted butter**, cubed

1 Preheat the oven to 350°F. Grease the bottom and sides of a 12 × 16-inch baking dish with the butter.

2 Make the filling: In a large bowl, whisk the lemon zest, lemon juice, and cornstarch together until smooth. Stir in the blueberries, granulated sugar, flour, and salt. Then stir in the jam.

3 Prepare the topping: In another bowl, whisk together the flour, brown sugar, cinnamon, and salt. Add the butter and break it up with your fingers, integrating the butter with the flour.

4 Assemble and bake the crisp: Spoon the blueberry filling into the prepared baking dish and cover it evenly with the topping. Bake until the top is golden brown, 25 to 30 minutes. Let the crisp cool slightly before serving it warm.

RHUBARB STRAWBERRY PIE

I love the kind of pie where you bake the crust in the oven and make the filling on the stovetop. The filling here sets up thanks to the addition of some cornstarch. I like to cook some of the strawberries a bit longer so that there is a jammy texture to the filling, leaving the remaining fruit firmer and less cooked as a contrast.

2 tablespoons **unsalted butter**
1 large stalk **rhubarb**, peeled and cut into ½-inch-thick pieces
6 cups fresh **strawberries**, hulled and quartered
¼ cup **cornstarch**
1½ cups **sugar**
Grated zest and juice of 1 large **lemon**
½ teaspoon **kosher salt**
Lemony Pie Crust (page 314)

1 Preheat the oven to 375°F.

2 Make the filling: Heat a large skillet over medium heat and melt the butter in it. Add the rhubarb, a handful of the strawberries, the cornstarch, and ½ cup of the sugar. Cook until the rhubarb becomes tender and the strawberries start to fall apart, 8 to 10 minutes. Stir in the remaining 1 cup sugar, the remaining strawberries, the lemon zest and juice, and the salt. Cook over medium heat until the strawberries are tender, 5 to 8 minutes.

3 Assemble the pie: Pour the filling into the pie crust. Allow the filling to set up before serving, at least 2 hours.

RASPBERRY CRISP
WITH CRUNCHY CINNAMON TOP

When making a crisp with a delicate fruit like raspberries, I like to cook the topping separately. That way, the raspberries don't become overcooked while waiting for the topping to brown and crisp.

13 tablespoons (1½ sticks plus 1 tablespoon) **unsalted butter**, cubed
1 cup **all-purpose flour**
1 cup packed **dark brown sugar**
1 teaspoon **kosher salt**
½ teaspoon ground **cinnamon**
½ teaspoon ground **ginger**
⅛ teaspoon grated **nutmeg**
4 pints **raspberries** (about 6 cups)
Grated **lemon zest** for serving

1 Preheat the oven to 350°F. Grease the bottom and sides of an 8-inch square baking dish with 1 tablespoon of the butter.

2 Prepare the topping: In a bowl, combine the flour, brown sugar, salt, cinnamon, ginger, and nutmeg. Add the remaining 12 tablespoons butter, and break up the butter cubes with your fingers until the ingredients are mixed.

3 Bake the topping: Spread the topping out in a single layer on a baking sheet and bake until it is golden brown, 15 to 20 minutes.

4 Assemble and bake the crisp: Layer the raspberries in the prepared baking dish and cover them with the cooked topping. Put the dish in the oven and bake until the raspberries are tender, 20 to 25 minutes. Allow the crisp to cool slightly, and top with a few grates of lemon zest before serving.

RASPBERRY CRISP WITH
CRUNCHY CINNAMON TOP

BLACKBERRY
CINNAMON TART

STRAWBERRY ICE CREAM
PIE WITH BALSAMIC

BOURBON PECAN PIE

There is no shortage of bourbon or sugar in this filling. The result is a super-nutty pie that's addictive. I like to serve this slightly warm from the oven.

2 tablespoons **unsalted butter**, cold

¼ cup packed plus 1 tablespoon **dark brown sugar**

3 tablespoons **granulated sugar**

2 teaspoons **kosher salt**

Scant ¼ cup **bourbon**

2 tablespoons **blackstrap molasses**

½ cup **light corn syrup**

1 **vanilla bean**, split lengthwise, seeds scraped out

3 large **egg yolks**, lightly beaten

½ cup **heavy cream**

2½ cups **pecans**, toasted

Basic Pie Crust (recipe follows)

1 Preheat the oven to 325°F.

2 Make the filling: Heat a small skillet over medium heat and add the butter. Cook the butter until it melts and turns golden brown, 3 to 5 minutes, and then immediately pour it into a large bowl to stop the cooking. Whisk in the brown sugar, granulated sugar, salt, bourbon, molasses, corn syrup, vanilla seeds, egg yolks, heavy cream, and pecans. Pour the filling into the pie crust.

3 Bake the pie: Put the pie pan in the oven and bake until the top browns lightly, 40 to 45 minutes. To test for doneness, gently shake the edge of the pie pan: the filling should be fairly solid. Let the pie cool at least slightly before serving so the filling can finish setting.

BASIC PIE CRUST

MAKES 1 (9-INCH) CRUST

13 tablespoons (1½ sticks plus 1 tablespoon) **unsalted butter**, cubed and chilled

3 cups **all-purpose flour**, plus more for rolling the dough

1½ teaspoons **kosher salt**

1 tablespoon **sugar**

⅓ cup solid **vegetable shortening**, cold

1 Preheat the oven to 350°F. Grease a 9-inch pie pan with 1 tablespoon of the butter.

2 Make the dough: In the bowl of a food processor, pulse the flour, salt, and sugar. Sprinkle the remaining 12 tablespoons cubed butter and small spoonfuls of the shortening over the dry ingredients. Pulse 10 to 12 times to blend. Pour in a scant ½ cup cold water and pulse just until the ingredients come together to form a dough. Do not overmix.

3 Roll the dough: Lightly flour a flat surface. Use a rolling pin to roll the dough into a flat round about 10½ inches in diameter and ¼ inch thick. Roll the dough gently around the pin and unroll it over the prepared pie pan. Press the dough against the bottom and sides so it adheres to the pan.

4 Bake the pie crust: Put a piece of parchment or foil on top of the pie dough and fill it with pie weights or dried beans. Bake until the crust is light golden brown, 12 to 15 minutes. Remove the weights and parchment, and bake until it is golden brown, another 5 to 8 minutes. Let the pie crust cool completely.

LEMONY PIE CRUST

Add the grated zest of 1 lemon with the sugar.

ROASTED SWEET POTATO PIE

I love the floral taste of sweet potatoes when they are baked into a pie. You cannot overcook the potatoes for this recipe. In fact, the more tender the potatoes, the easier it will be to make the pie. Every sweet potato is different. Bake the potatoes and taste the flesh for sweetness and rich flavor. If they seem bland, substitute half of the potatoes with canned pumpkin. Try this with maple ice cream or even a scoop of green apple sorbet.

3 pounds medium **sweet potatoes**

8 tablespoons (1 stick) **unsalted butter**, cold

2 tablespoons **dark brown sugar**

2 tablespoons **blackstrap molasses**

1 teaspoon **ground ginger**

1 tablespoon grated **fresh ginger**

½ teaspoon ground **cinnamon**

2 large **eggs**

1 cup **whole milk**

Basic Pie Crust (page 314)

1 Preheat the oven to 350°F.

2 Cook the sweet potatoes: Put the sweet potatoes in a single layer on one or two baking sheets. Bake until the sweet potatoes are tender when pierced in the center with the tip of a knife, 1 to 1¼ hours.

3 Make the filling: In a small saucepan, melt the butter completely over medium heat. Continue to cook until it starts to turn a light brown color. Remove the pan from the heat and immediately stir in the brown sugar and molasses. Cut the sweet potatoes in half and use a large spoon to scoop out the flesh into a large bowl. Whisk the potatoes to remove any large lumps; you should have about 2 cups. Whisk in the browned butter, ground ginger, fresh ginger, cinnamon, eggs, and milk. Pour the filling into the pie crust.

4 Bake the pie: Put the pie pan in the oven and bake until the top browns lightly and the filling sets, 40 to 45 minutes. Cool completely on a wire rack.

PUMPKIN PIE

How does that crack in the pumpkin pie appear? It happens to me most often when I overbake a pie. To avoid it, bake a pie with a custardy filling for a longer time and at a slightly lower temperature. The egg whites here make the pie lighter and fluffier without diluting the pumpkin flavor.

Nonstick cooking spray

CRUST

2½ cups **all-purpose flour**, plus more for rolling the dough

1 tablespoon **confectioners' sugar**

1½ teaspoons **kosher salt**

1 cup **solid vegetable shortening**, cold

8 tablespoons (1 stick) **unsalted butter**, cubed and chilled

⅓ cup plus 1 tablespoon **ice water**

FILLING

1 (15-ounce) can **unsweetened pumpkin puree**, preferably Libby's

1 cup **full-fat sour cream**

1 cup **granulated sugar**

½ teaspoon **kosher salt**

3 large **egg yolks**

1½ teaspoons ground **cinnamon**

1 teaspoon ground **ginger**

½ teaspoon grated **nutmeg**

¼ teaspoon ground **cloves**

3 large **egg whites**

¼ teaspoon **cream of tartar**

1   Grease a 9-inch pie pan with cooking spray.

2   **Make the dough:** In a medium bowl, whisk together the flour, confectioners' sugar, and salt. Work the shortening and the butter in with your fingers until the mixture is almost smooth. Add almost all of the ice water and continue to mix with your fingers until the dough comes together. Add the remaining water if the dough feels too dry or crumbly.

3   **Roll the dough:** Put the dough on a lightly floured surface and roll it out until it is at least 2 to 3 inches wider than the pie pan. Roll the dough around the rolling pin and gently unroll it in the prepared pie pan. Press it onto the bottom and up the sides. Pinch off any excess at the top. Refrigerate the dough for at least 30 minutes or up to 6 hours

4   Preheat the oven to 350°F.

5   **Bake the pie crust:** Put a piece of parchment or foil on top of the pie shell and fill it with pie weights or dried beans. Bake until the pie shell is light golden brown, 12 to 15 minutes. Remove the weights and parchment, and bake until golden brown, another 5 to 8 minutes. Let the crust cool completely.

6   **Make the filling:** In a large bowl, whisk together the pumpkin puree, sour cream, ¾ cup of the sugar, salt, egg yolks, cinnamon, ginger, nutmeg, and cloves. Do not overmix. In the bowl of a stand mixer fitted with the whisk attachment, beat the egg whites on high speed until they double in volume, 2 to 3 minutes. Add the cream of tartar and continue to beat until soft peaks form, 3 to 5 minutes. With the mixer running, gradually add the remaining ¼ cup sugar and whip until the whites become stiff and shiny, 3 to 5 minutes. Using a rubber spatula, gently fold the egg whites into the pumpkin filling. Do not overmix.

7   **Assemble and bake the pie:** Pour the filling into the pie crust and bake until the top browns lightly, 40 to 45 minutes. To test for doneness, gently shake the edge of the pie pan: the filling should be fairly solid. Let the pie cool completely on a wire rack before serving.

CHOCOLATE CROSTADAS

Many desserts need time to cool or rest before serving. This one, however, is a burst of chocolate that you can fully assemble ahead of time. Then just bake and serve it hot out of the oven. Vanilla or caramel ice cream and a pinch of flaky Maldon salt are my favorite additions.

GANACHE

1½ cups **heavy cream**

2 cups **semisweet chocolate chips**

½ teaspoon ground **cinnamon**

Grated zest of ½ large **orange**

DOUGH

2 cups **all-purpose flour**, plus more for rolling the dough

¼ cup **sugar**

½ teaspoon **kosher salt**

Grated zest of 1 large **lemon**

½ pound (2 sticks) **unsalted butter**, cubed

¼ cup **ice water**

Nonstick cooking spray

1 Make the ganache: Pour the cream into a small saucepan. In a heatproof bowl that fits over the pan containing the cream, combine the chocolate with the cinnamon and orange zest. Set the bowl on the saucepan, and using the pan of cream as the bottom of a double boiler, melt the chocolate in the bowl over the cream. When the chocolate is melted and the cream is heated, transfer the cream to a bowl and allow the chocolate and the cream to cool slightly, separately. When they are somewhat warm, combine them and whisk them together. Refrigerate until cool.

2 Make the dough: In a medium bowl, whisk together the flour, sugar, salt, and lemon zest. Add the butter, and toss to coat the cubes. Transfer the mixture to a food processor and pulse until crumbly. While pulsing, pour the ice water through the top of the processor and continue pulsing just until the dough comes together. Roll the dough into in a ball, flatten it, and cover it with plastic wrap. Refrigerate for 10 to 15 minutes.

3 Roll the dough: Roll the dough out on a lightly floured surface until it is ¾ inch thick, making sure you flour lightly under and on top of the dough as you roll it. Cut out eight 2- to 3-inch rounds. Cover with plastic wrap and refrigerate until they are cold, at least 30 minutes.

4 Preheat the oven to 350°F. Grease a baking sheet with cooking spray.

5 Bake the crostadas: Scoop a generous tablespoon of the cooled ganache onto the center of each dough round and fold the sides up around it, making the chocolate the center of a small money purse. Arrange the crostadas in a single layer on the prepared baking sheet and bake until golden brown, 10 to 15 minutes. Spoon any remaining ganache into the center of each crostada. Serve warm.

QUICK BREADS

CREAMY BISCUITS

This is my basic recipe for a cream biscuit. They are really all about cream and flour coming together with little else. But they welcome additions: here cayenne and mustard add a tingly heat. You can stir anything you like into the dough, from chopped dried fruit to grated Parmigiano-Reggiano or sharp cheddar.

3 cups **all-purpose flour**, plus more for rolling the dough

¼ teaspoon **cayenne pepper**

½ teaspoon **dry mustard**, preferably Colman's

1½ tablespoons **baking powder**

2 teaspoons **sugar**

2¼ teaspoons **kosher salt**

3 cups **heavy cream**

1 Preheat the oven to 350°F. Line a baking sheet with parchment paper or use a nonstick baking sheet.

2 **Make the dough:** Into a large bowl, sift together the flour, cayenne, mustard, baking powder, sugar, and salt. Stir in the cream. Take care that there is no flour remaining at the bottom of the bowl, but do not overmix.

3 **Form the biscuits:** Turn the biscuit dough onto a lightly floured surface, and with floured hands, pat it down to form a 6-inch square that is about 1½ inches thick. The edges should be mostly straight. Lightly flour a knife (to avoid sticking) and cut the dough into 1½-inch squares. Arrange the biscuits (with some distance between them) on the baking sheet and refrigerate for 15 minutes.

4 **Bake the biscuits:** Put the baking sheet in the oven and bake the biscuits for 6 minutes. Rotate the pan halfway in the oven and bake until the biscuits brown lightly, an additional 6 to 8 minutes. If their centers seem a bit moist, that's good! Remove the baking sheet from the oven. Let the biscuits cool at least slightly before serving them warm or at room temperature.

DARK CHOCOLATE MUFFINS

These muffins have that deliciously bitter note of chocolate mixed with just the right amount of sweetness. I love them with a scalding hot cup of coffee. While one might relegate them to breakfast only, they are really tasty in the afternoon, too.

Nonstick cooking spray (optional)
8 tablespoons (1 stick) **unsalted butter**
1 cup packed **dark brown sugar**
1 large **egg**, lightly beaten
2 ounces **unsweetened chocolate**, melted
1 cup **buttermilk**
1 teaspoon **vanilla extract**
1¾ cups **all-purpose flour**
1 teaspoon **baking soda**
½ teaspoon **kosher salt**
1½ cups **semisweet chocolate chips**

1 Preheat the oven to 350°F. Line a standard 12-cup muffin tin with paper liners or spray it with cooking spray.

2 **Make the batter:** In the bowl of a stand mixer fitted with the paddle attachment, beat the butter and brown sugar together until smooth, 5 to 8 minutes. Add the egg. With the mixer on low speed, mix in the melted chocolate, buttermilk, and vanilla. Remove the bowl from the mixer and use a rubber spatula to stir in the flour, baking soda, and salt. Stir in the chocolate chips.

3 **Bake the muffins:** Divide the batter among the muffin cups. Don't be afraid to fill them to the top. Put the muffin tin in the oven and bake until a toothpick inserted in the center of a muffin emerges clean, 20 to 25 minutes. Unmold and cool on a wire rack.

PARKER HOUSE ROLLS

These are a great American classic, the result of an accident in a Boston hotel. The story is that rolls were formed, but the tray fell over and left the rolls misshapen. They were baked as is and the Parker House roll was born. I could grab a stick of butter and eat my way through a roomful of these. They are perfect for mini sandwiches, lobster or shrimp rolls, or even a great hot dog. At the restaurant, we bake and cool them, then pull them apart and toast them individually.

1 packet (2¼ teaspoons) **active dry yeast**

½ cup **warm water** (between 110°F and 120°F)

½ cup **sugar**

6½ cups **all-purpose flour**, plus more as needed

12 tablespoons (1½ sticks) **unsalted butter**, melted, plus more as needed

2 cups **whole milk**, at room temperature

2 large **eggs**

2 teaspoons **kosher salt**

2 to 3 tablespoons **Maldon sea salt**, to taste

1 **Activate the yeast:** In a medium bowl, gently whisk the yeast into the warm water. Whisk in the sugar. Allow the mixture to sit for a minute; it should bubble and froth slightly. Using a wooden spoon, stir in 1 cup of the flour. Cover with plastic wrap and set the bowl aside in a warm spot.

2 **Make the dough:** In the bowl of a stand mixer fitted with the dough hook attachment, blend the melted butter and the milk on low speed. Add the eggs, one by one. Add the yeast mixture, the remaining 5½ cups flour, and the kosher salt. Mix until the mixture forms a ball, 2 to 3 minutes. If the dough seems wet or sticks too much to the sides of the bowl, add more flour in ¼-cup increments. Grease a large bowl with a little butter. Put the dough in the bowl, cover it with a towel, and allow it to rest in a warm place until it doubles in volume, 1½ to 2 hours.

3 Preheat the oven to 375°F. Line a baking sheet with parchment paper.

4 **Make the rolls:** Lightly flour a flat, clean surface and turn the dough out onto it. Flour your hands and gently press the dough to form an 8 × 16-inch rectangle between ½ and ¾ inch thick. Flour a large knife and cut the dough lengthwise into 2 equal strips. Cut each strip into 12 pieces, making 24 individual strips of dough.

5 Take a piece of dough and fold it unevenly in half so the top part overhangs slightly. Tuck the overhang underneath and put the roll, seam side down, on the prepared baking sheet. Repeat with the remaining dough, lining up the rolls right next to one another so that you have 3 tightly packed rows of 8 rolls each. (It helps if you imagine gently pulling the rolls apart after they have baked!) Cover the rolls with a kitchen towel and allow them to rise again until they increase in volume by about half, 45 minutes to 1 hour.

6 **Bake the rolls:** Put the baking sheet in the oven and bake for 12 minutes. Then rotate the sheet and continue to bake until the rolls are golden brown, another 10 to 12 minutes. Remove the baking sheet from the oven and brush the rolls with melted butter. Sprinkle them with Maldon salt. Serve immediately. Note: You can freeze the dough, formed and uncooked, and bake the rolls just before serving. You can also bake the rolls and serve any left over the next day by pulling them apart, and toasting them in a 350°F oven until golden brown, 5 to 8 minutes. Brush them with butter.

BANANA WALNUT BREAD

As everyone knows, banana bread takes bananas that are way past their prime and turns them into something irresistible. Here whole-wheat flour adds extra body, and vanilla and salt accentuate the flavor of the bananas. This bread is great as is, and it also makes tasty French toast or a decadent dessert sandwich with chocolate ice cream.

½ pound (2 sticks) plus 1 tablespoon **unsalted butter**, softened

½ cup plus 3 tablespoons **sugar**

1¼ teaspoons **kosher salt**

2 large **eggs**

7 very ripe **bananas**: 5 mashed by hand, 2 thinly sliced

½ cup **whole-milk plain yogurt**

¾ cup **buttermilk**

2 teaspoons **vanilla extract**

1 cup **all-purpose flour**

1 cup **whole-wheat flour**

1 teaspoon **baking powder**

1 teaspoon **baking soda**

½ cup **walnut halves**, toasted and chopped

1 Preheat the oven to 375°F. Grease the bottom and sides of a 4½ × 8½-inch loaf pan with the 1 tablespoon butter.

2 Make the batter: In the bowl of a stand mixer fitted with the paddle attachment, beat the remaining 2 sticks butter, sugar, and salt on medium speed until fluffy, 1 to 2 minutes. Turn the speed to low and add the eggs, one at a time, and then the mashed and sliced bananas, yogurt, buttermilk, and vanilla. In a separate medium bowl, whisk together the all-purpose flour, whole-wheat flour, baking powder, and baking soda. Gently mix the dry ingredients into the banana mixture until just combined. Do not overmix or the banana bread will be tough. Stir in the walnuts.

3 Bake the bread: Fill the prepared loaf pan with the batter. Put it in the oven and bake until a cake tester or paring knife emerges clean when inserted into the center, 25 to 30 minutes. Unmold the bread and let it cool on a wire rack.

IRISH SODA BREAD

When I started working in professional kitchens, I experimented with a lot of quick breads and really fell in love with this one in particular. The textures of the fennel seeds and raisins make this bread great as is and also super-tasty when toasted and slathered with butter. The bread really brings cheese to life: serve toasted slices with a cheese platter, or use it for a grilled cheese sandwich made with Gruyère or sharp cheddar.

5 tablespoons **unsalted butter**, melted

1½ cups **all-purpose flour**

2 tablespoons **sugar**

1 teaspoon **baking powder**

½ teaspoon **baking soda**

½ teaspoon **kosher salt**

1 large **egg**

⅔ cup **buttermilk**

1 cup **golden raisins**

1 teaspoon **fennel seeds**

1 Preheat the oven to 375°F. Grease the bottom and sides of a 4½ × 8½-inch loaf pan with 1 tablespoon of the butter.

2 **Make the dough:** In a large bowl, whisk together the flour, sugar, baking powder, baking soda, and salt. In a medium bowl, whisk the egg and buttermilk with the raisins and fennel seeds. Stir the buttermilk mixture into the flour mixture, and then stir in the remaining 4 tablespoons melted butter. Mix just until combined. The dough will be stiff.

3 **Bake the bread:** Transfer the dough to the prepared loaf pan and use a small knife to slash a line down the length of the dough. Bake until a toothpick inserted in the center emerges clean, 35 to 40 minutes. Unmold the loaf and let it cool completely on a wire rack.

QUINOA BREAD

I like the idea of a bread made without wheat flour and feel better when I take a break from my favorite neighborhood sourdough to eat a few slices of this whole-grain loaf. The nutty aspect of quinoa is something I love. I usually bake this loaf, cool it, slice it, toast it, and butter it before devouring. It is also great with some tangy marmalade or with slices of turkey and Swiss cheese.

1 tablespoon **unsalted butter**

2 cups **almond milk**

2 teaspoons **cider vinegar**

4 large **egg yolks**

2 tablespoons **maple syrup**

2 tablespoons **extra-virgin olive oil**

2 cups **quinoa flour**

1 cup **tapioca starch**

1 cup **sorghum flour**

2 teaspoons **baking powder**

1 teaspoon **baking soda**

1 teaspoon **kosher salt**

4 large **egg whites**

1 Preheat the oven to 350°F. Grease the bottom and sides of a 9 × 5-inch loaf pan with the butter.

2 Make the batter: In a large bowl, whisk together the almond milk, cider vinegar, egg yolks, maple syrup, and olive oil until smooth. In a separate large bowl, whisk together the quinoa flour, tapioca starch, sorghum flour, baking powder, baking soda, and salt. Gently stir the dry ingredients into the wet ingredients.

3 Finish the batter: In the bowl of a stand mixer fitted with the whisk attachment, whip the egg whites on high speed until stiff peaks form, 3 to 5 minutes. Use a rubber spatula to fold the whites into the batter. Pour the batter into the prepared loaf pan.

4 Bake the bread: Put the pan in the oven and bake until a toothpick inserted in the center of the bread emerges clean, 45 to 50 minutes. Unmold the loaf and let it cool on a wire rack.

JAMS
& FRUIT CONDIMENTS

PEAR AND GINGER CHUTNEY

Most chutney has both a savory side and a sweet and acidic side. In this case, I pit garlic and shallots against golden raisins and pears. There is both salt and sugar in this chutney, and there are important textural subtleties as well, including mustard seeds that crackle under your teeth as you bite into the flavors of pear and ginger. I love this on chicken, a thick steaky fish, or roasted eggplant.

1 tablespoon **canola oil**

2 medium **shallots**, thinly sliced

3 medium **garlic cloves**, thinly sliced

1 tablespoon **kosher salt**

2 tablespoons **yellow mustard seeds**

1 tablespoon **coriander seeds**, crushed

2 teaspoons **ground ginger**

¾ cup **cider vinegar**

½ cup packed **dark brown sugar**

1 dried **chile**, such as a guajillo, soaked in cool water until soft, drained

1 cup naturally sweetened **apple juice**

4 large underripe **Anjou pears**, peeled, cored, and thinly sliced

½ cup **golden raisins**

2 tablespoons grated **fresh ginger**

Heat a large saucepan over medium heat and add the oil. When it begins to smoke lightly, add the shallots, garlic, and salt. Stir in the mustard seeds, coriander seeds, and ground ginger. Cook until the shallots become translucent, 3 to 5 minutes. Add the cider vinegar, brown sugar, and the whole chile, and continue cooking over medium heat until the sugar dissolves, 3 to 5 minutes. Stir in the apple juice, pears, and raisins. Cook for 10 to 12 minutes to allow all the ingredients to meld together. Then stir in the fresh ginger and remove from the heat. Allow the chutney to sit for about 10 minutes. Transfer the chutney to a clean container with a tight-fitting lid and refrigerate it for up to 2 weeks. Remove and discard the whole chile before serving.

ROASTED BRAEBURN APPLE JAM

This jam has a deep caramelized flavor from the honey and a slightly spicy note from cinnamon sticks and cloves. Braeburn apples are one of my absolute favorites because they have a great fruity taste, almost like the fruit candy I ate as a kid, combined with a crisp flesh and a slight tartness. Fuji or Royal Gala would be great here, too—or try an apple variety you've never eaten before and see what happens . . .

3 pounds **Braeburn apples**

¼ cup **clover honey**

1 teaspoon ground **cinnamon**

Grated zest and juice of 1 large **lemon**

2 cups **apple cider**

2 (3-inch) **cinnamon stick**s

8 whole **cloves**

1 tablespoon **sherry vinegar**

1 Cook the apples: Peel and core the apples. Cut them in half and then into thin slices. In a large skillet, heat the honey over low heat until it begins to foam and turns a very light brown. Remove the skillet from the heat and add the ground cinnamon and the apple slices. Return the skillet to medium heat and cook, stirring from time to time with a wooden spoon, until the apples are cooked through and the cider has reduced, 30 to 35 minutes. Add the lemon zest and juice.

2 While the apples are cooking, flavor the cider: In a medium saucepan, combine the cider, cinnamon sticks, cloves, and vinegar and bring to a simmer over high heat. Cook until the liquid is reduced by half, 10 to 12 minutes.

3 Make the jam: Strain the cider mixture over the cooked apples (discard the cinnamon sticks and cloves). Simmer the apples over medium heat until all of the flavors meld together, 3 to 5 minutes. Remove the skillet from the heat and set it aside to cool. Transfer the jam to a clean container with a tight-fitting lid and refrigerate for up to 2 weeks.

BOSC PEAR VODKA JAM

I love to make jam on the stove and watch the fruit bubble and go from often imperfect (under- or overripe) to a delicious jam. On the other hand, baking the fruit in the oven lends a roasted flavor that's offset nicely here by the clean acidity of vodka. This is the tastiest companion to morning yogurt (the alcohol cooks off in the oven) or to after-dinner ice cream that you will ever meet.

1 cup whole blanched **almonds**

3 pounds **Bosc pears**, peeled and cored

½ cup **vodka**

1½ cups packed **dark brown sugar**

Grated zest of 1 large **lemon**, plus more for sprinkling

Juice of 2 large **lemons**

¾ teaspoon **kosher salt**

½ teaspoon ground **cinnamon**

⅛ teaspoon grated **nutmeg**

8 tablespoons (1 stick) **unsalted butter**, cut into cubes

1 Preheat the oven to 350°F.

2 Roast the almonds: Spread the almonds on a baking sheet and roast them in the oven until golden brown, 8 to 10 minutes. Allow them to cool, then chop them.

3 Prepare the pears: Put the pears on a flat surface. Cut them in half and then into thin slices. Put the slices in a large bowl and add the vodka, brown sugar, lemon zest, lemon juice, salt, cinnamon, nutmeg, and 7 tablespoons of the butter. Toss to blend.

4 Bake the pears: Grease the bottom and sides of a shallow 8-inch square baking dish with the remaining 1 tablespoon butter. Layer the pears in the dish and top them evenly with the almonds. Put the dish in the center of the oven and bake until the pears are completely yielding when pierced with the tip of a knife, 45 to 50 minutes.

5 Finish the jam: Sprinkle additional lemon zest over the pears. Set the baking dish aside to cool for a few minutes; then stir so the almonds loosely mix with the fruit. Fill a clean 12-ounce jar with the jam and let it cool completely. Then cover it with a tight-fitting lid and refrigerate for up to 2 weeks.

GRAPE
MOSTARDA

SPICED PINEAPPLE
CHUTNEY

GRAPE MOSTARDA

I like to make this sour and fruity condiment with tiny champagne grapes when they are in season, but it is also delicious made with red seedless grapes. In addition to serving as a classic cheese plate condiment, this mostarda can enrich a salad dressing, a cheese platter, cold cuts, or a simple piece of roasted fish.

2 pounds seedless **red grapes**, stemmed (about 7 cups)

1 cup **sugar**

½ cup **red wine vinegar**

2 tablespoons **yellow mustard seeds**

2 tablespoons **coriander seeds**, toasted

2 tablespoons **Dijon mustard**

In a large stainless steel saucepan, combine the grapes, sugar, vinegar, mustard seeds, coriander seeds, and mustard. Bring to a simmer over medium heat. Then lower the heat and simmer, stirring, until the sugar dissolves, the grapes start to fall apart, and the juices thicken slightly, 25 to 30 minutes. Remove from the heat and set aside to cool. Transfer the mostarda to a clean container with a tight-fitting lid and refrigerate for up to 4 weeks.

SPICED PINEAPPLE CHUTNEY

While I associate most types of chutney with Indian cooking, this one is more Indonesian in inspiration. It's super-simple and is great with any form of pork or a steaky fish. I omit about 90 percent of the seeds in the chiles, but if you're looking for a spicier chutney, leave them in.

1 large **pineapple** (2 to 2½ pounds)

1 tablespoon **canola oil**

3 tablespoons **clover honey**

2 red **serrano chiles**, most seeds removed, minced

1 small **jalapeño**, seeded and minced

1 tablespoon **kosher salt**

1 teaspoon ground **cinnamon**

1 teaspoon **Madras curry powder**

¼ teaspoon ground **cloves**

1 Prepare the pineapple: Cut a slice off the bottom and top of the pineapple and stand the pineapple up on a cutting board. Using a large sharp knife, slice down along the sides of the pineapple, taking care to cut off all the brown spiny skin. Quarter the pineapple lengthwise and remove the core from each piece. Cut each quarter into small chunks.

2 Make the chutney: In a large stainless steel skillet, heat the canola oil over medium heat until it smokes lightly. Add the pineapple and cook until browned, 3 to 5 minutes. Carefully add the honey and allow it to froth and foam as it cooks briefly with the pineapple. Stir in the serrano and jalapeño chiles, the salt, cinnamon, curry powder, and cloves, and continue cooking until the pineapple is tender, 15 to 20 minutes. Remove the skillet from the heat and set it aside to cool. Transfer the chutney to a clean container with a tight-fitting lid and refrigerate for up to 2 weeks.

RASPBERRY PEPPER JELLY

Raspberries and black pepper are a great combination: raspberries are tart, black pepper slightly floral and spicy. I use this jelly as a condiment with a platter of cheeses or cured meats. I also love a little with ham or duck and even sneak a spoonful into berry pie.

3 cups **sugar**

2 pounds fresh **raspberries**

1 (8-ounce) jar seedless **raspberry jam**

2 teaspoons freshly cracked **black pepper**

2 teaspoons **red wine vinegar**

1 Preheat the oven to 250°F. Spread the sugar on a rimmed baking sheet and put it in the oven to warm through.

2 Cook the raspberries: In a large stainless steel saucepan, bring 1 cup water, the raspberries, and the jam to a boil over high heat. Cook until the raspberries fall apart and give up their juice, 10 to 12 minutes. Strain the fruit through a fine-mesh sieve into a medium stainless steel saucepan, pressing on the fruit to extract the maximum juice. You should have about 1½ cups of juice.

3 Make the jelly: Add the warm sugar to the strained juice, and bring it to a simmer. Continue to simmer, stirring, over medium heat until the sugar dissolves and the texture thickens, 5 to 8 minutes. Then stir in the black pepper and red wine vinegar. Remove the pan from the heat and set it aside to cool. Transfer the jelly to a clean container with a tight-fitting lid and refrigerate for up to 2 weeks.

ROASTED TOMATO AND FRESH CHILE JAM

This jam rides the line between savory and sweet. I love it on meats and fish, and also spread on grilled bread with a wedge of cheese. This could make a cool BLT with some lettuce and cooked bacon. The heat is pretty intense, though it mellows some in the fridge over time.

2 tablespoons **extra-virgin olive oil**

1 medium **red onion**, minced

2 **jalapeños**, thinly sliced

1 teaspoon crushed **red pepper flakes**

Kosher salt

2½ pounds medium **tomatoes**, cored and halved crosswise

½ cup **sugar**

2 tablespoons **sherry vinegar**

In a large stainless steel saucepan, heat the olive oil over medium heat. When the oil begins to smoke lightly, add the onion, jalapeños, red pepper flakes, and a generous pinch of salt. Cook, stirring, until the chiles soften, 2 to 3 minutes. Add the tomatoes and the sugar, and continue cooking until the tomatoes become tender and are starting to fall apart, 12 to 15 minutes. Stir in the sherry vinegar. Taste for seasoning. The jam should not be too liquidy; if it is, let it cook for a few more minutes. Remove it from the heat and set it aside to cool. Transfer the jam to a clean container with a tight-fitting lid and refrigerate for up to 2 weeks.

PEACH AND BOURBON JAM

This is a jam that I love to spread on thick slices of Easy Beer Bread (page 325) or super-seedy rye bread. The bourbon note is bold, but it mellows and melds with the peaches and the background flavor of the apricot jam the longer you let it sit in the fridge. Adding a little apricot jam provides a natural thickener, giving the jam great body.

1 tablespoon **canola oil**
5 large yellow **peaches**, halved, pitted, and sliced ½ inch thick
¼ cup packed **dark brown sugar**
¼ cup **bourbon**
8 ounces **apricot jam**

Heat a medium skillet over medium heat and add the canola oil. When the oil begins to smoke lightly, remove the skillet from the heat and add the peaches and brown sugar. Stir to blend, return the skillet to the heat, and cook until the peaches start to brown and soften, 3 to 5 minutes, Remove the skillet from the heat and add the bourbon. Return the skillet to medium heat and simmer until the peaches are tender when pierced with the tip of a knife, 5 to 8 minutes. Stir in the apricot jam and warm it slightly until the jam melds with the peaches. Taste for sweetness. Remove the skillet from the heat and set it aside to cool. Transfer the jam to a clean container with a tight-fitting lid and refrigerate for up to 2 weeks.

BARELY COOKED BLUEBERRY JAM

I love the texture of a raw blueberry, but I also want the deep flavor of blueberries that have been cooked down and their flavor intensified. This jam gives us the best of both. Because there is raw fruit in it, this jam won't keep as long as fully cooked fruit jams—so cook it and eat it!

1 cup **Concord grape juice**
½ cup **confectioners' sugar**, plus more if needed
Grated zest and juice of 1 **lemon**
Pinch of **kosher salt**
2 pints fresh **blueberries**
2 teaspoons **red wine vinegar**
1 tablespoon **balsamic vinegar**
2 tablespoons **granulated sugar**

In a medium stainless steel saucepan, simmer the grape juice over medium heat until it has reduced by half, 3 to 5 minutes. Add the confectioners' sugar, lemon zest and juice, salt, and 1½ pints of the blueberries. Bring the mixture to a boil over high heat. When it begins to simmer and bubble, reduce the heat and allow the blueberries to cook down gently, 10 to 12 minutes. Taste for sweetness. If the mixture is slightly tart, add an additional ¼ cup confectioners' sugar and cook until smooth, 2 to 3 minutes. Remove the pan from the stove, transfer the mixture to a bowl, and let it cool for 10 to 15 minutes. Then stir in the remaining ½ pint raw blueberries, red wine vinegar, balsamic vinegar, and the granulated sugar. Set the jam aside to cool completely. Then transfer the jam to a clean container with a tight-fitting lid and refrigerate for up to 2 weeks.

KUMQUAT CHILE MARMALADE

I make huge batches of this and take it out when I need to give some flavor to anything from a duck breast, roasted chicken thighs, a simple slice of toast, or some fresh fennel. The mellow background heat and earthy note from the chile is so tasty with kumquat! I find that this marmalade also benefits from sitting in the fridge for a bit before serving.

1 dried **pasilla chile**
1½ to 2 pounds **kumquats**
½ cup **clover honey**
½ teaspoon crushed **red pepper flakes**
½ teaspoon **kosher salt**
Juice of 1 large **lemon**

1 **Prepare the chile:** Put the pasilla chile in a bowl, add warm water to cover, and set it aside to hydrate and soften, 15 to 18 minutes. Drain the chile, cut off the top, and slice the chile, with the seeds, into thin strips.

2 **Prepare and cook the kumquats:** Thinly slice the kumquats crosswise, discarding the pits as you slice. Pour the honey into a large skillet and heat it gently over medium heat until it starts to foam, 2 to 3 minutes. Add the red pepper flakes, kumquats, and chile strips, and bring to a boil over high heat. Stir in the salt and lemon juice.

3 **Make the marmalade:** Reduce the heat and cook until the liquid thickens, 15 to 20 minutes. Taste for seasoning. Remove the skillet from the heat and set it aside to cool. Transfer the marmalade to a clean container with a tight-fitting lid and refrigerate for up to 2 weeks.

STRAWBERRY JAM

I love the texture of the little seeds in strawberry jam. In this one, the lemon and balsamic add acidity and sweetness at the same time. Macerating the fruit (sugaring the fruit and allowing it to sit so the juices emerge) and then cooking it is a great way to create a light, flavorful jam.

2 large **lemons**
1 cup **sugar**
1 teaspoon **kosher salt**
2 tablespoons **balsamic vinegar**
2 pounds fresh **strawberries**, hulled and halved

1 **Macerate the strawberries:** Using a vegetable peeler and a light touch, remove the zest in strips from one of the lemons. Juice both of the lemons and combine the juice and the zest in a bowl with the sugar, salt, vinegar, and strawberries. Toss to mix well. Allow the fruit to sit at room temperature for about 1 hour so the juices start to emerge.

2 **Cook the jam:** Transfer the strawberry mixture to a large stainless steel saucepan, and cook over medium heat, stirring from time to time, until the fruit starts to fall apart, 10 to 15 minutes. Use a slotted spoon to scoop out the fruit and transfer it to a bowl to cool. Simmer the remaining juices and errant bits of fruit over medium heat until the liquid thickens slightly, 3 to 5 minutes. Pour the thickened juices over the fruit, and set it aside to cool. Transfer the jam to a clean container with a tight-fitting lid and refrigerate for up to 2 weeks.

CANDIED GRAPEFRUIT

I have grown to love the pleasant bitterness of grapefruit skins. I like them on toast, on roasted poultry, even chopped and mixed into a salsa. Imagine dipping these in dark chocolate. Or putting them over tangy plain frozen yogurt . . .

3 large **pink grapefruits**, halved and juiced
3 cups **sugar**, plus more for sprinkling
4 whole **cloves**
Grated zest of ½ small **lemon**

1 Prepare the grapefruit skins: Bring a large pot of water to a boil over medium heat, add the grapefruit halves, and simmer for about 10 minutes. Drain off the water, refill the pot with cold water, and bring to a simmer. Cook the grapefruit for an additional 10 minutes. (This makes the grapefruit skin tender and removes any bitterness in the process.) Drain, and let the grapefruit halves cool. Use a sharp knife to scrape out some of the white pith and cut the peel into ¼-inch-wide strips.

2 Candy the grapefruit skins: In a medium pot, combine the sugar, 2 cups of the grapefruit juice, 1 cup water, and the cloves. Bring to a simmer over medium heat and cook until the sugar dissolves. Add the grapefruit strips and simmer until the syrup bubbles and reaches about 230°F, 25 to 30 minutes. Let the mixture cool. Then drain the strips and arrange them on a baking sheet. Sprinkle sugar over the strips, turn them over, and sprinkle the other side so they are well covered. Then sprinkle the grated lemon zest over them. Allow the strips to dry out for a few hours or overnight. Put the candied grapefruit in a container with a tight-fitting lid and refrigerate for up to 2 weeks.

SUGARED LEMONS

I love salted preserved lemons and often have a few jars of them in the fridge. But what about sugared ones? The bitter and sour notes are still there and are perfect for enhancing desserts. Slice the peel into strips or small pieces and use them everywhere from pie crusts to cheesecake to fruit salads, even as a garnish on top of ice cream.

6 medium **lemons**, scrubbed clean
4 cups **sugar**
2 tablespoons **kosher salt**
1 **vanilla bean**, split lengthwise, seeds scraped

Use a paring knife to make a few incisions in each of the lemons. (This will allow the sugar to penetrate the lemons as they sit.) In a medium bowl, stir the sugar with the salt, vanilla seeds, and vanilla bean. Mix the lemons with the sugar mixture. In a jar with a tight-fitting lid that is large enough to hold the sugar and lemons, pack some of the sugar on the bottom, arrange the lemons on the sugar, and then top with the remaining sugar. Seal the jar and let it sit on a shelf at room temperature for 3 days. The sugar will appear to be melting as it mixes with the escaping lemon juice. Then refrigerate and allow the lemons to sit for another 7 to 14 days before using. This will keep in the refrigerator for 3 to 4 weeks.

COCKTAILS

SPICY BLOODY MARY

This has the power of canned tomato juice mixed with juicy bits of cherry tomato. I love getting some of the shallot, garlic, and tomato in each sip. The bitters round out all of the flavors, too. For the best results, make the mixture in advance, without the vodka, and let it sit overnight. Stir in the chilled vodka the next day. Want it even spicier? Add ¼ teaspoon crushed red pepper flakes to the tomatoes.

1 small **shallot**, diced small

½ small **garlic clove**, minced

12 **cherry tomatoes**, quartered

½ teaspoon **Maldon sea salt**

1 teaspoon freshly cracked **black pepper**

¾ cup (6 ounces) **vodka**, chilled, plus more for serving

½ cup (4 ounces) **tomato juice**, preferably Sacramento brand, chilled

Juice of 2 large **limes**

1 teaspoon **Angostura bitters**

2 tablespoons prepared **horseradish**

2 teaspoons **Worcestershire sauce**, preferably Lea & Perrins brand

6 drops **Tabasco**

10 to 12 thin slices fresh **serrano chile**, to taste

1 Prepare the vegetables: Put the shallot in a small strainer or colander and rinse under running cold water. (This will remove some of the raw flavor but retain the crunchy texture.) Drain, pat dry with a kitchen towel, and combine in a small bowl with the garlic and tomatoes. Season with the Maldon salt and cracked black pepper.

2 Make the tomato base: In a small pitcher, combine the vodka, tomato juice, lime juice, bitters, horseradish, Worcestershire, and Tabasco. Stir to blend. Taste for seasoning.

3 Pour the drinks: Put a little crushed ice into each of two highball glasses. (I don't overload a Bloody Mary with ice because I want the flavors to remain intense, not diluted.) Add a hearty spoonful of the fresh tomato mixture. Fill the glasses almost to the top with the tomato juice mixture, leaving a little room. Add another spoonful of the fresh tomato mixture and 5 to 6 slices of chile to each glass. Add a splash of vodka on the top, like a floater, and serve.

NEGRONI

It took me a while to find the Negroni: I had my first one when I was thirty-five years old. It also took me a while to fall properly in love with a Negroni. Now the bitter and sweet notes always make me hungry for good food as I sip. I honestly love a cocktail that is refreshing and gets me thinking about dinner. While Negronis are not traditionally shaken, I like when the ingredients are really combined and slightly aerated. I also like the addition of grapefruit juice to the classic trio of gin, Campari, and sweet vermouth.

1 **lemon**
3 tablespoons (1½ ounces) **gin**
3 tablespoons (1½ ounces) **Campari**
3 tablespoons (1½ ounces) **sweet vermouth**
¼ cup fresh **pink grapefruit juice**

Remove 3 strips of lemon zest, using a vegetable peeler. Run one of the strips over the rims of two small glasses. Fill each glass with a few ice cubes. In a shaker or jar with a fitted lid, combine the gin, Campari, sweet vermouth, and grapefruit juice with a few more ice cubes, and shake until the ingredients are mixed and chilled. Strain out the ice as you divide the Negroni between the two glasses and garnish each one with a strip of lemon zest. Drink.

TEQUILA LIME SUNRISE

This is such a throwback drink for me. I remember watching the traditional grenadine form a strangely appealing pool in the bottom of the glass, and the ritual of stirring it with my straw and getting ready for that first sip. Here I have made a slightly fresher version—with the brightness of cherry juice—that I think improves upon the original.

Grated zest and juice of 1 **lime**
¼ cup (2 ounces) **silver tequila**
½ cup (4 ounces) fresh **orange juice**, chilled
¼ cup (2 ounces) **tart cherry juice**, chilled

In a shaker or jar with a fitted lid, combine the lime zest and juice, tequila, and orange juice with a few ice cubes and shake until the ingredients are mixed and chilled. Put 3 ice cubes into each of two cocktail glasses. Strain the ice out as you divide the tequila mixture equally between the glasses. Next, stretch a bandanna or a thin cloth napkin over the rim of a glass, and pour half of the cherry juice through the cloth into the glass. It should settle on the bottom. Repeat with the second glass.

DIRTY BLUE CHEESE OLIVE MARTINI

This is a grown-up drink, not to be trifled with. I make this cocktail only when I have time to kick off my shoes and really enjoy it. The olive and blue cheese are a chef's salt bomb that I love. Make sure the details are right: the olives are stuffed before making the drink, the glasses are chilled, and the hammock is ready . . .

2 tablespoons crumbled **blue cheese**, such as Danish blue or Gorgonzola
6 large pitted **green olives**, plus ¼ cup (2 ounces) olive brine
1 tablespoon (½ ounce) **dry vermouth**, preferably Noilly Prat
½ cup plus 3 tablespoons (6 ounces) **Plymouth gin**

1 Stuff the olives: Push some of the blue cheese into the crevice of each olive where the pit once lived. I like to fill them solidly so the bite of olive is the proper balance of cheese to olive.

2 Make the drink: Put some crushed ice into a shaker or jar with a fitted lid. Add the vermouth and swirl it around in the ice so it coats the shaker and chills in the ice. Add the gin and the olive brine. Shake to blend. Strain out the ice as you divide the gin mixture between two chilled martini glasses. Add 3 olives to each.

SALTY AND SOUR MARGARITA

I love passion fruit and salt in a margarita. This can be a dangerous drink because there is an addictive quality to it. Sometimes I serve them in slushie form if I'm feeling extra-fancy. The perfect combination? I gravitate toward a handful of pretzels or slices of fresh avocado alongside this drink. Or chips and guacamole . . .

2 large **limes**
1 tablespoon **kosher salt**
½ cup (4 ounces) **silver tequila**
¼ cup (2 ounces) **passion fruit juice**
¼ cup (2 ounces) **Cointreau**
Pinch of **Maldon sea salt**

1 Prepare the glasses: Remove a strip of lime zest from one of the limes using a vegetable peeler. Juice the limes; you need 2 tablespoons (1 ounce) juice. Spread the kosher salt on a small plate. Run the lime zest and a little of the juice around the rims of two margarita glasses and then dip the rims in the salt.

2 Spice the tequila and make the margaritas: In a shaker or jar with a fitted lid, combine the tequila with the passion fruit juice, Cointreau, lime juice, and a few ice cubes; shake to blend. Fill the salt-rimmed margarita glasses with crushed ice. Strain the ice out as you divide the drink between the two glasses. Sprinkle the Maldon salt directly on the drinks, and serve.

SPICY MARGARITA

While I love a fancy cocktail with boutique ingredients, I will admit that I often order or make myself a margarita. Sometimes I like a classic and sometimes, when it's hot outside or I am about to dig in to some chips and salsa or some smoky barbecue, I make a spicy one. Really spicy.

3 large **limes**
1 tablespoon **kosher salt**
½ cup (4 ounces) **silver tequila**
12 very thin slices fresh **serrano chile** (seeds and ribs included)
¼ teaspoon crushed **red pepper flakes**
¼ cup (2 ounces) **Cointreau**

1 Prepare the glasses: Remove a strip of lime zest from one of the limes using a vegetable peeler. Juice the limes; you need 2 tablespoons (1 ounce) juice. Spread the salt on a small plate. Rub the lime zest and a little of the juice around the rims of two margarita glasses and then dip the rims in the salt.

2 Make the margaritas: In a shaker or jar with a fitted lid, combine the tequila, chile slices, and red pepper flakes. Shake to blend. Add a few ice cubes to the shaker, along with the Cointreau and lime juice. Shake until the ingredients are mixed and chilled. Strain out the ice as you divide the drink between the two salt-rimmed glasses.

HERBED VODKA SODA

I love adding herbs and vegetal notes to the simplest cocktails. It's so refreshing—and makes the cocktails seem healthier. I serve this with some cheese and crackers or when sitting outside for a relaxing moment.

1 medium **hothouse cucumber** (about 8 ounces), cut into 1-inch-thick rounds
Leaves from 4 sprigs fresh **mint**
Leaves from 4 sprigs fresh **basil**
2 tablespoons **clover honey**
¾ cup (6 ounces) **vodka**, chilled
¼ cup **seltzer**, chilled

1 Prepare the cucumber-herb puree: In a blender, combine the cucumber slices, mint and basil leaves, and the honey. Blend until completely smooth. Refrigerate the puree until cold.

2 Make the cocktails: Fill two highball glasses with ice and divide the vodka equally between them. Stir in the cucumber puree until the glasses are almost full. Stir in a splash of seltzer to finish.

SALTY GREYHOUND

This is my absolute favorite brunch drink and, quite honestly, hangover drink. I love the salt and pepper against the bitter grapefruit. The colder the ingredients, the better.

½ cup **sugar**
1 small **cucumber**, thinly sliced
1 medium **pink grapefruit**, sectioned (see page 129)
8 ounces **grapefruit vodka**, preferably Belvedere or Absolut
Juice of 4 **limes**
1 tablespoon **Maldon sea salt**
Freshly ground **black pepper**

1 Make the simple syrup: In a small saucepan, combine ⅓ cup water with the sugar. Bring to a boil, stir until the sugar dissolves, and then remove from the heat. Transfer the syrup to a bowl to cool, and then refrigerate until cold.

2 Mix the cocktails: In a medium bowl, combine half of the cucumber slices with the grapefruit segments. Muddle them by pressing down on them with a whisk to extract the juices and lightly crush the cucumbers. Add the syrup, vodka, lime juice, and 1 cup lightly crushed ice. Pour the mixture into four rocks glasses, and sprinkle the salt and pepper to taste over the top. (Alternatively, serve in a pitcher and add the seasoning as you pour individual drinks.) Garnish with additional cucumber slices.

RASPBERRY AND LIME BRUNCH COCKTAIL

This is my brunch pitcher cocktail. Instead of mixing one or two drinks at a time, I make a batch of this and serve it up to my friends.

¾ cup **sugar**
Leaves from 16 sprigs fresh **mint**, torn into small pieces
3 pints fresh **raspberries**
1¼ cups fresh lime juice (from 10 to 14 **limes**), chilled
½ cup (4 ounces) **vodka**, chilled
1 to 1½ cups **seltzer**, to taste, chilled

1 Make the simple syrup: In a small saucepan, bring 1 cup of water to a boil and add ½ cup of the sugar. Stir until the sugar dissolves, then remove from the heat and transfer the syrup to a small bowl to cool. Then stir in the mint leaves and refrigerate until cold.

2 Mix the cocktails: In a large bowl, combine the raspberries with the remaining ¼ cup sugar and the lime juice. Stir with a spoon to blend, crushing some of the raspberries so the juice begins to meld with the lime juice and sugar. Stir in the vodka, and refrigerate.

3 Finish the cocktails: Stir the mint syrup into the vodka mixture. Transfer the cocktail to a pitcher, and stir in the seltzer just before serving.

VODKA SNOW CONE

This is really just an excuse to drink vodka ice that is super-slushy and refreshing. I love a slushy Moscow Mule and this drink is its more easygoing cousin. I also love chewing the ice. Sometimes I put out a platter of fresh watermelon alongside this drink. It's perfect on the patio . . .

1 cup **sugar**
2 tablespoons grated fresh **ginger**
Grated zest and juice of 2 **lemons** plus 4 thin slices from a whole lemon
1 cup (8 ounces) **vodka**, chilled

1 Make the simple syrup: In a small saucepan, combine 1 cup water with the sugar. Bring to a boil, stir until the sugar dissolves, and then remove from the heat. Transfer the syrup to a bowl to cool. Then stir in the ginger and the lemon zest and juice, and refrigerate until cold.

2 Make the cocktails: Fill four small glasses with finely crushed ice until slightly overflowing. Pour ¼ cup of the simple syrup and ¼ cup of the vodka over the ice in each drink. Garnish each glass with a lemon slice.

BOURBON SOUR CHERRY SLUSH

I really love sour cherries and ginger with bourbon; it's one of my favorite combinations. Make the ginger beer ice in advance and use a fork to scrape and flake it. This cocktail is addictive. Note: The ice can melt quickly, so make and drink immediately.

3 cups **ginger beer**
1 tablespoon grated fresh **ginger**
Grated zest and juice of 1 **lemon**
1 tablespoon **clover honey**
¾ cup (6 ounces) **bourbon**
12 fresh **cherries**, pitted and chopped, or 12 bourbon cocktail cherries (see Note)

1 Prepare the ginger ice: Pour the ginger beer into a clean rimmed baking sheet or large shallow baking dish. Stir in the fresh ginger, lemon zest, and honey. Freeze overnight or until completely frozen.

2 Make the cocktails: Pour 3 ounces of the bourbon into each of two highball glasses. Add a few cherries to each glass. Use a fork to scrape the ice into shavings, and fill the glasses to the top (and slightly overflowing) with the shaved ice. Sprinkle with the remaining cherries and lemon juice.

NOTE: These cherries are available in jars from bourbon houses like Woodford Reserve and Maker's Mark. You can find them online and at some specialty stores.

HOT BUTTERED RUM LIFESAVER

This is about combining a few strong flavors that end up collaborating instead of eclipsing one another: salted butter, dark rum, and spices. I make this because I truly love this flavor of Life Savers candy. Takes me back! This is rich but not too rich: bone-warming on a chilly night. I always serve this drink in a clear mug, so I can see it as I sip it!

2 tablespoons **salted butter**, softened
¼ cup packed **dark brown sugar**
1 tablespoon **blackstrap molasses**
½ teaspoon ground **cinnamon**
½ teaspoon ground **ginger**
1 pack **Butter Rum Life Savers candy** (optional)
1 cup (8 ounces) **dark rum**, preferably Myers's
2 (4-inch) **cinnamon sticks**

1   Prepare the butter: In a large heatproof bowl, whisk together the butter, brown sugar, molasses, cinnamon, and ginger until smooth.

2   Make the cocktails: In a medium saucepan, bring 1½ cups water and the Life Savers candies (if using) to a boil over medium heat. Stir until the candy dissolves. Pour the boiling water over the butter mixture and whisk to blend. Stir in the rum, and divide the drink between two mugs. Garnish each mug with a cinnamon stick.

HOMEMADE EGG NOG

This is so simple to make from scratch and so much fresher tasting and more satisfying than store-bought. Although rum is a classic, eggnog is also great with bourbon. Make a double batch and serve it old-school-style in a punch bowl with a ladle.

2 cups **sugar**
2 cups **dark rum**, preferably Myers's, chilled
2 cups **whole milk**, chilled
2 cups **heavy cream**, chilled
1 tablespoon **vanilla extract**
½ teaspoon ground **cinnamon**
¼ teaspoon grated **nutmeg**
Grated zest of ½ **orange**

In a bowl, gently whisk together the sugar and rum until smooth. Whisk in the milk, cream, vanilla, cinnamon, nutmeg, and orange zest. Serve cold.

ACKNOWLEDGMENTS

Everything I do will always be for my daughter, Ava: She keeps me on the straight and narrow with her painfully honest comments and unwavering love. She always tells me whether I am "chopped" or not . . .

I would not be here without my parents and their love of food. My dad made broccoli with balsamic the other night and my mom cooked some simple breaded veal cutlets. Eating that meal with them made me realize where my love of simplicity done brilliantly comes from. That table. That plate of food. Thanks, Mom and Dad.

Thanks to my aunt Agnes Pearson for being such an amazing force in my childhood. Everyone should be lucky enough to have an "Aunt Aggie."

My most important food mentors, without a doubt, are Guy Savoy and Bobby Flay. I would not have found any confidence had they not both whispered the right words in my ear countless times and at crucial moments. They also stood silently waiting for me to get it together. That kind of belief from other people is one of my great motivators and I'm lucky to have found people who give that to me. Especially when it means believing in my ability or just adding some more salt to a dish. I am so lucky to have crossed paths with them both.

To the group of incredible kitchen staff who made a little joint on Lafayette Street and a scrappy midtown restaurant so special: Alvaro Buchely, Michael Jenkins, the incredible Jamaal "Edward 40hands" Dunlap, Antonio Morales, Eligio Morales, Kevin O'Brien, Miguel Angel Cruz, Flaviano Sosa, Deborah Caplan, Alexandria Ventrella, DJ Sergei Ramirez, and Manuel Duarte.

To amazing purveyors and friends: Pat Lafrieda, Mark Pastore, and Louis Rozzo.

Thanks to my editor, Rica Allannic, and the staff at Clarkson Potter for hatching the idea for this book and inspiring me to do it. Thanks to Stephanie Huntwork for the design of the book and to Chris Tanigawa, Heather Williamson, Kelli Tokos, Jana Bramson, and Carolyn Gill for their support for it along the way.

Thanks to Irika Slavin and Lauren Mueller at Food Network for their amazing support and patience.

Thanks to Josh Bider, Jeff Googel, Bethany Dick, Jon Rosen, Strand Conoverm, and Andy McNichol at William Morris Endeavor.

Thanks to the farmers at the Union Square Greenmarket: Alex Paffenroth, Rick Bishop, and the folks at Northshire Farms, Windfall Farms, Stokes Farms, Cherry Lane Farm, She Wolf Bakery, and Keith's Farm.

Thanks to Johnny Miller for his great passion for the photography. He is a joy to work with. Thanks to Justin Conly for the digital piece of this equation. Thanks to Rebecca Jurkevich for the amazing cooking and food styling. Thanks to Jacob Spector and Judi Mancini for their assistance with the food. Thanks to Bette Blau and Steph Becker for the "pop o color" prop styling. Thanks to Joshua Fennell for assistance with the photography.

Thanks to Colleen Grapes, Bruce Seidel, Annie Washburn, Emily Giske, Patti Jackson, Daniel Boulud, Missy Robbins, Michael Symon, Lee Schrager, Ted Allen, Geoffrey Zakarian, Scott Conant, Chris Santos, Marcus Samuelsson, Amanda Freitag, Marc Murphy, Maneet Chahuan, Alton Brown, Giada De Laurentiis, Anne Burrell, Mikey "Bagels," Vivian Sorenson, Dave Mechlowicz, Madi Clark, the precious Michael Castellon, and fellow chefs everywhere.

Thanks to Jeffrey Chodorow, Cobi Levy, Jackie Akiva, Lauren Basco, Tony Ramirez, and Ashley Marshal for working with me at Butter and keeping the dream alive.

Thanks to Jaret Keller and Tara Halper for being amazing publicists, therapists, and support systems all rolled in one . . .

Thanks to my great friends, patrons of the arts Bruce and Karen Bronster, for allowing me to basically live at their house in exchange for some plates of food. And thanks to Peter Cook for the champagne and jokes.

Lastly, a shout-out to dishwashers and short-order cooks. Some of the toughest jobs to have. Respect.

INDEX